Creeds, Councils and Christ

Gerald Bray

Mentor

© Gerald Bray
ISBN 1 85792 280 8

First published in 1984. This edition published in 1997.

Cover design by Donna Macleod

Mentor
is an imprint of
Christian Focus Publications.
For details of other Mentor titles please write to
Mentor,
Geanies House, Fearn, Ross-shire,
IV20 1TW, Great Britain.

Printed and bound by J. W. Arrowsmith Ltd, Bristol

CONTENTS

PREFACE

Anyone who is an active churchgoer and practising Christian will not need to be told that more changes have taken place in the churches in the past thirty years than in any comparable period of time since the Reformation. Attitudes towards these changes vary from enthusiastic acceptance to an equally enthusiastic rejection, although it seems that most people have a sliding scale of preferences which adjusts to particular needs and circumstances. At the most popular level, a man may surrender the Authorized Version on the ground that its archaic language is a hindrance to evangelism, yet resist modern versions of the Lord's Prayer, which jar his religious sensibilities.

Of course, in one way such an attitude is inconsistent and unlikely to be permanent, but it demonstrates the unsettled condition in which all the major denominations, including even the Roman Catholic Church, now find themselves. 'The old order changeth, yielding place to new' and men confuse themselves in many ways, not least in the field of dogmatic theology. At a time when Christian commitment is lower then ever before, and when all branches of the Church have admitted the need for clear, incisive evangelism, it seems that the leading theologians of our colleges and universities are engaged in a kind of competition to see which of them can deny the greatest number of central Christian doctrines without being disciplined. As the title of a well-known book by the Dean of Emmanuel College, Cambridge, puts it, *Taking Leave of God*, is now possible without taking leave of the Church. Jonathan Swift's prediction that the abolition of Christianity would scarcely affect the Church has seemingly been fulfilled in our own generation.

In such circumstances, it is hardly surprising that the man in the pew is often scandalized by academic theology, and prefers to regard it as irrelevant, or even hostile to his own beliefs. Matters are complicated by a tendency among theological specialists to take refuge in technicalities. We are told, for example, that a word like 'myth' does not mean what most people assume it to mean, but that since its technical meaning is too complicated for an ordinary layman to understand and since the specialist's academic integrity must be

7

preserved at all costs, the word must continue in use and the public's bewilderment be dismissed as a tiresome irrelevance.

Theologians of the liberal kind frequently picture themselves as the advance-party of the Church, busily exploring the frontiers of faith and unbelief in the hope of discovering some new El Dorado of the mind which will eventually enrich the whole People of God. Like stout Cortez on his peak in Darien, they gaze into the blue, whilst lesser mortals hack their way through the overgrown jungle of traditional faith, hoping somehow to find the secret trail which leads to the top of the mountain. The appeal of conservative Christianity to those struggling below is sometimes acknowledged, but it is explained as a subconscious longing for a sense of security which the true pilgrim of faith must forgo. Traditional piety is a brake on progress, and its eventual, if painful, demise can be confidently assumed.

It is hardly necessary to say that conservative Christians have a rather different picture of the current theological scene. For them, the recent statements of liberal theologians are aberrations, in line with the general decay of the social order. In their wilful abandonment of traditional wisdom and authority, they herald not a new era of progressive discovery, but a return to the Dark Ages of chaos and unreason. Against this possibility only the faith once delivered to the saints offers a sure and lasting bulwark. Heretics come and go, but Christian orthodoxy is a solid bedrock of belief which will remain long after today's controversies have vanished into the footnotes of Church history books.

Which side is right? Conservative Christians tend to assume that history is on their side and that the current wave of unbelief will pass, leaving the Church unscathed. There is a good deal of precedent to support this view, but there are certain factors in the present situation which differ from those of earlier periods, and these may turn out to be more influential than is sometimes supposed. Crucial elements in the equation are the following:

Conservative Christians have lost a sense of worship. It has generally been assumed that modern translations of the Scriptures and freer forms of service would make it easier to worship God. In fact, the reverse has proved to be the case. It is no longer possible to use one version of the Bible as a common point of reference, and different translations of the same passage are just as likely to cast doubt on the text as they are to illuminate it. Enforced spontaneity in worship has led to awkwardness and confusion, and contributed to an atmosphere in church which many find painfully irreverent. At a deeper level, many otherwise conservative Protestants have accepted these changes in complete ignorance of the fact that the Authorized Version of the Bible and the Book of Common Prayer were composed after the Reformation with the express purpose of conveying the Reformed understanding of biblical doctrine. One may agree that they are far from perfect, and accept that their modern substitutes are often superior on many points of detail, but the latter come nowhere near the classical texts in their desire to promote the distinctive teaching of the Reformation. On the doctrinal level they often fall down badly, though most conservatives have hardly noticed.

This is because conservative Christians have also lost a sense of doctrine. The confusion and uncertainty surrounding our public worship has its roots in a widespread failure to appreciate the importance of Christian doctrine. The modern Church has been so concerned to extol the virtue of love that it has ignored the claims of truth, and conservatives too have fallen into this trap. Our churches can proclaim a gospel which too often is grounded in personal experience and is only vaguely related to theological principle. There are exceptions of course, but our most gifted evangelists are more likely to be noted for their repertoire of memorable anecdotes than for their deep grasp of Christian truth, and this tendency is reflected in popular tastes. Lightweight biographies and potted commentaries far outsell serious works of theology, and those who preoccupy themselves with the latter are liable to be branded as bigots or bores (or both!).

Conservative Christians cannot escape from the charge that they have replaced instruction in the things of God with religious entertainment, and that the doctrinal backbone to their preaching is decidedly weak. Many have no idea that creeds and confessions are an essential aid to Christian growth, and that the quality of our spiritual life is directly dependent on our understanding of spiritual truth. They do not know that the great centuries of the Church have been marked not by an aversion to doctrine and theological controversy, but by a passion for these things. Of course, controversy can be unpleasant and divisive, but the New Testament is full of it, and the great arguments of the past have seldom diminished our respect for the truths for which men fought and died. Conservative Christians need to recover a sense of their heritage, both in order to be able to defend it more intelligently and in order to be able to enjoy it as a living reality in their spiritual experience today.

Liberal theologians likewise need to take the Christian heritage more seriously than they have done of late. It is intrinsically unlikely that a series of lectures or a couple of popular paperbacks will overturn the wisdom of the ages, especially in matters which are not subject to empirical verification. A twentieth-century commentator on the resurrection of Christ is not better placed or more highly qualified than a first-century eye witness to interpret the meaning of the event for the future of mankind. In matters spiritual we owe a debt to the past which cannot be ignored or derided in one-sided polemic. We cannot debate with Athanasius or Augustine, with Calvin or Luther, as if our opinions were on a par with theirs. The reputation of these giants is assured, and it behoves us to respect that fact, even if we wish to disagree with them or modify their points of view.

Whether we incline towards acceptance or towards rejection of our Christian inheritance, its study remains of fundamental importance. Unless we understand what it is and how it came to have the shape in which it was transmitted to us, we are very poorly placed either to criticize or to defend it.

The present book is a fresh examination of this vital subject from the standpoint of the defence. Criticisms have not been ignored, but it is the author's conviction that the creeds and councils of the Early Church remain the unique historical basis for our present understanding of Christian truth. They have proved their worth in centuries of turmoil, and it was to their teaching that the great Reformers appealed in their efforts to purify the Church.

Those who believe in the communion of the saints, who share the conviction of the Book of Common Prayer that it is with angels and archangels and all the company of heaven that we laud and magnify the glorious Name, will concur in this judgment and use this book for refreshment and instruction. Those who do not will find in these pages what I hope is a fair treatment of their views, as well as much meat to chew on. Theological students, clergy, pastors and educated laypeople of every persuasion are invited only to ponder what is written here, to choose what is good, and to use it for their own edification and for the upbuilding of the Body of Christ.

It remains for me to thank those who have assisted me in the writing of this book. Mrs Teresa Atkins has kindly typed the manuscript, and in the process uncovered a number of errors which she has happily corrected. I must also thank the late Reverend Professor Eric Mascall who kindly gave me an afternoon of his time at a particularly crucial moment and whose influence will be apparent in many parts of the book. The Reverend Roger Beckwith, Warden of Latimer House, Oxford, and the Reverend Timothy Wilson read the book in manuscript form and made a number of helpful suggestions, for which I am most grateful. Lastly special thanks are due to my long-suffering students, who have endured both the exposition of the contents in class, and their lecturer's periodic absence during the course of preparation. It is to them that the work is respectfully dedicated.

Gerald Bray

PREFACE TO THE SECOND EDITION

It is a great joy to me that *Creeds, Councils and Christ*, after having been out of print for a number of years, has been chosen as one of the first volumes to appear in the new *Mentor* Series. The need to re-format the text has made it possible to make a number of minor alterations, but it is quite remarkable to note how well the book has weathered the test of time. When it was written, it was quite clearly intended to speak to the contemporary doctrinal crisis in the Church. Sadly, that crisis continues, and it has now produced a series of delicate ethical issues which threaten to split many of the major denominations in two. The need for a book like this one is greater than ever, and I am especially grateful to Malcolm Maclean and his colleagues who have made a second edition possible.

I dedicated the first edition to my long-suffering students at Oak Hill College, London, where I was privileged to teach the contents of this book – among much else – to four generations of budding theologians. Unfortunately, the College was put through its own crisis, which in some ways reflected that of the wider Church, and the happy years which produced this book were brought to an end. In the mercy of God there are now signs that, after a period of wandering, the College may be returning to its first love, and that future generations of its students may once more be exposed to the compelling claims of Christian orthodoxy. It is in that hope that this second edition is dedicated to those students, and to others like them everywhere, who long for the outpouring of God's Spirit in our midst, and for the true revival of the faith once delivered to the saints.

Gerald Bray
January, 1977

1

Modern Theology and Christian Doctrine

'Don't study theology, it will put you off!' This advice offered in different guises to many young Christians today really sums up the crisis of doctrine in the modern Church. 'Don't study theology.' Why not? Because theology, at least as it is taught in the majority of universities and colleges, appears to interpret critical analysis of the Christian faith as a licence to destroy any form of belief. Christians full of the warmth of the saving power of Christ and secure in the confidence of his Word find their cherished beliefs assailed and ridiculed by learned professors, who see it as their duty to expose such simple-mindedness as obscurantist and untenable in the light of modern research. Academic theology, it soon appears, has little interest in or connection with the worshipping life of the average congregation.

Faced with this surprising discovery, a theological student may react in a number of ways. He may be stung by the mockery of his teachers and some of his peers, and this may make him determined to prove himself the equal of the best academics. Soon he will be immersed in long books by leading German scholars and be imbibing their views. At first he may attempt to share these new discoveries with his friends, but their hostile reaction and 'I told you so' disapproval of theological study will drive a wedge between him and his former fellowship. Before long he will begin to appreciate what his teachers mean when they talk of anti-critical fundamentalism, and will start to sympathize with them. Prayer and devotional Bible study will be pushed to one side, in a compartment by themselves, untouched by the new learning, or else abandoned altogether.

Another student may react very differently. Instead of absorbing academic theology, he may cut it off in his mind and isolate it from the wider interests of his Christian life. If he is training for the ministry, he may have his goal fixed firmly in his mind and look upon theology as a dangerous hurdle to be surmounted. Like Christian in *Pilgrim's*

Progress, he will aim for the Celestial City and regard anything encountered en route as a potential distraction from the main business in life. Others may try to shake him, but he will stand firm and in the end absorb as little academic theology as he possibly can.

Yet another student may approach his subject with a clear mind and few illusions. He knows that the academic world will challenge and oppose his basic convictions and that he can expect only limited support from his church and his Christian friends. He knows that a Christian must grapple with every challenge to his faith, and is confident that in the end he will find an answer which satisfies both the mind and the soul. Yet even he can hardly avoid wondering why it is that such a tension should ever be felt in the first place. Luther and Calvin were respected scholars and the leading theologians of their day, yet their preaching and teaching moved the masses and led to religious revival. Why does this not happen today? Why does academic theology seem so remote from the life of the Church and inspire fear, rather than faith, in the hearts of ordinary people?

The dilemma of the theological student highlights a crisis in the contemporary church which gnaws at its vital organs and sucks away its lifeblood. Whatever our own attitude may be, we cannot escape it, because it affects us at every level and in every aspect of our Christian life. Academic theology has been estranged from spiritual experience. Instead of complementing and enriching each other, each struggles for supremacy in the hearts and minds of men.

When we take a closer look, however, we discover that both sides in this battle are in serious internal crisis. Academic theology is finding itself increasingly on the margins of university life, no longer even on the defensive because no-one takes much interest in it. It seems like a survival from an earlier age, and has often to restructure itself as Religious Studies. Speculative theology, where it still exists, is not certain that it has any subject-matter to speculate about. Critical study of the Bible has reduced its value as a theological authority and the modern philosophical climate is not particularly hospitable to religion. John Kent's study of modern theology is provocatively titled *The End of the Line?* Don Cupitt has gone even farther. In *Taking Leave of God* he virtually abandons theism and leaves theology, in the strict sense, with nothing to talk about!

Cupitt undoubtedly represents an extreme view, but his work brings out the fact that modern theology is faced with the problem of finding reliable source material. If the Bible cannot be trusted, and natural science is not interested in theistic explanations of causality, where can the theologian turn? How is his study distinguishable from philosophy, and a discredited type of philosophy at that? Perhaps it is not surprising that most works of theology today are concerned to prepare the ground for theological construction by tearing down the systems and models of the past, but do not advance very far with the projected rebuilding programme.

On the other side, the spirituality of the churches is not in much better shape. Christians today are fed on a simple diet of basic truths, but are given little encouragement to grow into a deep understanding of the Faith. Basic Bible knowledge, which is the indispensable foundation for serious reflection, is at an all-time low. Friendliness and fellowship are emphasized to the point where doctrinal correctness is regarded as a potentially divisive force. If a Roman Catholic and a Baptist share a common experience of Christ, how can it not be sinful to emphasize the doctrinal differences which separate their respective churches? Within the charismatic movement in particular, the experience of speaking in tongues is often a badge of acceptability which cancels out other factors, not least doctrinal convictions.

The present mood in the churches is fed by the spirit of ecumenism which deplores the divisions of the past and looks for a new unity transcending ancient (and therefore old-fashioned!) barriers. It is impossible not to welcome a spirit of charity in place of strife, and it is undoubtedly true that past divisions have often provoked a quite *un*-Christian bitterness over petty issues which should never have stood in the way of fellowship between true believers. But having said that, there is still a core of truth which cannot be surrendered if the credibility of the gospel is to be maintained. We cannot allow a spirit of charity to become a tolerance rooted in indifference. The Church is not a society of men of good will but a fellowship of the redeemed, who worship Christ as Saviour and Lord. This vital truth is in danger of being lost in today's tolerant climate, which is eroding the knife-edge of Christian spirituality and blunting the witness to Christ which the Church exists to maintain.

The challenge of the Enlightenment

How have we reached the present state of affairs and what should we try to do about it? The so-called 'modern' period in theology begins with the Enlightenment in the eighteenth century. Philosophers who were tired of religious warfare between churches preaching mutually exclusive versions of the truth began to suspect that the base on which the various doctrinal systems rested was itself faulty. To the claims of revelation they opposed the logic of reason. Truth could only be found in the abstract world of mathematics, which gave the key to unravelling the secrets of the natural order. In the minds of the early rationalists, the system was self-contained and needed no God to sustain it, though they were willing to admit the possibility of a divine creator.

Such an outlook obviously made miracles, prayer and the spiritual life either unnecessary or impossible. Human logic was sufficient for understanding the universe, and scientific criteria were the only measurement of truth. Rationalism of this type was much more than an attack on traditional religion. In purely philosophical terms it was a revolt against the metaphysical, and it is this aspect which is still powerful today. Metaphysics is by definition that type of knowledge which transcends the order of nature and is, therefore, unverifiable by scientific means. In a world which was determined to regard scientifically demonstrable fact as the only form of truth, metaphysics had no logical place. It was in fact irrational, and the rationalistic mind has always waged war against it.

The effect of this anti-metaphysical urge on theology was devastating. The Christian faith is grounded upon the belief that there is a God who dwells in eternity and who has revealed himself to men within the space-time framework. It is, therefore, primarily metaphysical, and regards the natural world as the creature of supernatural forces who are at liberty to use it as they might choose. With this outlook, miracles and the like were not only possible but actually to be expected, a notion which the rationalistic mind could not contemplate.

By the middle of the eighteenth century, dogmatic Christianity was everywhere in retreat. Educated people despised it and sought to remove creeds and confessions from the churches, whilst at the popular level a non-intellectual pietism was spreading over Protestant Europe. In Britain this pietism took the form of the Evangelical Revival, which produced a great outpouring of spiritual power in the lives of countless individuals without doing much to counter the philosophical influence of the Enlightenment, which remained entrenched in intellectual circles.

Pietism did, however, produce some modification of the pure rationalism of the early eighteenth century. David Hume in Scotland, and after him Immanuel Kant in Germany, both recognized that logic could not explain everything. Man possessed feelings and a creative genius which did not obey the strict rules of reason. He had a spiritual dimension to his nature which could not be satisfied by mathematical constructions alone. In England this new way of thinking made its appearance just at the moment when scientific development was launching the Industrial Revolution. Faced with the reality of sooty chimneys and terraced houses, men began to ask whether there was not more to life than industrial production. William Blake did not hesitate to connect this inner feeling with the apocalyptic vision of New Testament Christianity:

> And was Jerusalem builded here
> Among these dark Satanic mills?

Blake portrayed the relationship between the spirit and science as a struggle in which he was quick to take sides:

> I will not cease from mental fight,
> Nor shall my sword sleep in my hand
> Till we have built Jerusalem
> In England's green and pleasant land.

Blake was far from being an orthodox Christian, and his vision of Jerusalem was a long way from that of St John the Divine. But he did at least see that Christianity offered an escape from the machine culture of rationalism, and it was on this basis that a new theological system would eventually be built.

Liberal Protestantism in the nineteenth century

The architect of modern theology in this sense was Friedrich Schleiermacher (1768-1834), a disciple of Kant and one-time pietist.

Schleiermacher seized on the supposedly irrational element in man – his feelings and his spirit – and said that religion was the force which governed and developed this side of the human personality. Every nation had its religion, which gave it the power to produce a cultural synthesis of beauty and meaning. Without such a force, civilization would not exist. At the same time it was obvious that not all religions were equal in this respect. Protestant Germany had reached the heights of human achievement because it possessed a form of Christianity which was a higher type of religion than anything hitherto known to man.

What distinguished Protestantism, in Schleiermacher's mind, was its commitment to spiritual freedom. It was Martin Luther who led the revolt against dogma, tradition and ecclesiastical authority, and the Enlightenment was the spiritual descendant of the Reformation. Schleiermacher understood that Luther never went as far as his deistic 'successors' and he may have realised that the Reformation was nothing like the kind of revolt he was picturing. But the propaganda value of his claims was immense, and determined the character of Lutheranism for friend and foe alike. Gospel instead of law, grace instead of nature, Scripture instead of tradition – these were the antitheses which governed Schleiermacher's theology, for which he claimed precedent in the works of Martin Luther.

Schleiermacher maintained that the pure teaching of Jesus had been corrupted by Greek philosophy and Roman legalism, which between them had produced the great theological systems of classical orthodoxy. How this had come about was the subject of research undertaken by Schleiermacher's disciples, in particular August Neander (1789-1850). Neander was one of the principal founders of Church History (*Kirchengeschichte*) as a separate discipline, and he set out to demonstrate the process which Schleiermacher claimed had taken place. After his death, his work was taken up and worked out more thoroughly by Adolf von Harnack (1851-1930), the leading church historian of his day and the most prominent spokesman for German liberal Protestantism. Harnack's reputation rests above all on his massive History of Dogma (*Dogmengeschichte*) which appeared in 1894. In this great work he sought to demonstrate just how the simple moral teaching of Jesus had been corrupted into a theological system far removed from the original message. The following passage (Book II, chapter 1) gives some idea of his thought:

How great the innovations actually were, however, may be measured by the fact that they signified a scholastic tutelage of the faith of the individual Christian, and restricted the immediateness of religious feelings and ideas to the narrowest limits .... The fixing of the tradition under the title of apostolic necessarily led to the assumption that whoever held the apostolic doctrine was also essentially a Christian in the apostolic sense. This assumption, quite apart from the innovations which were legitimised by tracing them to the apostles, meant the separation of doctrine and conduct, the preference of the former to the latter, and the transformation of a fellowship of faith, hope and discipline into a communion *eiusdem sacramenti*, that is, into a union which, like the philosophical schools, rested on a doctrinal law, and which was subject to a legal code of divine institution.

It is clear from this that Harnack believed that the teaching of the Apostles did not correspond, as a matter of historical fact, to the tradition which had been handed down as apostolic. To some extent, this view was undoubtedly justified. There is no reason to believe that the Apostles' Creed or the *Apostolic Tradition* (usually attributed to the third-century Roman writer Hippolytus) were orginally composed by the Apostles themselves. Similarly, it is well known that the claims of certain Churches, like that of Rome, to apostolic origin, are open to question and were not generally pressed before the fourth century.

The question becomes more complex when we turn to the evidence of the New Testament. Already before Harnack, the great Tübingen scholar, F.C. Baur, had discovered that certain of the Epistles in particular contained elements of doctrine and discipline which did not conform to the picture of the apostolic church as presented by Schleiermacher and his disciples. The Pastoral Epistles appeared to assume the existence of a fixed church order. 2 Peter referred to the Epistles of Paul as Scripture. In 1 John, right belief was a condition of Christian love and fellowship. In other words, said Baur, the New Testament itself contained a form of Early Catholicism, which was later to expand and take over the entire church.

The main architect of Early Catholicism was thought to have been Luke. Not one of the original twelve, Luke was both a Gentile and a disciple of the apostle Paul, whose own teaching was widely held to diverge significantly from that of Jesus. Of all the Evangelists, Luke showed the greatest awareness of Roman power and civilization, and the greatest willingness to link the coming of Christ to the destiny of the empire. In the Acts of the Apostles he recorded the progression of Christian witness from the charismatic assembly at Jerusalem to the court of the Caesars at Rome – a progression which was paradigmatic of what was happening to the Church in general. The emergence of a fixed system of doctrine could not be found as early as Acts, which suggested that Luke was not wholeheartedly committed to the development of a Catholic order, but of course it followed naturally in the wake of the events he described.

The discovery of Early Catholicism in the New Testament was an event of major importance, because it weakened the classical Protestant opposition between Scripture and tradition. As Baur pointed out, Scripture was itself part of the Church's tradition, and large parts of it reflected post-apostolic developments. This did not make Baur and his followers more inclined to accept the authority of tradition, however. On the contrary, its corrupting influence could be traced right back to the New Testament itself, which necessitated a purge of this secondary material from the sacred texts. Baur maintained that it was not the New Testament but the teaching of Jesus, which the Gospels contained and to some extent concealed, which was the true source of Christian faith.

The result was a furious search for the authentic words of the historical Jesus, in an attempt to recover the pure gold of his teaching from the dross of interpretation, even apostolic interpretation, which surrounded it. The idea that Jesus' followers must have distorted his message became so powerful that even today it is a basic assumption of much New Testament study. When it was pointed out that *all* the sayings of Jesus have been transmitted through others, the conclusion was drawn that the historical Jesus was inaccessible and that everything we know about him is somehow distorted. More recently this rather extreme view has been modified. It is now generally conceded that the New Testament documents must bear some relation to the teaching of the historical Jesus, since otherwise it would be hard to explain why he plays such a central role in them, but confidence in the text as a historical record is still regarded as impossible by the majority of critical scholars.

Developments in the twentieth century

In the twentieth century various new developments have taken place which have both extended and challenged the assumptions of nineteenth-century scholars. In the field of Church history, Walter Bauer has tried to show that the first Christian communities embraced a plurality of beliefs and practices, traces of which can be seen in the New Testament. Gradually, in the course of the second century, the Hellenized élite of the Church elaborated the elements of Early Catholicism and imposed them on the congregations. The teaching authority of the bishop was emphasized, and a form of credal orthodoxy began to appear. In some places, like the Syriac-speaking area of northern Mesopotamia, this process was never really completed, and an archaic form of Christianity survived much longer. By looking at these backwaters, we can get a picture of what the New Testament churches must have been like.

Much more recently the hypothesis that the churches of the New Testament were much more diverse in faith and practice than has usually been assumed has been taken up and developed by James Dunn in his book, *Unity and Diversity in the New Testament*. Dunn restricts the confessional unity of the New Testament churches to the slogan 'Jesus is Lord', which he believes testifies to the common conviction among the early Christians that the Risen Christ was the same Jesus of Nazareth who had taught the disciples around the Sea of Galilee. This confession was born of experience and was the living force which drew diverse and often disparate elements together into a common body of people. Only later was a theological system erected, a process which entailed the suppression of the more primitive charismatic features of church life and the introduction of a Catholic order buttressed by philosophical arguments and legalism.

On a rather different track, the twentieth century has witnessed a new approach to the question of the historical Jesus. In 1906, Albert Schweitzer published his famous study on this theme in which he criticized his predecessors for their false religious and cultural assumptions. The historical Jesus was not the prototype of the liberal German Protestant but a prophetic figure wrapped in the popular apocalyptic Judaism of his own time. Heaven, hell and the final judgment were realities to him, and the surviving documentary evidence represents, if anything, a toning down of his original message to make it acceptable to the wider Greek world. This suggestion led to a renewed interest in the messianic types of Judaism current in Jesus' day, and to a whole new understanding of Christology.

Following the lead given not only by Schweitzer but also by Bousset and Wrede, whose research led them in similar directions, modern scholarship has focused strongly on the titles given to Jesus in the Gospels. These titles – Son of man, Messiah, Lord, Son of God, *etc.* – all have a prehistory in Jewish apocalyptic literature which has been drawn upon and adapted in the New Testament. It thus transpires that Jesus must be seen not so much as an original teacher in his own right, towering over his contemporaries, but as a typical first-century Jew around whom the messianic hopes of his nation were later gathered.

These hopes were not an aberration, despite some extreme manifestations on the sectarian fringe, but the logical outcome of the Old Testament revelation. The work of God in Israel could best be understood as salvation history (*Heilsgeschichte*), which culminated in a saviour-redeemer figure who was God's anointed Messiah. That this Messiah would also be the Paschal Lamb and the suffering servant of Isaiah 53 was implicit in the Old Testament but not at all clear to the Jews of Jesus' day. It was the sacrificial death and resurrection of Jesus which brought the two themes together and laid the foundation for a new religion of Christ, the fulfilment of Israel's hope.

One of the chief exponents of this type of Christology was Oscar Cullmann. Unlike many of his predecessors, he took a remarkably conservative line and was broadly sympathetic to classical orthodoxy. Even so, he refused to accept its validity for New Testament interpretation. In his *Christology of the New Testament* (p.3) he wrote:

> The later so-called Christological controversies refer almost exclusively to the *person* or *nature* of Christ. They refer on the one hand to the relation between his nature and that of God; on the other hand, to the relation which exists in Christ himself between his divine and his human nature. If we are to avoid the danger of seeing the Christological problem of the New Testament in a false perspective from the very beginning, we must attempt first of all to disregard these later discussions. It must be acknowledged from a historical point of view, of course, that it was necessary for the Church at a certain period to deal with the precise problems resulting from the Hellenizing of the

Christian faith, the rise of Gnostic doctrines, and the views advocated by Arius, Nestorius, Eutyches and others. That is, it was necessary for the Church to deal with the question of the natures and attempt to answer it. We may say, however, that although the Church attempted a solution to the problem by reference to the New Testament, its statement of the problem was nevertheless oriented all too exclusively in a direction which no longer completely corresponds to the manner in which the New Testament itself states it.

Cullmann's assessment of classical Christianity was cautious and he guarded himself against a wholesale condemnation of dogmatics in a way which was calculated to offend almost nobody. But at the same time he carefully excluded the dogmatic approach from the study of the Scriptures. Ontological questions implied by the terms *person* and *nature* were regarded as fundamentally irrelevant. The Christology of the New Testament was functional, in that Jesus of Nazareth was the man chosen by God to fulfil Israel's destiny. Who he was in himself was secondary; what really mattered was what he did on behalf of the people.

The emphasis on Jewish apocalyptic influence was taken one step further by Rudolf Bultmann, perhaps the leading New Testament scholar of his day. Bultmann went further than his predecessors and contemporaries in assigning a philosophical dimension to the Christology of the New Testament. According to him, the Gospels were rooted in a metaphysical outlook on reality which the scientific mind has rejected. This metaphysic Bultmann calls myth, following the great tradition of German Romanticism. If the message of Christ is to be translated into language a twentieth-century rationalist can understand, it must be *demythologized*. The apocalyptic overtones must be removed, so that the kernel of Jesus' teaching can stand out in a form which scientific thought can recognize.

Bultmann's understanding of myth in the New Testament has made an enormous impact on contemporary theology. Not only are there demythologizers of the New Testament, but the process has been extended to take in classical orthodoxy as well. In a notorious symposium which appeared in 1977, a number of leading British theologians sought to expose what they claimed was *The Myth of God Incarnate*. The book has been severely criticized, particularly for its rather ambiguous use of the term *myth*, but its gist seems clear enough. What the writers are saying is that the early Christians accepted the myth-soaked Gospels as scientific fact, and on that basis systematized them into the classical credal system, of which the doctrine of the incarnation is the centrepiece. They did not, as a rule, doubt that *if* the Gospels were historical fact the doctrine of the incarnation would be implied in them. Their complaint was that the wrong method had been used to analyse the data, so that the end-product was a systematized myth posing as scientific truth.

Can the New Testament be demythologized though, and still remain the foundation document of Western religion? A very radical theologian like Dennis Nineham would answer, No. The world of the New Testament is so foreign to our experience that no amount of reconstruction can bring it back to life. The teaching of Jesus, perfectly adapted as it was to the world-view of his time, represented a great spiritual and moral advance, but now it must be superseded by a new vision of equal power and influence. It is the prophetic task of the theologian to point out this need and look for signs of a development which might meet it.

Few scholars follow so radical a line as Nineham, however. Most continue to believe that Jesus can speak meaningfully to the modern world, though they insist on the need for some kind of demythologization. Not all would agree, though, that stripping away an outdated metaphysic is enough. Influenced by such diverse disciplines as behavioural psychology and comparative anthropology, some theologians maintain that the gospel message must be *remythologized*, i.e. cast in a metaphysical mould which is credible in the scientific age. To those who argue that science is anti-metaphysical, they point out that such a position is unsatisfactory and untenable. Any attempt to systematize, explain or evaluate data involves using standards of judgment which of their very nature employ metaphysical categories. Even a secular and naturalistic philosophy like Marxism cannot escape this tendency. Marx sought to discredit the supernatural, but in its place he erected a dialectic of historical inevitability into a metaphysical principle. This produced a fatalism which has led to monstrous immoralities in the name of progress and the virtual enslavement of large parts of the human race.

Anthropological influence has been felt in the work of Structuralist interpreters like Paul Ricoeur, which has highlighted the symbolic richness of biblical language and imagery. At a more prosaic level it has led to the search for 'dynamic equivalents' in translating the Scriptures. These are expressions and symbols which can convey the original force of the Greek New Testament in contemporary idiom. Ideas of this kind have been influential among missionary translators attempting to bridge the enormous gap between a primitive culture and the relatively sophisticated world of the New Testament. It is by no means confined to these circles, however, and its implications for translating the Bible into our own language and culture are now matters of serious study.

Generally known as the New Hermeneutic, the process of finding a modern metaphysic for the gospel message assumes that each culture is bounded by a horizon of perception which defines its world-view and outlook. It is therefore necessary to deconstruct the Biblical horizon and refashion its message according to criteria acceptable today.

This is in fact what is supposed to have happened in the early centuries of the Church. Classical orthodoxy came into being because the biblical data were adapted to the cultural norms of the Graeco-Roman world. What makes it unacceptable today is the loss of this classical culture. Just as we no longer live in a world dominated by the philosophical principles of Plato or Aristotle, so we can no longer subscribe to a type of theology which is basically Platonic or Aristotelian.

The demise of traditional orthodoxy is therefore not a catastrophe but a necessity, so that a new synthesis can be worked out. Perhaps it would be better to speak of new syntheses, since each culture must make its own adaptation. In the new world of emerging, theological pluralism, Indian Christianity will look very different from the African variety, and each will bear little resemblance to its Western counterpart. One can almost see the development of a new science of comparative Christian theology, seeking to align one cultural area with another and reveal the universal element underlying them all!

The Orthodox response

That, in brief, is the history of the development of the liberal Protestant theological tradition, in which German scholars and ideas have played the leading role. In many ways it has been the dominant force in academic theology for nearly two centuries, and its influence has been felt well beyond the confines of Protestantism. Since the Second Vatican Council (1962-65) its spirit has triumphed in large parts of the Roman Catholic Church as well. Indeed, the ecumenical movement now seems to be moving towards a super-Church whose order will be Catholic but whose theology will be liberal-Protestant, albeit with as much deference as possible to traditional creeds and confessional formulae.

But if this tradition has been dominant at the academic level, the situation in the Church at large has been very different. As has been mentioned already, there is in the modern church a split between the spiritual life of ordinary people and the speculations of academic theology. To the extent that the latter have had any impact at all, it has been to encourage the wider trend towards secularism and indifference.

A classic example of this was John Robinson's *Honest to God*, published in 1963. Those who followed Robinson into rebellion against traditional ways of thinking did not break away to form a new church; they merely stopped or reduced their religious commitment. From 1963 to 1980, the number of men ordained annually in the Church of England fell by over half – from 636 to 309. But for the dramatic rise in the number of Evangelicals in the same period, the situation would be even more serious than it is. The survival, and even revival, of 'fundamentalism' is a phenomenon which has perplexed and even annoyed the theological intelligentsia, who see it undoing everything they have tried to achieve. Whether this will happen remains to be seen. What is certain is that the tradition of opposition to liberalism, that modern conservatives have inherited, while less prominent, is intellectually not less powerful than the trends it has tried to combat.

One of the first men to perceive the direction being taken by Schleiermacher, and to be alarmed by it, was E.B. Pusey (1801-1882). Pusey was one of the few English divines of his day who knew German well, and who could argue against German theology on its own ground. He accepted Schleiermacher's claim to stand in the tradition of Luther and as a result he turned against Protestantism in all its forms. Pusey was the leading Anglo-Catholic of his day, not a Romanizer like John Henry Newman, but a conservative who sought his intellectual salvation in the classical theology of the Early Church.

In many ways it was fortunate that he did so, since his influence attracted some of the best theological minds in England to the cause of patristic orthodoxy. To this day there remains a tradition of historical scholarship closely associated with Anglo-Catholicism and maintaining in England a living respect for the Early Church and its achievement. The names of H.P. Liddon, H.B. Swete, G.L. Prestige and J.N.D. Kelly stand out as those of major contributors in the field. Nor should one forget the work of O.C. Quick or R.V. Sellers, less broad or less brilliant perhaps, but nevertheless worthy of respect and admiration. These English scholars, ably supported by others of a broader outlook like H. Bettenson, J. Stevenson, H. Chadwick and H.E.W. Turner, have done so much to keep the study of the Fathers alive. Their often meticulous scholarship has overturned the broad and hasty judgments of Harnack at any number of points, so much so in fact that Harnack's *History of Dogma* can no longer be treated as a serious work of historical scholarship.

The Anglo-Catholic tradition was less successful in its defence of Christian orthodoxy at a philosophical level. Its traditionalism was often more romantic than reasonable, and it displayed a strong tendency to prefer details of form and ritual to matters of philosophical and doctrinal substance. The result was that many Anglo-Catholics drifted into a liberalism scarcely distinguishable from that of German Protestantism, by which they were influenced as much as anyone. They were certainly less prepared to abandon the ancient creeds, which to them remained a part of Catholic tradition, but they lost any deep understanding of their meaning. This growing indifference to the nuances of classical dogmatics, a phenomenon now apparent among some Roman Catholics as well, can be seen in the version of the Nicene Creed found in the *Alternative Service Book 1980*. Although this book reflects a strong commitment to patristic tradition, we can still read that Christ was 'conceived by *the power of* the Holy Spirit'. The italicized words are an unjustified interpolation of the original text which could have serious consequences for the doctrine of the incarnation, yet they appear to have slipped by unnoticed.

A more consistently theological reaction to liberalism came from the German-speaking world itself. When Harnack and his colleagues openly supported the Kaiser's war aims in 1914, one of his students, Karl Barth (1886-1968), was so shocked that he began to question the whole basis of the theology which he had been taught. A term as a pastor in Switzerland convinced him that liberalism had little to offer the ordinary Christian, and set him on his life-work, which was to be the resurrection of Protestant orthodoxy and the reinstatement of dogmatics at the heart of theology. Barth's achievement was so massive and went so much against the trend of his time that even now it has not been fully digested by the theological world.

Barth's *Church Dogmatics* is both a denunciation of nineteenth-century liberalism and a restatement of classical orthodoxy, upholding the creeds and confessions of the Church and trying to show how they are both true to Scripture and relevant to the concerns of the present day. As such his work is without parallel and will undoubtedly remain as a monumental expression of traditional Christianity in the first half of the twentieth-century. Having said that, however, it must be recognized that Barth was not uninfluenced by the liberalism he rejected, and that has left serious flaws in his work. The most important of these is that Barth accepted the Christocentric emphasis of liberalism and tried to link this with a doctrine of revelation. There is obviously a close connection between these two, as the polyvalent expression 'Word of God' makes plain, but Barth failed to follow through the logic of classical orthodoxy in two areas of fundamental importance.

First, he did not identify the revealed Word of God with the text of Scripture. For Barth, the Bible remained a primary witness, but revelation could not be contained in propositional statements made in human language. The distance between God and man was too great for this; God in his essence must forever remain 'wholly other' than man in his creaturely finitude. The revelation of the Word of God was uniquely given in Jesus Christ, whose life and work remained immeasurably greater in scope and in power than anything the Bible could express. At best it could only be a vehicle to a knowledge of God which lay above and beyond a written text.

Second, Barth maintained that in Christ God had revealed himself fully and finally. We have no mandate as Christians to seek the divine in nature, in other religions or in mystical experience. Jesus Christ is the complete statement of everything God has to say to us, and all theology must use him as its fundamental point of reference. As a result, Barth was inclined to regard the whole of dogmatics as an extension of Christology. In particular, only in and through Christ was it possible to have any knowledge of the Trinity. Barth was a strong defender of Trinitarianism in an age which had almost abandoned it as a serious element in theology; but this should not blind us to the fact that his Trinity is different from that of the Augustinian tradition which he sought to uphold. Augustine had developed a Trinity of Love, in which the actions of the Persons flowed of necessity from their innermost essence. Barth excluded the essence from consideration and offered instead a Trinity of Revelation, in which the action was everything. Augustine looked to the Trinity to discover the *source* of God's saving work; Barth looked to it to explain its *result*, in the life and death of Jesus Christ.

Differences of this kind are subtle and easily missed. But they are of fundamental importance. Barth has not been recognized as the orthodox theologian he wanted to be, because his fundamental principles were derived from the liberalism he was trying to combat. On the other hand, the dogmatic superstructure which he proceeded to build has struck many liberal theologians as anachronistic and without foundation. The assumption that Jesus Christ can be known by means of the Scriptures has received such a battering in scholarly circles that, even when the truth of Barth's claim is conceded in principle, it turns out to be virtually impossible to give it any practical substance which will not be shifted by the next wind of scholarly inquiry.

A very different approach to dogmatics, but which, like Barth's, seeks to justify the position of classical orthodoxy, is associated with the work of the Jesuit scholar Bernard Lonergan. Lonergan belonged to a Catholic tradition which traces its origins to John Henry Newman. In Protestant circles Newman is regarded as a renegade who abandoned the Evangelical faith of his youth for the ecclesiastical traditionalism of Rome. But in Roman Catholic terms, Newman was a liberal who tried to introduce a new way of thinking into that church. He rejected the standard Roman view that the system of dogmatic theology proclaimed by the Counter-Reformation Council of Trent was no more than a definitive exposition of the teaching of Holy Scripture in the light of tradition. Newman insisted that there had been a development of doctrine during the course of the centuries, and that New Testament Christianity was therefore not the same as nineteenth-century Roman Catholicism. But Newman certainly did not regard this development as a progressive corruption of the pure teaching of Jesus. On the contrary, for him it was the ongoing work of the Holy Spirit, bringing illumination to the Church at different times in its history, and enabling it to fulfil its mission in changing circumstances. The process of development was neither smooth nor easy, as the history of dogmatic controversy made clear; but its ultimate direction and validity was assured by the apostolic ministry given to St Peter and held by his

successors, the Bishops of Rome and Primates of the Universal
Church.

Newman's views were revolutionary at the time, but they have
been accepted by the Roman Catholic Church and have even come to
be seen as a powerful buttress to the claims of the papacy, regarding
which Newman himself was rather lukewarm. Lonergan inherited this
way of thinking and pursued it at the philosophical level, taking into
consideration the findings of modern psychology as well. He explained
the development of doctrine as a differentiation of consciousness
affecting the human race as a whole. In earlier times, men thought
primarily in terms of naïve experience, and this is reflected in the
undifferentiated character of the scriptural revelation. Later, the human
mind became progressively more analytical, separating out reason
from emotion and experience. The growth of theoretical thought
necessitated a similar differentiation of the biblical material, and this
process produced the creeds of Catholic Christendom. As he said in
The Way to Nicea (p.3):

> The gospels are addressed to the whole person, on all levels of
> operation. The dogmas, on the contrary, demand a subject who
> can focus attention on the aspect of truth alone, so that other
> powers are under the sway of intellect, or else are somehow
> stilled.
>
> Dogmatic development, therefore, not only presents an
> objective aspect, which is grasped by comparing earlier with
> later documents; it also demands a certain subjective change
> involving a transition from undifferentiated common sense,
> which is what is most widespread and most familiar, to the
> intellectual pattern of experience. And this transition does not
> occur spontaneously; it comes about only through a slow
> learning process, sustained by serious effort.

Thus the Church, guided by the Holy Spirit, learned to express its
faith in a way which would speak to the intellectual climate of the
age. Lonergan did not deny that further developments have occurred
since the fourth century, and in that sense he would not have regarded
the classical creeds as the fixed and immutable formulae of orthodoxy.
But change, if it is to come, will come always as a further development,
building on the past and extending it, not as a revolution overthrowing
everything which has gone before.

Lonergan's theory has attracted widespread interest, even among non-Roman Catholics, because it offers a positive approach to the tradition based on a theory which is compatible with modern knowledge. As such it is a remarkable achievement, worthy of close study and attention. Nevertheless, it has certain features which are debatable and which must stand in the way of uncritical acceptance of it. Chief among these is that Lonergan does not seem to have appreciated the importance of the written medium as a force for intellectual thought, or as he says, for differentiation of consciousness. It is hard to see how the gospel, in its written form, is any less 'theoretical' than the propositional statements of the creeds, or for that matter of the Old Testament law. If there was a progression from one level of consciousness to another, surely it occurred at Mt Sinai, when God wrote the Ten Commandments on tablets of stone, thereby inaugurating the Judeo-Christian tradition of sacred writing. The power inherent in the very writtenness of Scripture (*graphe*) comes across strongly in the teaching of Jesus, where 'It is written' carries the same solemn force as 'Thus saith the LORD'.

However much Lonergan may be criticized, his insistence that propositional discourse is an appropriate means of conveying religious truth marks him out as a staunch defender of orthodoxy at the much-neglected but all-important level of theological method. Over-emphasis on myth and feeling in theology has led to a crisis for the academic discipline, which at the end of the day has to explain itself in propositional terms. Writing in *The Problems of Theology* (p. 145), Brian Hebblethwaite has this to say:

If we are to distinguish the doctrinal dimension from the mythical dimension in religion, we shall have to resist this conflation of myth, symbol, parable, and doctrine. Without denying that religious truth is often conveyed most graphically by myths and parables, we should have to show that it is possible to state, more prosaically in non-parabolic form, at least something of what was being conveyed pictorially or dramatically in the myths and parables. It can be argued that this was what the early Fathers of the Christian Church were doing as they hammered out the doctrines of the Trinity and incarnation, though the process goes right back to the New Testament writers too.

If this admission becomes more generally recognized in theological circles, it could mean the return of a way of thinking much closer to that which produced the great formulations of Christian doctrine, even if we should not expect it to lead automatically to a general acceptance of orthodoxy as such.

Traditional Orthodoxy today?

The general picture of modern theology as presented here is hardly encouraging for an exponent of traditional Christian orthodoxy. Even those theologians with the greatest sympathy for it are inclined to reject it at certain crucial points. Biblical scholars continue to regard it as an appendix to their own discipline. It is hard to imagine any of the major Protestant churches embarking on doctrinal definition in the present theological climate; all the emphasis is on unbridled pluralism and the tolerance of any kind of faith or unbelief. Roman Catholicism has a living dogmatic tradition, but even its own adherents are inclined to admit that it has less and less connection with the New Testament witness. In modern times, there have been three major dogmatic pronouncements – the Immaculate Conception of Mary (1854), the Infallibility of the Pope (1870), and the bodily assumption of Mary into heaven (1950) – none of which has any support in the New Testament. The Eastern Churches proudly call themselves Orthodox, but here too doctrinal definition is unlikely in the near future. For them the most recent authoritative dogmatic statements date from the Second Council of Nicaea in 787!

Another difficulty is the diversity of the theological systems which claim to be orthodox. A major argument of the eighteenth-century rationalists was that conflicting dogmatic tenets cannot both be absolutely true, and they used the divisions of Christendom as evidence that Christianity itself was an absurdity. There is substance *behind* (if not so much *in*) this argument, and it needs to be faced squarely. If we return to a period of doctrinal definition and conviction, will it not lead to the kind of religious warfare which existed in Reformation Europe and which still apparently lingers in Ireland? Religious prejudice can be a lethal weapon, and seems to be quite out of line with the teaching of Jesus, who was himself the victim of narrow-minded bigotry and sectarian strife.

In answer to this, it must be said that the existence of truth and the possibility of knowing it must also imply the existence of falsehood. Certainly we must deplore any recourse to violence to determine which is which, but the principle must surely be admitted. If God is a Trinity of Father, Son and Holy Spirit, then he cannot also be an impersonal force ruling the world by blind fate. Those who take the second view will be wrong and should not be allowed to air their views from positions of authority in the Church, any more than a Christian Scientist would be allowed to proclaim and implement his views if he were the head of a large hospital. Holding unorthodox views should not invite persecution, but neither should it be tolerated as a valid option within the Christian fellowship.

As far as the main traditions of Christendom are concerned, differences of opinion demand consideration and respect, with a clear recognition of fundamental principles and a willingness to work together as much as possible. In this respect, it is important to maintain a clear distinction between the creeds of the Early Church and the confessions of the Reformation era. The former are intended to express the content of belief necessary for salvation. Because of this, they are as brief and as comprehensive as possible. Every Christian in full possession of his rational faculties is expected to subscribe to them, as their traditional place in public worship makes plain.

The Reformation confessions, by contrast, were intended for a different purpose. They belong exclusively to the different strands of Protestantism within which they were formulated, and are meant to clarify the position of a particular denomination on matters of controversy. They are generally preoccupied with details of church organization and sacramental practice, which were major issues in dispute in the sixteenth and seventeenth centuries. Of course it is true that these questions are related to doctrinal issues, especially to the sufficiency of Holy Scripture for establishing points of belief and to the doctrine of justification by faith. At this level, however, all Protestants are agreed, and have usually felt that their differences are not great enough to stand in the way of co-operation and communion. Protestant unity has never taken an institutional form, but even so, it has always been felt to be a living reality.

Much more serious is the divide which separates Protestants from Roman Catholics and both these from the Eastern Orthodox. Here, intercommunion has never been possible, and even intermarriage has been fraught with difficulties which would be unthinkable between members of different Protestant denominations. Both the Roman Catholics and the Orthodox believe that theirs is the one true Church from which others have departed, and for them ecumenism can only mean reintegration into the traditional fold.

Protestants, who believe that the true Church is an invisible, spiritual reality, have always rejected this claim, though usually without denying that Roman Catholics and Orthodox may be true Christians, with valid sacraments and ministry. A baptized member of one of these churches would not be rebaptized on becoming a Protestant, because Protestants hold that their picture of the Church is the traditional one, purified of the legalism and false teaching which they believe has crept into the older bodies. In fact, Protestants sometimes express their views by saying that they hold firmly to orthodox doctrine and catholic (universal) tradition, on the understanding that these terms refer to beliefs and practices in accordance with the teaching of Scripture. The common inheritance which this foundation provides is much greater than the apparent divisions would suggest, and for Protestants it offers the only solid foundation for an eventual reunion of the Churches.

It may seem odd at first sight, but a renewed emphasis on Christian doctrine and systematic theology may be the best way to build unity across the denominations of Christendom. If we begin from fundamental principles on which all are agreed, we can proceed to a fresh examination of the ways in which the different strands of theology have developed. In this way it may be possible to isolate the causes of particular divisions and even to heal them. By contrast, a non-dogmatic ecumenism, which emphasizes friendly co-operation and puts doctrinal differences to one side, is liable to suffer a rude awakening when serious proposals for ecclesiastical reunion are made. Then the cracks which have been papered over by diplomacy will reappear and destroy the work of reconciliation. The failure of recent Church unity schemes should be a reminder and a warning that lasting fellowship can only be built on a foundation of agreed principles, a common confession of Christian truth.

The argument that doctrinal differences invalidate dogmatic thought as the appropriate means of expressing biblical truth is a weak one and bound to fail, if only because the advocates of a non-dogmatic religion are obliged to put their case in terms of propositional logic. Much more serious is the charge that this kind of logical discourse is inappropriate or inadequate to convey truth of a religious nature. Those who reject the metaphysical altogether will naturally laugh at Christian claims to make pronouncements about a God who by definition cannot be known; but although scientific atheism of this type is fairly widespread today, its very crudeness and sterility as a philosophy render it less serious as a challenge to religious belief than might be thought. Where it was imposed by force, as in Communist countries, it failed to carry conviction, and underground religious revivals became a standard feature in Marxist societies, long before they finally collapsed.

More subtle and more serious is the compromise solution characteristic of liberal humanism in the West. This accepts that propositional logic must be restricted to the scientific domain, and to that extent rules out religious dogmatism. At the same time it is prepared to admit the possibility of non-rational experience, thereby opening the door to religious mysticism. What it cannot accept is the traditional Christian claim that the same logical process used in the natural sciences may be applied to theology as well. In other words, it refuses to accept that theology is a science in its own right, whose fundamental data are found in the biblical revelation.

Various attempts have been made in modern times to overcome this prejudice. In Roman Catholic circles there was a revival of the natural theology of Thomas Aquinas (1226-1274). Neothomism sought to bring back the principle of analogy as a means of demonstrating the existence and nature of God. Analogy involves taking examples from the natural world, *e.g.* the existence of parent-child relationships, and extrapolating from them a universal principle of relationship inherent in the universe. According to this way of thinking, basic reality must contain within itself every principle observable in the natural world. Putting it the other way round, the creature gives some clue as to the nature of the Creator. From this, exponents of neothomism have sought to develop a complete natural theology to explain even such things as the doctrine of the Trinity.

Natural theology is a bold attempt to bridge the gap between the physical and the metaphysical, but it is open to serious objections. For a start, it is by no means obvious that a creature must reflect the nature of his Creator. Man can make a computer, but he can also make a rubbish heap. Which of these reveals his nature? Even if a computer might legitimately require the creative power of a rational mind, there is no evidence that the being which made it necessarily possesses moral qualities, for example. Logically speaking, what is true of man's work in relation to man may also be true of God's work in relation to God. There is no logical reason why man must *reflect* the divine being; the view that he is created in the image and likeness of God is a datum of revelation which cannot be tested by scientific means. Then again, there is no guarantee that this method will produce an accurate picture of the God of the Bible. Even if a capacity for relationship is required by analogy with humanity, it does not automatically follow that there is a Godhead of three Persons, all of whom are described as being masculine!

Natural theology has made some impact in Protestant circles, but it was severely attacked by Karl Barth and has never been very widespread. Protestant theology is by definition a theology of revelation, which at the most basic level is preoccupied with the question of whether or nor God can speak to mankind in terms which can be regarded as valid at the level of human thought and experience. Protestants are certainly not the only Christians to believe in propositional revelation (Roman Catholics and Orthodox share this belief), but they are unique in making it the *sole ground* of a dogmatic theology.

Maintaining this claim means asserting that man as a creature has a spiritual dimension to his being which sets him apart from the rest of creation and unites him to God. In the Bible this is the fundamental characteristic of Adam, who was created 'in the image and likeness of God'. In classical orthodoxy it is described by the term *Person*, which belongs to both God and man, but not to any non-spiritual being. This word does not occur in the Bible itself, but it serves as a common term for the image of God, the spiritual character of man and the ability to enter into relationship with others who share spiritual qualities, which may be either good or evil, though they are never morally neutral.

It also means asserting that the unity of man as a creature makes it inevitable that this spiritual quality will be active in every aspect of his nature. The human mind may be no more than a brain, subject to the laws of decay in the physical world, but its functioning is constantly subject to the working of spiritual powers. The two must be distinguished – a brilliant intellectual is not necessarily close to God, any more than a mentally handicapped person is for that reason cut off from him. Confusion at this point is fatal and must never be pushed to the point of complete separation. The mind of man cannot be cut off from the workings of spiritual forces, any more than the latter can be divorced from the intellect's capacity for theoretical thought.

The fundamental assertion of the Bible is that God can and does speak to mankind in a way which enables us to make an intelligent response. God and man are not so much cut off from each other by their mutually incompatible natures as united by spiritual characteristics which make communion between them possible. The need of all mankind to find a purpose in existence, to create a metaphysic, is the testimony of nature to this fundamental reality. The Christian revelation is God's answer to this need, fulfilling and replacing the aspirations half-hidden in the mythologies and cosmologies of the world. In this sense it is related to them by a kind of generic affinity, but at the same time it is radically different. The message of the Bible is a message of spiritual truth addressed to the human mind. Dogmatic definitions of its content are not an aberration, but the logical outcome of the process of revelation itself. Salvation for the whole man cannot bypass the mind, but must use it for the powerful weapon which it is.

Properly understood in this way, Christian dogmatism is the greatest force for freedom which mankind has ever known. By claiming the mind for God, dogmatism shatters the bounds of the natural world which imprison the creative imagination and distort scientific analysis. It makes a relapse into sentimentality and vagueness in the name of religion impossible. It attacks the philosophies of the world and denies the claims of atheistic and amoral logic to rule the lives of men. Dogmatism abhors indifference and agnosticism, and demands considered commitment from those who would follow Christ. The early centuries of the Christian Church were a time of great hardship for those who followed the way of the cross. Christians had little cause to indulge in activities which might sidetrack them in their race for the prize of eternal salvation. Yet it was in those very centuries that the dogmatic foundation of Christian theology was laid, to be built upon later in the great struggle against paganism and Greek philosophy. Today, a dispirited and non-dogmatic Church is in retreat everywhere in the Western world. It is time we looked again at our heritage and re-examined our attitudes toward it, so that we too, like our forefathers in the faith, may bear a true witness to the God who has spoken to mankind and sent his Son into the world to save us from our sins.

2

The Canon of Scripture and Christian Doctrine

We have seen from our brief survey of the leading trends in modern theological thought that there is a strong tendency to distinguish and even to divorce Scripture from the dogmatic tradition of the Church. The latter may be accepted as a legitimate development or criticized as a corruption of the faith, but either way it led to something essentially *different* from the Bible.

This difference is seen partly as one of style and partly as one of content. Dogmatics has occasionally gone beyond (and therefore away from) Scripture, either by canonizing beliefs which have no biblical basis, *e.g.* the immaculate conception of the Virgin Mary, or by attempting a rigid systematization which squeezes Scripture into a particular mould which does not quite fit. This charge is frequently laid, for example, at the door of the English Puritans, whose theology sometimes tended towards legalism and towards causing division in the Church. More recently, the disciplines of anthropology, comparative religion, and literary analysis have combined to raise the question of style, or genre in the Bible. Scripture is seen to belong to a pre-critical stage of human thought in which science and myth blended without conscious distinction, whereas classical dogmatics is an attempt to analyse these data, albeit on the (false) assumption that the text may be treated as scientific history.

Defenders of Christian orthodoxy cannot accept such interpretations. It is axiomatic to the whole concept of 'right belief' that propositional statements can be made concerning the teaching of the Bible and that these statements can be arranged in a way which is coherent, comprehensive and internally consistent. Systematic theology is the exposition of the core of common teaching which gives the Bible its unity.

No-one would deny that systematization can be pushed too far, or that doctrinal statements can be made without sufficient evidence.

Nor is it possible to deny that a particular doctrine may conceivably represent only one aspect of biblical teaching and be framed in such a way that it effectively denies some other truth. A good example of this would be the statement that God is love, if this is then interpreted to mean that God is unable to punish the wicked by eternal damnation. The orthodox theologian recognizes the strength of such objections to the framing of dogmatic *statements*, but he insists that they highlight abuses which do not invalidate the dogmatic *method*. On the contrary, they are a constant challenge to the systematic theologian to ensure that his statements and constructions have the firmest possible foundation in Scripture, so that they may serve their purpose of illuminating the text without distorting it.

Bible and canon

This task has been made more difficult by the modern distinction between systematic theology and biblical studies. This distinction has now been pressed to such extremes that Old and New Testament scholars can appear to be exponents of comparative religion in their treatment of different strands *within* the canonical texts. Protests against over-analysis of this kind have not proved very effective and many scholars are at a loss to explain how the Bible came to be regarded as a single book, or even how parts of it like Isaiah came to be accepted as the work of a single author!

These questions are of fundamental importance to the dogmatician because they determine his approach to the source material. If the canonical texts are not all equally trustworthy or if parts must be relegated to a second tier of validity (thereby creating a canon within the canon), the theologian can hardly feel free to use the texts indiscriminately. Likewise, if it can be shown that data supporting an incarnational Christology are late additions to the primitive core, he will be under considerable pressure to minimize such a concept in his thinking, or even to delete it entirely.

Against such tendencies, the orthodox theologian must argue from the *canon* of Scripture, claiming that it establishes the normative bounds of the source material for the construction of a systematic theology. It does not necessarily mean that all parts of the canon have the same function in this regard, nor does it remove the need for careful exegesis of the text. But it does say that certain documents, whatever theories one might entertain as to their authorship and composition, constitute the fundamental data of the Christian faith, and that no amount of criticism can overturn this basic fact.

This argument has been strongly advocated by Brevard Childs, whose massive *Introduction to the Old Testament as Scripture* is a scholarly plea for the importance of the underlying unity of the textual corpus against the fissiparous tendencies of modern critical analysis. A similar line was also taken by Donald Guthrie in his *New Testament Theology*. Like Childs, Guthrie argued that the unity of Scripture is ultimately more important than its internal diversity, and he exposed the overemphasis on literary analysis which has broken the text up into numerous strands and schools of thought. A little more attention to context and greater allowance for the creative freedom of the writer would produce very different results, argued Guthrie, and differences of emphasis seldom, if ever, reach the point where they are mutually incompatible.

How legitimate is this emphasis on the canonical tradition as normative for our understanding of what Scripture is? Roman Catholic scholars have sometimes pointed out that it tends to undermine the Protestant emphasis on the sufficiency of Scripture, since it makes the extent of the sufficient texts dependent on the authority of ecclesiastical tradition. How fair is this claim?

In favour of the canonical approach is the indisputable fact that the Scriptures have come down to us in this form from earliest times. In both Testaments there have been queries about certain books and portions of books, but there has never been any hint of making a collection of books from scratch. The only question has been which books should be added to, or separated from, the core material, and on what grounds.

The Old Testament canon

In the case of the Old Testament, the core is the Torah, or the Five Books of Moses, to which Joshua has sometimes been added. The other books, grouped into Prophets and the Writings, are built around this core and depend on it. Scholarly research has confirmed this in remarkable ways, notably in the recognition that the historical books of the Old Testament, which everyone recognizes are the most likely to contain eye-witness accounts of the events they describe, are dependent on Deuteronomy for their emphasis and general orientation.

This is very important from the standpoint of the canon. It reinforces the belief that these books were composed and recognized as authoritative because they were seen to serve the religious tradition already laid down in the Torah. We have no way of knowing the precise details of this process, but two things seem reasonably clear. There was never a council of Jewish leaders called to establish the authority of particular books, nor was there resistance among the Jews to an expansion of the basic Torah. The Five Books of Moses have always held a special place within Judaism, but not to the exclusion of the rest of the Old Testament, which Jews regard as a single collection (the Tanach) and sometimes even refer to collectively as Torah.

This does not mean that there are no difficulties in the tradition of the Old Testament canon. On the contrary, there are several books which to this day have remained on the edge of Scripture, and at least three canonical books (Ecclesiastes, Song of Solomon, Esther) were still being disputed in the time of Jesus. Some books, like Esther and Daniel, had additional portions which were not recognized by the Jews but which crept into the Greek versions of the text. They had been added for edification, which was a common practice of the time, but were not read in the synagogue. Still other books, like Tobit, Judith, Wisdom, Ecclesiasticus and the two Books of the Maccabees, were customarily linked to the canon, especially in the manuscripts of the Greek Septuagint (c. 200 BC), though their status remained unclear.

For Christians the problem arose when these books came to be regarded as part of the Old Testament. The Church used only Greek translations of the original text, and hardly anyone was competent in Hebrew. Those who were, like Origen, noticed the problem and tried to grapple with it, though without lasting success. The so-called deutero-canonical, or apocryphal, books became embedded in the canon and remained there, largely undisturbed, until the fourth century.

Trouble arose only when Damasus, bishop of Rome, asked Jerome to make an official translation of the Bible into Latin. Jerome took the trouble to learn Hebrew, and in the process discovered that the original text was both shorter and occasionally different from the Septuagint, which had been in use for centuries. As a scholar he seized on this discovery, and maintained that the Latin text should be based on the Hebrew original. It must be said that he was also motivated by

a certain Roman chauvinism which made him somewhat antipathetic
to things Greek.

Jerome's views caused a sensation not unlike the reaction provoked
by the higher criticism in the nineteenth-century. The Bible was under
attack from a scholar who appeared to be a latter-day Judaizer! The
cause of tradition was taken up by Augustine, who knew no Hebrew
and surprisingly little Greek, but who possessed the finest theological
mind of his age. Augustine pointed out that the Septuagint was the
Church's Scripture, used as such by the Apostles themselves. Most
of the quotations in the New Testament are taken from it, including
not a few which differ from the Hebrew original. Since the New
Testament was the Word of God and in matters of controversy was to
be preferred to the Old Testament which was a partial and incomplete
revelation, it was clear to Augustine that the translators of the
Septuagint were as inspired as the original authors! His views prevailed
and the medieval Church continued to regard the Apocrypha as an
integral part of the Old Testament.

The matter raised its head again at the Reformation, when the
ancient conflict between the scholar and the theologian was resolved
by recognizing each man's contribution for what it was. The work of
the Reformers is an interesting blend of Jerome's scholarship and
Augustine's theology, tempered by the circumstances and learning
of the sixteenth-century. Even the Roman Catholic Church is now
obliged to admit that the apocryphal books are deutero-canonical,
though officially it still holds to the decree of the fourth session of the
Council of Trent (8 April 1546), according to which all the apocryphal
books are included in the Old Testament canon. The Reformers
satisfied themselves that the New Testament never quotes one of these
books directly, and gives no indication that they possess any authority.
The use of the Septuagint is more problematic, however, and the whole
question of the relationship between the Testaments has become one
of the major areas of controversy in modern biblical studies.

The New Testament canon

In comparison with this, the New Testament canon presents relatively
few difficulties. Partly this is because it is much shorter than the Old
Testament and more compact. It would not have been impossible for
a man who had known Jesus in the flesh to have read the entire New

Testament before his death; John Robinson argues, in *Redating the New Testament*, that the entire corpus was in existence by AD 70. Partly also it is because all branches of the Christian Church accept the same 27 books.

There was a time when some of these were not universally received as Scripture. We know that Hebrews, 2 Peter and Revelation in particular suffered from uncertainty about their apostolic origin. Eventually it was decided that Hebrews was written by Paul, 2 Peter by Peter, and Revelation by the apostle John, though today Hebrews is universally regarded as anonymous (as it was by the Geneva Bible of 1560) and the other two are widely contested. James, Jude, 2 John and 3 John were also slow to gain universal recognition, though the majority of churches accepted them from the beginning.

When the New Testament as a collection of books first made its appearance is unknown, as is the date when it was first recognized as Scripture on a par with the Old Testament. The first list of books which corresponds exactly with our New Testament dates from the fourth century, but a canon was certainly in existence long before that. 2 Peter 3:15-16 refers to the letters of Paul as Scripture and places them within a wider canon, though we do not know whether the Gospels or other New Testament books would have been included in this. This fact is used by many scholars as evidence that 2 Peter is late in date, but even if was written about AD 140, it would still be the earliest indication that the apostolic writings had canonical status. On the other hand, if 2 Peter is the work of the apostle himself, as scholars like Michael Green and Donald Guthrie believe, or of one of his immediate circle, as John Robinson argues, the evidence goes right back to the lifetime of Paul.

External evidence for a New Testament canon is scarce before the end of the second century. Justin Martyr (100-156) does not appear to have recognized it, though he used the Synoptics and he may have made limited use of John's Gospel. In part this could be explained by the fact that his work was mainly apologetic and directed towards Hellenized Jews and pagan Romans who would not have accepted the apostolic writings as Scripture. Much the same could be said for other early writers, like Ignatius of Antioch and Athenagoras of Athens, though difficulties arise when there is no reference to these writings in letters addressed primarily to Christians. The immediate successors of the Apostles carried on their tradition of writing letters to the churches, and this practice did not die out until about 150. These letters are comparable to those written by the Apostles themselves and speak with a similar tone of authority, yet they were never regarded as canonical in the way the apostolic letters were.

Why was this? It seems that the Church reached a major turning-point in its history about 150. It had already faced the challenge of Marcion (c. 144) who had denied the authority of the Old Testament and tried to expunge all Jewish tendencies from the New. This in itself indicates that a New Testament canon of sorts must have been in existence by 140 at the latest, and it was probably considerably older, if Marcion could dare to exalt it over previously recognized texts. About the same time a Syrian Christian known to us as Tatian was attempting to harmonize the four Gospels in parallel columns. This work, known as the *Diatessaron*, indicates that the Gospels were recognized as authoritative and that a need was felt to iron out apparent discrepancies among them. The search for consistency would probably not have been carried this far if no canonical authority attached to the texts concerned. Finally about 180-200 Irenaeus and then Tertullian refer quite happily to the New Testament as Scripture and appear to treat the canon as closed, at least in principle. Tertullian may have recognized the sayings of Montanus (c.171) as revealed by God, and he quotes them as authoritative; but he never goes so far as to put them on exactly the same plane as the New Testament writings, from which he quotes extensively. Indeed, the only books of which he may have been ignorant are 2 and 3 John, though their absence from his writings may be due to their extreme brevity.

It is thus possible to say with certainty that the New Testament canon was recognized and in use by the end of the second century. Moreover, although its earlier history is obscure, the evidence which does exist points to canonical acceptance of the Gospels and Paul's Epistles long before this date. The year 150 marks a crucial turning-point, in that it represents the end of the apostolic age. Until then there were people in places of authority who had known at least one of the Apostles personally and who had received instruction directly from them. After that, the teaching was second-hand and the need for a recognized canon became much more pressing. It was no longer possible to carry on the work of the Apostles in an unselfconscious way, and the appearance of false Gospels and the like made discrimination essential. The emergence of the canon in a formal sense was the Church's answer to changing circumstances. It was not a break with previous practice but an attempt to ensure that traditional beliefs and practices would continue unhindered by novel ideas masquerading as apostolic.

Canon and Church

Who made these decisions and on what grounds? Here we enter a minefield of controversy which goes back at least to the Reformation. Roman Catholics (and Eastern Orthodox) believe that the Church, acting through its bishops and synods, fixed the canon. There is no doubt that there is some truth in this assertion, since the precise limits of the New Testament were in dispute for some centuries and common agreement of this kind was the only possible answer.

Unfortunately, however, Catholics and Orthodox infer from this that the Church has the power to determine the contents of Scripture and interpret its meaning. Protestants have traditionally disagreed with this by claiming that the Church recognized the books which ought to belong to the canon and accepted their authority as normative for its faith and practice. The Bible is self-interpreting, not in the sense that everything it says is perfectly clear to everybody, but in the sense that the clearer passages provide the context for interpreting the more obscure parts, on the assumption that the Bible is basically one book with one world-view and one message.

One of the ironies of modern scholarship is that although it has been carried out largely by Protestants, many of whom have worked with a strong anti-Catholic bias, the conclusions they have reached favour the traditional Catholic view much more than the traditional Protestant one. The idea of fundamental unity in Scripture is scarcely taken seriously among Protestant scholars of the liberal type, and the notion that the New Testament is a collection of insights and recollections of the first Christians is very popular. Jesus in particular is seldom portrayed as an original teacher in his own right. It is much more usual for him to be regarded as the object of the Church's veneration which has created a religious Christ only partially connected to the historical Jesus. Roman Catholics are certainly not happy with the findings of liberal scholarship, but they have seized on the emphasis on the Church as a creative source of Scripture to bolster their own position.

An honest look at the situation in the late first and early second centuries reveals a rather different picture from the one painted above. Much of the detail is obscure of course, but some salient features are reasonably clear. First, there was never a council which debated the content of the New Testament canon until the late fourth century, by which time its broad lines had long been settled. No ancient writer ever suggests that the Church's reception of the canonical books was due to anything other than their intrinsic value as apostolic documents. Second, there is no indication that the canon represents a compromise between different schools of thought or the victory of one school over another. The idea that there was a Pauline circle and a Johannine circle of thought, each of which regarded its own texts as fundamental and used them to determine the validity of the rest, cannot be sustained from the available evidence. It belongs to the hypothetical universe of critical New Testament scholarship rather than to the history of the Early Church. Such disputes as did arise had nothing to do with 'Paul vs. John', nor were they connected with anything remotely like a struggle between 'Early Catholicism' and a primitive, 'charismatic' Church.

The criterion of acceptability, on which all were agreed, was *apostolicity*. The role of the Apostles as teachers of the Church was recognized from the start, as we can see from the career of Paul. Shortly after his conversion he made contact with Peter, James and John at Jerusalem, and it was their acceptance of him as their equal which certified his claim to be an apostle. Even so, it remained in some dispute because of its apparent irregularity, and we know that Paul was attacked on these very grounds. The controversy, which he alludes to in 1 Corinthians 9, shows how important it was to the early Christians that their teachers should have impeccable credentials. It is, therefore, not surprising that the Apostles' own writings should be regarded as supremely authoritative. In 1 Corinthians 7, Paul even goes so far as to make pronouncements on Christian marriage without a direct command from the Lord, but he justifies this by saying that he has the Spirit of God (7:40). We are left to conclude that this is sufficient; his commission as an apostle allows him to teach – a view which evidently was accepted by the Church.

Matters were slightly more complicated in the case of non-apostolic books. These include at least two Gospels (Mark and Luke), Acts, Hebrews, James and possibly Revelation. We have already seen that controversy lingered about the latter for a long time, and that the question of authorship was the major point at issue. In the end it was agreed that a book could be admitted if its teaching had apostolic authority and its author was a close associate of one or more of the Apostles. Mark was said to have written down the reminiscences of Peter, Luke was a close associate of Paul, as was the writer to the Hebrews, and Revelation was ascribed to John the Evangelist. No vote was taken, nor pronouncement made, to this effect; once more, the weight of external testimony and the fact that the vast majority of Christians had always accepted them stilled the opposition, which in any case had never been very vociferous. The consensus of opinion is perhaps best indicated by the fact that nobody has ever disputed it. Even Luther, who had serious reservations about Hebrews, James, Jude and Revelation, partly because they had been queried in ancient times, managed to accept them.

The closing of the canon requires some comment, because it raises another bone of contention, that of apostolic succession. Roman Catholics believe that the Pope, as Bishop of Rome, is the living counterpart of Peter, and they invest him with the same apostolic authority as Peter supposedly had. In particular, this is meant to give the Pope the right to pronounce on doctrine and even to formulate dogmas which have no scriptural support. If Peter could speak with the authority of the Word of God, the Pope must also be able to do so. To be fair, this extreme view of papal authority, though official, is not widely or enthusiastically supported today even among loyal Roman Catholics. Nevertheless, the concept of an apostolic succession remains alive and separates them from Protestants and (to a lesser extent) from the Eastern Orthodox as well.

In favour of a doctrine of apostolic succession it can be said that the Apostles ordained men to succeed them in the care of churches. Paul left elders behind in the churches he founded, and both Timothy and Titus were specially commissioned to carry on his work. At the same time, their commission was to guard the deposit, to hold fast the form of sound words which they had received from Paul (2 Timothy 1:13-14). There is no suggestion of ongoing revelation, and this was quickly recognized in the Church itself. The second-generation leadership – Clement, Ignatius and others – continued the apostolic *style* to some extent, but they never claimed, nor were they given apostolic *authority*. Modern scholars have frequently cited the Pastoral Epistles as evidence of a hardening of the arteries in the life of the early Christian communities. Perhaps they would be nearer the mark if they recognized that here we find the apostolic understanding of the future teaching and ministry of the Church. From the age of revelation the Church was passing to the age of defence and confirmation of the gospel – a new situation demanding new skills and attitudes, but one in which in terms of faith and doctrine the Church aimed to remain in the strictest continuity with apostolic times.

The fixing of the canon of Scripture was a long, slow process, but the end result is a remarkable consensus. The extent of the New Testament is universally agreed, as are the 39 books of the Hebrew (and Protestant) Old Testament.

The so-called apocryphal or deutero- canonical books are generally not used to establish points of doctrine. No Christian doctrine depends on their witness alone, though it has often been pointed out that some New Testament ideas, like the resurrection of the body, appear in them much more explicitly than anywhere in the Hebrew canon. Students of the history of religion are thus inclined to regard these books, most of which date from the inter-testamental period, as a kind of bridge between Israelite faith and Christianity. Some even conclude from this that the early Christians did little more than create a new synthesis out of post-exilic Jewish ideas.

It should be said immediately that in earlier times *nobody* – certainly no Christians and almost certainly no Jews – ever regarded the deutero-canonical books in this way. Traditional theology on all sides has treated Scripture as a unit in which all the parts are of equal value and authority in questions of doctrine. The idea of a development was never seriously entertained, not even by Christians seeking to justify the claims of Christ and the consequent rupture with Judaism. For them everything revealed in the New Testament was already contained in the Old, and even the Apostles themselves regarded much of their teaching as primarily expository. That is to say, they applied their understanding of Christ to the Old Testament, which for them was simply 'Scripture', and claimed that he was the hermeneutical key to understanding the text. The difference between Christians and Jews is thus not a question of the canon, but of its *interpretation*.

An enormous amount has been written on the question of biblical interpretation, or hermeneutics, from almost every angle and embracing most points of view. It is impossible to do justice, in a paragraph or two, to all the literary, historical, philosophical and religious theories which have been advanced to explain either particular passages of Scripture or the existence of a sacred text in the first place. Yet some attempt must be made to grapple with the problem, since the interpretation of the Bible is crucial to both the form and the content of a systematic theology. For that purpose, the issue needs to be looked at under three separate headings.

The interpretation of the Old Testament

First comes the meaning of the Old Testament. The early Christians accepted the Jewish Scriptures as divinely inspired, but interpreted them in a completely different way. They did not regard the Old Testament as a prelude to Christianity, which the new revelation in Christ augmented or displaced. The only Christian who said anything like this was Marcion (d. c.144), who tried to expunge the New Testament of all reference to the Jews on the ground that the Jewish God was an inferior being to the God of Jesus Christ, and therefore did not deserve Christian worship. Christians generally believed that the Old Testament spoke about Jesus Christ, not merely prophetically but in types and allegories which the Holy Spirit revealed to Christians.

Where did this idea come from? According to the Gospels, it was initially part of the teaching of Jesus himself. His words about 'fulfilling the law and the prophets', his freedom in interpreting the Ten Commandments, his claim that a true understanding of Moses would have led the Jews to be his disciples, and above all his exposition of the Scriptures to the men on the road to Emmaus, all point in this direction. Moreover, it should be made clear that Jesus put as much emphasis on *himself* as he did on his *mission*. This may seem like a small point, but it is crucial in modern New Testament interpretation. Whatever role Jesus may have been playing in the unfolding drama of salvation history, there can be no doubt that he realized that what he did depended on who he was, and that he went to the Scriptures for support on this point as much as any other.

What Jesus taught was taken up by Paul and the other apostles as a central ingredient in their proclamation. The Jews could not understand the Scriptures because their faces were veiled (2 Corinthians 3:13-16); in other words, they were blind to the truth which the Scriptures contained. Paul claimed that they had made the law an end in itself, with the tragic result that what should have been a living witness to Christ had become a barren and lifeless religion, a form of slavery instead of freedom.

The implications of this teaching need to be firmly grasped if we are to understand what the Christian claim really is. In contrasting the law with the gospel, Paul was not drawing a historical lesson of promise and fulfilment, nor was he saying that the latter had supplanted the former. The key to his mind at this point is the understanding that what he was really getting at was the *attitude* of the Jews to their sacred texts.

It was this more than anything else which divided them from Christians. For the Jews, the law was an external code, but for Christians it had become an internal principle of life in the Spirit. Whereas the Jews continued to explore and extend the law as a means of achieving righteousness, as well as separation from the rest of the world, Christians found themselves forced, in the power of the Holy Spirit, to break down the old barriers and preach God's free gift of forgiveness in Jesus Christ to all people everywhere. Without Christ, so radical a change of direction would hardly have been conceivable. He not only sent his followers off in a new direction, but changed their whole way of reading the Scriptures. This was apparent immediately, and it is highly significant that it was the nature of their expository preaching which first alerted the Jews to the radical message of both Jesus and his disciples.

From this basic principle we can understand the motivation behind the Christological exposition of the Old Testament which we find in the Gospels and Epistles. It is surely mistaken to link this too closely to rabbinical exegesis or to develop theories as to which texts were interpreted in this way and why they were chosen in preference to others. This kind of thinking betrays a narrowly analytical mind working from hindsight and trying to figure out a system which the early Christians followed, consciously or otherwise. In this connection, it must be said that most of the speculation known as source and redaction criticism supposes a mental attitude which is quite improbable. However the Evangelists set about their work, they certainly did *not* reach for the scissors and paste, chopping up and rearranging fragmentary sayings of Jesus culled from earlier documents and oral tradition. As C.S. Lewis pointed out, creative literature of the power the Gospels have always exercised on the minds of men is not produced in such a mechanical way as this.

In all probability, the first Christians looked on *every* part of Scripture as Christological, and were prepared to see Christ in it by whatever exegetical means would produce the desired result. It did not worry them if the literal meaning of the text seemed somewhat distant from this concern, since in that case it was plain that the passage in question contained a revelation of Christ which was more difficult to grasp than simpler texts.

When the writer to the Hebrews complained that his readers had not advanced beyond the milk of the gospel to the meat of the Word, he almost certainly meant just this. The Christians to whom he was writing had mastered the basic principles of a Christological hermeneutic but had not penetrated its depths. The meaning of Melchizedek, for example, had escaped them, yet it was essential to understand Christ's atoning work as both priest and victim. It was to supply this lack that the Epistle was written. Chapter eleven is a checklist of Old Testament characters, all of whom could be used to illustrate the same basic principles. No doubt the author did this himself when preaching, just as his countless expositors have done ever since.

Modern critical scholarship, with its commitment to the historical perspective, cuts right across the Christian interpretation of the Old Testament, and raises the hermeneutical question in a way which has not happened since the time of Marcion. According to historical criticism, any specifically Christological interpretation of the Old Testament is necessarily from hindsight. The original writers could not have known to what use their texts would later be put, nor is it very likely that they intended anything remotely resembling what later occurred. The Law and the Prophets were written for the circumstances of the time and reflect the thinking of Israel at particular moments in its history. The exodus and the exile weighed more heavily with them than a future Messiah, and the concept of God becoming man was quite beyond them.

This approach to the text has had a devastating effect. At the level of textual criticism it has led to the dismembering of books like Isaiah and Zechariah, for which there is scant internal support. At a deeper level, it has cut the Old Testament off from the Church by making it appear as the first stage in a religious development which has now been superseded. As such, the Old Testament retains its historic interest and value, but it is no longer the Word of God for today's Christians, many of whom have not even read it through.

Today the historical approach is so firmly anchored in critical research that anything else appears almost inconceivable. Yet the systematic theologian must challenge it, because it calls into question the teaching of Christ and the validity of the New Testament. It is simply not possible to worship Jesus and regard the New Testament as God's Word if at the same time one denies the Christological interpretation of the Old Testament. The two go inseparably together, as Tertullian long ago demonstrated in his five books *Against Marcion*. We cannot have one without the other. Being a committed Christian demands a certain attitude towards the Old Testament Scriptures which has always been contested, first by Jews and then by rationalists, but which must be defended as an essential foundation of the Christian faith.

This can be done, first of all, by pointing out the limitations of the historical approach. We do not know, and can never hope to know for certain, what the original writers of Scripture intended. To presume to be able to read the author's mind from an examination of the text is a literary delusion of the first magnitude. What is more, students of literature like C.S. Lewis recognize this, and call it the *'intentional' fallacy*.

All we can legitimately go on is the text itself, the meaning of which has been determined as much by the use to which it has been put as by anything else. The idea that the documents of the Old Testament were primarily concerned with the immediate situation in which they were composed has a superficial validity, in the sense that the original readers must have made something of them; but to suppose that this exhausts their significance is ludicrous. What makes the Old Testament worth studying is the fact that it has demonstrated the power not only to survive but to dominate the lives of countless generations of men far removed from the original historical context. Under its hegemony a whole civilization has come into being, and missionary work is still winning converts to its teaching. Why is this? To speak of it as if it were no more than the collected remains of ancient Israel is to commit one of the grossest acts of philistinism in history, a fact which is readily recognized by literary critics.

Proper criticism of the Old Testament must rest on two fundamental principles, which are equally valid for other documents as well. First, a *manuscript is innocent until proved guilty*. If Isaiah comes to us as the work of an eighth-century BC prophet, that ascription must stand until and unless it can be convincingly demonstrated to be false. Had the book turned up for the first time in 1947 at Qumran, let us say, there might have been reason to suspect its authenticity, if only because it had not been brought into the open centuries ago. But a book which, as far as we know, has always been public, and whose author was perhaps the greatest of all the prophets, is so unlikely to be a forgery that the very notion borders on the incredible. Yet 'Second Isaiah' is now a well-established biblical writer, even though there is not a shred of hard evidence from any source to indicate that he ever existed. The whole theory is based on the assumption that much of Isaiah reflects the Babylonian exile and, therefore, cannot have been written 150 years before that date. On that slender basis, the witness of the entire manuscript tradition has been relegated to oblivion, which is surely one of the great scandals of modern biblical 'scholarship'.

Second, *a great text will survive any critic*. It is one of the tragedies of modern biblical scholarship that the pressure on scholars to produce original work has forced them either into obscure fields of research which have hitherto escaped serious investigation, or led them to rework familiar material from a new angle. In biblical studies the basic texts are so well known that genuine originality is most difficult to achieve. Yet the need to find something new to say is so pressing that the most improbable hypotheses are put forward to explain these documents, and theories thus developed are regarded as serious contributions to learning when they have not been properly examined in the light of other evidence in related fields. The classical historian, A. N. Sherwin-White, is not alone in expressing his amazement that biblical scholars could be so sceptical about their sources, and advance such improbable hypotheses about their origin and meaning. It is a common reaction among those who have studied the ancient world in any depth to think that most of what passes for textual analysis in the biblical field is more akin to scholarly mythology than it is to science.

More serious than this, however, is the ease with which the greatness of the text can be eclipsed by the shadow of criticism. It is all too easy for students to spend their time discussing various commentators and their theories, without ever really bothering to examine the text. Furthermore, very few commentators are truly expository in the sense of trying to elucidate the meaning of the text. Either they are too technical and abstruse, or they concentrate on general theories whose origins may have more to do with the so-called 'history of religions' than with the textual evidence itself. The question why such a compact set of documents should be given so much attention in the first place gets lost amid the clamour of rival theories and arguments.

Nevertheless, it is to this question that the Christian theologian presses for an answer. Was Jesus right to claim that the Old Testament spoke of him? Were the Apostles and their successors justified in their use of the Jewish Scriptures? Here the Christian must answer, Yes. Jesus made a shockingly radical claim about the Scriptures. Unlike other teachers either within or on the fringes of Judaism, he did not so much expound the text as appropriate it. The Jews were scandalized and rejected this claim, but Jesus justified it by rising from the dead and by sending the Holy Spirit to confirm the truth of what he said.

This second point is crucial. Calvin recognized that the ultimate criterion for interpretation is the inner witness of the Holy Spirit, and the same theme is found in the New Testament, both in John (*cf.* John 16) and in Paul (e.g. 1 Corinthians 2, *etc.*). The claims of Christ have been verified by the growth and expansion of the Church, by the power of Christianity to capture the hearts and minds of the most sophisticated as well as the most primitive of men. Judaism has never broken out of its ghetto. Islam is uncreative and even sterile, expanding as much by force as by persuasion but never developing a civilization of its own. Even the triumphs of the medieval Arabs were largely the work of Christian subject peoples in Egypt, Syria and Mesopotamia. When these converted to Islam in substantial numbers the *élan* was lost and decay set in. The great Eastern religions are similarly locked in a particular cultural setting from which they cannot emerge, in spite of their many spiritual achievements. Only Christianity has conquered on the strength of its own merits, and it alone is now capable of challenging everything from atheistic humanism to superstitious animism. What further proof is needed to satisfy the historian that the claims of Christ must be taken with the utmost seriousness?

The interpretation of the New Testament

A glance at history offers overwhelming support for the belief that Christ's interpretation of the Old Testament has carried more conviction over a longer period of time than has any rival view. This observation thus leads us naturally to the second part of our inquiry, which concerns the interpretation of the New Testament. The resources of literary, historical and theological criticism have not been spared in the investigation of these twenty-seven books; indeed all that was said above about Old Testament research could be multiplied several times over with respect to the New. There is certainly no comparable corpus of texts which has been studied as intensely as this one. To what effect?

On the one hand, New Testament scholarship tends to be more conservative in its findings, particularly at the textual level. The meaning of the words is clearer because we have a much better knowledge of Greek than of classical Hebrew, and the period during which the books were written was certainly less than a century, a fact which reduces the number of hypotheses available to the critic. Even so, there has been no consensus of opinion on the one crucial point – the relationship of Jesus and his teaching to the canonical text as we have it.

Most liberal scholars have assumed a religious development away from Jesus himself to a religion much more in tune with Greek philosophical ideas, though not identical with them. Jesus' own teaching, which in essence was a kind of spiritualized Judaism, is supposed to be contained (more or less obscured by the propaganda of the Evangelists) in the Synoptic Gospels. Paul subsequently develops this teaching in an anti-Jewish direction, making it more acceptable to the Gentiles. John goes even further than this and produces a Gospel which is almost a philosophical treatise. Later writers followed either a Pauline or a Johannine tendency and wrote under the name of one apostle or the other, leaving us the Pastoral Epistles, Hebrews and Revelation. The result is a picture something like the following. There are, or were, three main strands of early Christianity which can be defined as

> Palestinian Jewish (Jesus, Peter, James and Jude)
> Hellenistic Jewish (Paul, Hebrews)
> Hellenistic Gentile (John)

Of course a scheme as rigid as this cannot be applied in practice to the texts in their entirety. Matthew and Mark bridge the gap between Palestinian and Hellenistic Judaism, and Luke-Acts fits somewhere between Hellenstic Judaism and the Gentile world. John is not by any means purely Greek; many scholars have maintained that the Fourth

Gospel contains more authentic reminiscences of Jesus' early ministry than any other. Marcion chose to base his anti-Semitism on Luke rather than on John, and Revelation, which belongs to the Johannine corpus, can hardly be called a philosophical treatise in the style of Aristotle or Plato! Paul, too, is a more complex figure than this scheme allows. He wrote most of his letters before the Gospels were composed, which on the above reckoning would make the Gospels reactionary documents, retarding the evolution of Christianity by going back to Galilee. Of course, it can always be argued that the Evangelists were pre-empting the historical Jesus for their own ends, but the Gospels themselves are much too untidy to support such a theory in full. Jesus and his teaching somehow manage to come through in spite of all the supposed overlay.

Nevertheless, and in spite of all the reservations listed above, a threefold division of the kind just outlined has persisted in modern research. It is important, moreover, because Church history has also been interpreted according to this scheme. According to the mainstream of liberal biblical criticism, the historical development of theology centred on John and philosophical Christianity, which formed a kind of symbiosis with the 'early Catholicism' of Luke-Acts and the allegedly pseudo-Pauline corpus. Luther broke through this to the Paul of Romans, and established Protestantism on a Hellenistic Jewish base – closer to the Old Testament than Catholicism, yet still anti-Jewish. Israel was identified with the Church, and the religious experience of the Jews as the chosen people was simply appropriated by large numbers of Protestants. Modern scholarship has sought to go one better than Luther and take the Church back to Jesus himself. The only quarrel is whether this leaves us with an enlightened ethic based on a univerisalized, spiritual type of Judaism in which sacrificial love replaces burnt offerings, or with an apocalyptic, revolutionary code in permanent opposition to every kind of establishment. Both theories have had their advocates, and the fruits of each can be seen in the contemporary Church.

The dogmatic stance of traditional orthodoxy stands in stark contrast and open conflict with the above scheme and its results. Its basic principle makes this inevitable. Classical orthodoxy is synthetic and integrative in its approach to the New Testament, whereas modern criticism is analytic and divisive. For an orthodox theologian there is no conflict between John and Paul, still less between either of these and the teaching of Jesus himself. The New Testament is an authentic record of historical facts which can and must be seen in its entirety. The unity which governs it is sufficiently great to contain and reconcile any diversity which may appear.

In favour of this approach are the following considerations. First, from a literary point of view, the New Testament comes to us as the work of nine men who were close associates. It is always bound together as a single volume and is universally accepted as such. There is an *a priori* argument here for the principle of underlying unity.

Second, the period of composition is extremely short. Jesus died c.AD 30 and most of the New Testament – possibly, as John Robinson has argued, all of it – was in existence by AD 70. More radical scholars like James Dunn prefer a longer timetable, arguing that the Church cut its links with Judaism c.AD 80, after which there was a rapid development towards early Catholicism up to the end of the first century, which is as far as the New Testament takes us. Even so, we are dealing with a period of seventy years or so, which is well within the compass of a single lifetime. If it is true that John lived to the reign of Trajan (98-117), then he witnessed this development from beginning to end, as well as taking a considerable part in it himself.

One of John's disciples, Polycarp of Smyrna, was martyred in 156, having 'served Christ for eighty-six years'. We do not know the precise meaning of this. But if it means that he was eighty-six years old at the time of his death (and thus had been baptized in infancy as the child of Christian parents), he too would have witnessed the rapid development from 80 to 100 and taken part in its later stages. In this way, a living witness of the events would have been preserved up to and beyond the year 150, by which time the New Testament canon had already taken its basic shape. If the Church of this period had experienced the weeding-out process by which one, thoroughly Hellenized, interpretation of Christ became the standard orthodoxy from which any deviance was condemned, there ought to be some evidence of the struggle transmitted to us through these key figures. Where are the Jewish Christians, left behind by the alien tendencies which were supposedly creeping in? What about the Paulinists? The plain truth is that there is little trace of such organized groups. They simply did not exist, at least not in the way in which modern scholarship generally imagines them.

There is never any suggestion in any Christian writer of the first two centuries that the Church consisted of different theological schools which gradually coalesced into 'Catholicism' and forced out recalcitrants. Attempts to make the Montanists, who flourished as a sect in Asia Minor about 171, into the last of the charismatic, non-'Catholic' Christians are now known to be so wide of the mark that it is surprising to find anyone still entertaining the idea. Montanus was a visionary who prophesied the descent of the New Jerusalem and the ushering in of the reign of the Paraclete – both Johannine themes, which apparently caused some Church leaders in Asia Minor to question the authenticity of the Johannine corpus. But how could a sect, inspired by the most 'Hellenistic' part of the New Testament, be regarded as the last bastion of primitive, even Judaistic, Christianity? Such are the contradictions into which liberal scholarship falls when its theories are set in the wider context of the age which it is trying to describe.

The third factor which must be considered is the natural tendency of pluralistic groups to achieve conformity by splitting into their different components. One need only consider a modern movement like Communism, which has developed a sectarianism based on Trotsky, Mao, Lenin, *etc.*, each of which claims to be the authentic interpretation of Karl Marx. If early Christianity were in any way comparable, would it not be much more likely for the Paulinists, the Johannine circle and the like to have formed their own sects? The fact that the Church emerged as a single society, paying equal honour to all its apostles, is the best argument against primitive pluralism. Splits did occur, and there were rival groups of Christians in different places, but the church as a whole always maintained a sense of its own unity which could be tested and guaranteed by the consensus of the faithful throughout the world.

In sum, then, it can be said that the best argument against dividing the New Testament into its component parts is the fact that the Early Church did not think in that way. There is not a shred of evidence that the first Christians sought to pit one apostle against another by accepting only a part of the New Testament revelation. At Corinth there were factions of a sort, claiming a special link with Paul, Peter or Apollos, but we cannot deduce from that that there was open sectarianism in the church. Indeed, Paul counters such foolish behaviour by pointing out that *all* the Apostles are *equally* servants of Christ, so that to make such distinctions was a nonsense.

The Corinthian situation highlights another point which is of great importance in understanding the New Testament. Too often it is assumed that the text in its many parts must *reflect* the various elements in the Early Church, as if the Gospels (in particular) are really a kind of cumulative reflection on the life of Jesus, arrived at by some consensus among the conflicting groups which made up the Church. Such a theory is practically impossible on literary grounds, since works of genius do not appear as a result of compromises between warring factions. And the witness of Paul also tells against it.

There *was* great diversity in the Early Church, and there were many disagreements about what it meant to lead a Christian life in an essentially pagan society; but there is no sign anywhere that any kind of theological pluralism was tolerated. Those who differed from the Apostles were anathematised and excluded from the fellowship. From the start there was only one way and one recognized truth, however imprecisely it may have been formulated in the apostolic writings. When the Apostles disagreed with each other, as Peter and Paul did over the reception of Gentile converts (Acts 15), it was not a case of 'live and let live' in separate denominations. A council of the Apostles was called to debate the issue, and although a compromise solution was reached, all had to accept it. Furthermore, it was made clear that this compromise was made to soothe tender Jewish consciences. There is little evidence that its provisions were enforced for long, especially when there were no Hebrew Christians to take offence at Gentile behaviour.

There is, therefore, every reason, in orthodox eyes, to regard the unity of the New Testament and its continuity with the Old as fundamental principles to which elements of diversity must be related. When a discrepancy appears, one of two possibilities presents itself. Either it is due to an incomplete picture of the whole, or it is a matter of secondary importance, not binding on the Church as a fundamental belief. The purpose of dogmatic definition is to establish the framework which will define the limits of what is essential and put the isolated truths of Scripture in proper perspective, so as to avoid distortions and false emphases. Orthodox theologians would argue that the Bible itself makes this task necessary as a means to understand its message. Its ultimate judge is its ability to open the Scriptures in a deeper way to the believing Christian who needs them for a closer walk with God.

Scripture and theology

This brings us to the third and final point we must consider in relation to the interpretation of Scripture. Is it true that the New Testament invites us to engage in theological speculation and dogmatic construction? There are many who would argue that it does not. Protestantism, they say, maintains that the Scriptures contain everything necessary for salvation. They are the Word of God in a way that creeds and doctrinal statements are not. Christianity is the religion of a person and preaches a relationship with God based on mutual love. Yet doctrine sets up barriers and has caused untold harm to the body of Christ, by splitting it into countless fragments. 'The letter kills, but the Spirit gives life', a Pauline statement which some have taken to mean that the true Church consists of men and women who have shared a common experience, however they may choose to define it. Words are limited and limiting; only the power of the Spirit, moving beyond language into strange tongues or other forms of mystical experience, can authenticate Christian experience in a convincing way. These attitudes are widespread in the anti-intellectual climate of today, so much so that even those who held to traditional beliefs are reluctant to suggest that an understanding of Christian doctrine is an indispensable aid to learning from the Scriptures.

Modern thinking of this kind appears to be a long way from the historical liberalism of the nineteenth century, but in fact it is very closely linked to it. The great liberals also believed that religion was a matter of feeling rather than the intellect, and were prepared to accept the superstructure of Christian worship and doctrine as a channel along which these thoughts could be directed. They propounded, with great learning, a thesis which has now penetrated to the popular level and become very influential, even in conservative evangelical circles. Antidogmatism is a feature of the age we live in, and it affects us all whether we like it or not.

In response to this method, the orthodox theologian must say that it runs counter to the biblical witness to God and his saving work in Christ. The Bible is a revelation in *writing* – Scripture – and this fact is of supreme importance. Writing is fixed, objective, definable communication to an extent that no other means is. Of course it can be unclear; it may also be obscured or corrupted by faulty transmission. Textual criticism of the Bible has shown that this has sometimes been the case, and its task is to put right what has gone wrong. But the assumption on which textual criticism is based is that the original text *did* make sense, and that it is possible, given enough evidence, to recover that sense. It is a work of restoration similar to that carried out on old buildings and paintings. The underlying intelligible harmony is the incentive which gives textual criticism a purpose and a goal.

The task of the dogmatician is somewhat similar to that of the textual critic, but at a different level. When the two disciplines are functioning properly they feed each other in the accomplishment of their respective tasks. The textual critic is concerned with the detail of the documents in his care, whilst the dogmatician is concerned to elucidate the principles which govern the thought they contain and which led to their compilation in the form in which we now have them. Analytical studies of portions of the text are helpful only in so far as they reveal the underlying pattern which links the isolated unit to the wider whole. On its own, a verse or a chapter may be very interesting and even unique in its teaching and emphasis; but deprived of its context it loses its true meaning and is open to serious misinterpretation. It is this which is the bane of modern biblical studies, and which the science of dogmatics exists to correct.

It is true, of course, that the Bible is not a philosophical treatise, and that it deals with a great many things which most philosophers would regard as irrelevant, like genealogical tables and ceremonial laws of purification and sacrifice. The Bible has a much wider range than merely presenting a picture of the logical structure of reality. At the same time, however, this does not mean that it neglects the philosophical dimension, or fails to offer guidelines for understanding that are distinct from those of secular philosophy, consistent in themselves and compelling for those who would follow Christ. The fact that they are not set out in order does not mean that they are not there. The dogmatician's task is to lay bare the foundations on which the teaching of Scripture is built, both as an aid to Christian growth and as a means of evangelizing those who do not share the same principles.

A few examples must suffice to show how important this is. The Bible everywhere assumes the existence of God. This proposition is so obvious that it hardly needs stating, except that very few people in biblical times agreed with it! Either they were polytheists, for whom the term 'god' meant a spiritual force (but not necessarily the Supreme Being), or they were philosophical atheists who believed in a supreme

Reason or a first cause, but did not regard this as a personal, spiritual power which could be called 'God'. From the start, both Jews and Christians had to contend for the biblical notion of God against a world which rejected it.

But what *is* the biblical notion of God? Is the Bible monotheistic in the sense of teaching that there is only one God, or is it henotheistic, meaning that only one God should be worshipped, even though many may exist? What is the character of the biblical God? Is he personal or not? Is he a God of love, justice, wrath or what? All these elements are found in the Scriptures and used to describe the same Being. How is it that they fit together without a sense of contradiction? The answers to these questions are by no means obvious, but they must be found if Christianity is going to win and *retain* the allegiance of men and women.

Then again, it can be said that the Epistles of the New Testament are *ad hoc* compositions, designed to meet specific situations. They are not, and were never intended to be, manuals of theology. This is true, but so what? They may not be manuals of theology, but they very clearly operate on the assumption that the readers already possess a clear theological understanding. When Paul writes to correct or upbraid his congregations, he does so on the assumption that they have forgotten and turned away from his teaching. In some cases they have accepted the words but not drawn the logical conclusions for behaviour and worship. In this sense, the Epistles are supplements to a theological teaching which had been given orally and which is assumed in the documents we possess. It is the task of the dogmatician to uncover what the teaching was.

The relationship between the Bible and classical dogmatics is not simple, in the sense that the one does not simply contain the other, but in principle it is quite clear. Dogmatics is the study of the fundamental principles on which the teaching of Scripture is based *and which are necessary for a proper understanding of God's plan of salvation in Christ*. This last qualification is necessary, because there are aspects of biblical teaching which are *not* necessary for salvation. Some of these are clear and non-controversial, like the command to offer hospitality to strangers. Others are more difficult, and when attempts have been made to erect them into dogma, trouble and division has usually been the result.

This has been especially notorious in the field of church order.

The New Testament gives the strong impression that the churches founded by the Apostles were governed by presbyters (bishops) and deacons. The presbyters looked after spiritual affairs, whilst the deacons assisted them, dealing particularly with material needs. By the second century, the chief presbyter had become bishop over the rest, a development which has often been interpreted as necessary after the death of the Apostles, who had exercised this wider control. How the local congregations were related to one another we do not know, but they were certainly in close contact with each other, as Paul's letters indicate. It was also possible to take decisions, as at the Council of Antioch (Acts 15), which the entire Church would regard as binding.

The fledgling New Testament order developed in the course of time into the medieval system against which the Reformers revolted. All the churches of the Reformation recognized that the New Testament pattern had changed in the course of time. The Church of England accepted this, and retained the traditional church order in so far as it did not conflict with biblical principles. Others were more ambitious. Presbyterians were convinced that the New Testament enjoined a certain type of church government from which it was sinful to deviate. Others accepted this principle, but reached different conclusions from their reading of Scripture. As a result the Puritans in England found themselves at each others' throats, because they were all convinced that Scripture laid down as dogma something which was unclear in actual fact. Many of the divisions in English Protestantism stem from a failure to recognize that church order is not an essential part of the gospel.

Another obvious example of over-dogmatism is in the realm of sacramental practice. Should children be baptized? The New Testament is not clear on this point and it would appear that the issue was never raised. Christians have a long history of disagreement on the issue, the only solid result of which is that neither side in the debate can prove conclusively that it is right. When a particular line has been pressed, against scriptural testimony, it has usually resulted in division and bad feeling of a peculiarly ugly kind. On matters such as these, it is not only impossible but improper to be dogmatic. Nothing serves the cause of liberal religion more than a false application of theological principle, especially when it is accompanied by that curious lack of charity which convinced Christians can so often show to one another.

In evolving the dogmatic framework of the creeds, the councils and theologians of the ancient Church were obliged to concentrate on the fundamentals of the Christian faith in order to explain it to a hostile world and strengthen those converts whose intellectual outlook had been formed in an alien environment. Whether in the process they allowed that environment to obtrude on their thinking is a question we shall have to investigate with some care.

Their achievement, however, should not be underestimated. Whatever one may think of them today, the great creeds of Christendom established themselves as *the* authoritative expressions of biblical faith. Every Christian church accepts their teaching, explicitly or implicitly, in spite of all the criticisms which have been levelled against them. As such, their enduring power is unequalled by any subsequent theological thought. Thomas Aquinas, Luther, Calvin and Wesley belong to parts of the Church; the creeds, like the Scriptures themselves, are universal. How and why this came to be so is the theme of the succeeding chapters.

3

The Spread of the Gospel

From the point of view of a student of ancient religion, one of the great distinguishing marks of Christianity is its outgoing and remarkably successful missionary activity. Even sceptics who question the truth of its claims cannot deny that an obscure Jewish sect conquered the Roman Empire by the force of its message. Nor can they ignore the fact that this message was the promise of salvation from sin and damnation, given by Jesus Christ in his teaching and made effective by his work of atonement on the cross.

The message of salvation

Many books have been written to explain that a longing for salvation was characteristic of the world in which Christianity emerged. People had outgrown the folk religions of their native lands and had found the schools of Greek philosophy unsatisfying. More and more were turning to Persian or Egyptian mystery cults as a means of satisfying their spiritual hunger. Just as in recent years young people have hitchhiked to Kathmandu in search of enlightenment, earnest Greeks and Romans frequented the temples of Serapis or Mithras in the hope of finding some comfort for their inner longings. Even Judaism did not escape, and there were many foreigners – partially excluded and sometimes humiliated as 'Gentiles' – who sought moral purity and meaning in life from the law of Moses. Christianity met the needs of such people without imposing the restrictions and humiliations of Judaism, which is supposed to explain why it was able to 'capture the market' in religion!

This simple picture is now known to be untenable, but its assumptions are still commonly found in works of considerable learning. Lack of evidence makes it difficult to refute such an analysis in detail, and the obscurity which surrounds so much of the Early Church's growth can be used to support widely different hypotheses.

To assess the probability of a development like the one sketched above we can only return to the most basic principles of Christianity and work from there.

Serious students of religion will recognize at once that Christianity would never have got anywhere, indeed would never have emerged from Judaism, if it had not had something which the parent religion could not offer. This could not simply have been a breaking down of barriers between Jew and Gentile, for several reasons. Gentiles could observe the moral laws of Judaism without entering into its ceremonial aspects, and it appears that they did so without complaining. There is no evidence that they resented their exclusion from the nation of Israel. The first Christians were mostly Jews themselves, and they felt a strong compulsion to preach to their own people first. Indeed, some of them probably thought that the gospel was *only* for Jews, a feeling which would explain Peter's reluctance to visit Cornelius (Acts 10:14-15) and his later sympathies with 'Judaizing' elements (Galatians 2:11). Even Paul, who claimed to be the 'apostle to the Gentiles', based his missionary outreach on the synagogues of the Diaspora.

In such a context, the rise of Christianity can only be explained *vis-à-vis* the special claims of Judaism. A race which had clung to its ancestral faith despite every form of alien pressure, a nation which had even exchanged its sacred language (Hebrew) for two Gentile tongues (Aramaic and Greek) without abandoning its religious inheritance, would not easily be shifted to a new allegiance, especially if all that it promised was the dissolution of Israel in a kind of universalistic syncretism.

One of the distinguishing marks of Judaism was its belief in the efficacy of the work of atonement performed annually by the High Priest in the temple at Jerusalem. Even today, though the outward form has long since disappeared, Yom Kippur, or the Day of Atonement, is the most solemn day in the year for religious Jews. Other religions were capable of moral excellence, and it was not uncommon for high-minded pagans to regard Judaism as primitive and barbaric. This was the opinion of the Roman poet Horace, who may have known King Herod the Great personally, and it must have been a fairly common prejudice which we can discern in the contemptuous attitude of a man like Pontius Pilate. As for sacrifices, they were a universal feature of every ancient cult, so much so that some scholars have maintained that Christianity borrowed concepts of expiation and propitiation from pagan sources!

The only way large numbers of Jews could be persuaded to abandon their religion was by offering them something demonstrably better than what they had already. To do this, one of two approaches was possible. The Jews could perhaps have been persuaded to *reject* their faith in favour of something quite different, if it could be shown that another religion or philosophy was superior. Greek ideas came to the Jews with this claim, but they never made any serious impact because they had no effective substitute for the atonement. Jews could absorb Hellenism within their own traditions of law and wisdom without abandoning their ancient beliefs.

In the second century AD there were Christians who tried this approach. Marcion, who went to Rome from Pontus on the Black Sea sometime before 139, tried to abandon the Old Testament and expurgate the New of all reference to it. He was preaching at a time when Judaism, after the revolt of Bar-Kochba (AD 132-135), seemed to be on the point of extinction. The Roman Government had finally lost its patience, already somewhat thin after the Jewish revolt of AD 66-70, and was trying to expel the Jews from Palestine. In such a climate it must have seemed pointless to hang on to the remnants of a discredited religion, and the temptation to rid Christianity of its embarrassing family connections must have been strong.

Yet this did not happen. Furthermore, the opposition which Marcion encountered came not from Jewish Christians but from his fellow-Gentiles. Most of what we now know about him comes from five books written to refute his ideas by the Latin writer Tertullian (fl. c. 196–c. 212), who certainly was no friend of the Jews. Why? The reason is simple. Even when the Church had become largely Gentile in composition, it could not extricate itself from its Jewish roots. As a religion, Christianity was not and never had been a simple rejection of Mosaic law and practice.

The other possibility for a religion seeking to supplant Judaism was to *appropriate* it by demonstrating that it offered all that the temple worship could offer and much more besides. As a technique, appropriation is obviously more subtle than rejection. At the same time, it is also more difficult. In modern times it has been tried by a number of sects seeking to overthrow Christianity – Mormonism, Christian Science and so on – but, despite a certain power of persuasion, these sects cannot be said to have got very far. The main reason is that anyone who studies their origin discovers that the founders were highly unattractive figures with no special claim to found a religion apart from the ability to delude others as they had already deluded themselves.

The magnitude of the task facing a would-be deceiver or religious revolutionary in the time of Jesus should not be underestimated. Judaism could have been out-distanced only by the provision of an atoning sacrifice more efficacious than the one already being offered each year. It is not immediately clear that the victim of this sacrifice need have been anything more than a spotless lamb in the ancient Passover tradition. The attitude of both the Pharisees and the disciples as portrayed in the Gospels bears this out. When Jesus spoke of himself as the temple or foretold his death as the atoning victim, the reactions ranged from incomprehension to horror; but there is no indication that anyone took his words at face value and believed in him in this way.

Even more important from the Jewish angle were the credentials of the priest who purported to make the sacrifice. In terms of Mosaic law, Jesus the prophet and teacher from Galilee had no claim at all to such a dignity. Sacrifice was the privilege of the tribe of Levi, concentrated in the priesthood descended from Aaron. Jesus did not belong to this family and no claim was ever made to that effect. His lineage went back to David, which might have given him the right to claim quite a different inheritance – that of the Kingdom of Israel.

In fact, as the Gospels tell us, there *was* a great deal of speculation to that effect. Many Jews would have followed him, had he raised the banner of revolt, and probably nobody would have quarrelled with his messianic claims if he had driven out the Romans. But Jesus refused to play the part which popular legend and expectation tried to foist on him. Instead, he took the messianic promises of the Old Testament and joined them to the concept of an atoning sacrifice. Such a development was anathema to the Jews and could only be rejected by them. Lines had been crossed before, as when David had eaten the show bread (1 Samuel 21:6) or Uzziah had tried to burn incense at the altar of the LORD and been stricken with leprosy (2 Chronicles 26:19-21), but never on such a scale as this.

What gave Jesus the right to alter the God-given order of Israelite society? How could he arrogate to himself a role which was not his and at the same time reinterpret the messianic ideas of the people?

Who did this man think he was? The question is given more urgency by the nature of the intended sacrifice. Jesus was not going to take a lamb and kill it in the traditional manner. On the contrary, he was going to offer *himself* as the lamb and be the instrument of atonement. Nowadays many people interpret this act as a noble example of self-sacrifice, perhaps the most appealing of its kind in human history. For them the sight of a great moral leader giving his life for the sake of others is a powerful spur to take similar action themselves. The name of Jesus lives on in their minds as that of a great ideal, worthy of imitation and even worship.

Had Jesus claimed no more than this, it is possible that the Jews might eventually have honoured him as a great rabbi and national hero. The Greeks already had at least one martyr-for-truth in the person of Socrates, and they too might well have been amenable to more of the same. That things did not work out in that way was due to the nature of the lamb which the Jews prepared for sacrifice. It had to be spotlessly perfect as a token of its worthiness to stand before God without sin of any kind. The slightest blemish would have represented the lingering presence of sin and destroyed any possibility of effecting atonement.

But here, of course, was the rub. The Jews could sacrifice lambs, not because there was any virtue in sheep, but because it was possible to find ones which could convey the message of purity and holiness. A human sacrifice was not possible for precisely this reason – there was nobody who could claim the necessary sinlessness. The High Priest who performed the sacrifice had to conform as much as possible to the ideal, and it is well-known that a mutilated man could not perform the necessary task. But even so, he was still obliged to offer sacrifice for his own sins as much as for anyone else's (Hebrews 5:3).

In claiming the right to make the sacrifice by offering himself as the lamb, Jesus was doing nothing less than claiming to be God himself. Only God had *both* the right to combine the different traditions of Israel in this way *and* the sinless nature capable of making an atonement more effective than that made with sacrificial lambs. Only by claiming to be God could Jesus hope to overturn the traditions of Judaism.

It is for this reason that Jesus pressed his disciples to discern *who he was* (Matthew 16:15-16). Peter's famous confession, that Jesus was not only the Messiah, but the Son of the living God, is therefore not the product of a hyperactive imagination untainted by theological learning, but the foundation-stone of a new faith which could surpass Judaism and conquer the world. Only a man who could see that in Jesus he was coming face to face with God himself would have any reason to abandon the religion of his fathers. He alone would have any incentive to move into a realm of spiritual understanding whose gift of inner freedom far outweighed the external persecutions which such a claim would bring. In short, only a man who could make Peter's confession had any reason to bear the name of Christian.

We can now see that the message of salvation which the early Christians proclaimed was inescapably bound up with the claims made by and for the *Person of Jesus Christ*. Unless he were God in human flesh, there could be no final atonement and no Christianity. The line of development from the teaching of Jesus to the creeds of the Church was not a deviation from the original intention of Christ. On the contrary, it was the logical response to the question which Jesus asked his disciples in Matthew 16:15. The entire achievement of early Christian theology can be explained as the answer to this question – the answer which alone makes sense of the New Testament and gives an adequate explanation for the later progress and triumph of Christianity.

The point of Christology is to offer us a credible picture of the High Priest and Victim whose atoning sacrifice made the Jewish sacrificial system redundant and opened up the gates of eternal life for those who believe. It was the conviction of the early Christians that Jesus of Nazareth had performed this double task – a possibility which had not been previously envisaged – and that in order to do so he must have been God. Furthermore, the Apostles realized after the resurrection that Jesus had all along been teaching them precisely that. The Gospels show both that Jesus exposed his divinity to the disciples before the crucifixion and that the disciples failed to understand the true importance of what he was saying until after his work was accomplished. The person and work of Christ depend on each other for their full meaning, and the one could not be grasped without the other. In seeking to explain and transmit this record, the theologians of the Early Church undoubtedly gave priority to the former, and have been accused of minimizing the work of Christ, particularly when compared with the writings of the sixteenth-century Reformers.

There is a certain element of truth in this, but two points must be borne in mind. The Reformers would never have thought and written the way they did, had they not been imbued with the theology of the Early Church. They never repudiated their inheritance, but rather saw it as the indispensable foundation for their own work. If there is an imbalance in ancient theology, it was corrected, not rejected, by subsequent generations. The second point is that the Person of Christ is *logically* prior to his work, and this truth of the gospel is reflected in the progress of theological construction. The Christology of the creeds and councils of the Early Church is a necessary preliminary to further thinking, just as the teaching of the earthly Jesus about himself created the conceptual framework for what he later did. There is an order in the plan of salvation which is faithfully reflected in the progress of credal development.

The first Christians saw this order clearly and set about the difficult task of determining, in the light of Scripture, how Jesus could be God and man at the same time. As this involved not merely reconciling but uniting two incompatible beings in an indivisible whole, we need not be surprised that the process took many centuries, nor that it encountered some formidable difficulties *en route*. There were always people, both Jews and Gentiles, who refused to accept that a man could be God, or that God could enter the created order of time and space.

Philosophical difficulties of this kind lay at the root of most ancient heresies, though they were not always expressed with the greatest clarity. Leading heretics were often sincere Christians trying to explain the mystery of Christ within a conceptual framework which was unequal to the task. This does not excuse the errors they made, but it can help us to understand the deeper implications of evangelism in a society which had never heard the gospel before.

Without an adequate framework for their ideas, the early Christians were almost certain to fail in their attempts to explain their faith. The Early Church needed the right language in order to express its faith clearly, in exactly the same way that modern missionaries have to find the right concepts in which to preach the gospel to non-Christians. At the same time, however, they had to avoid compromising their essential beliefs. To achieve this dual purpose, Christians had to stake out the bounds of their faith both in the light of Scripture and against the background of contemporary non-Christian thinking.

The sanctification of the mind

The first principle which had to be established was that the human mind (*nous*) was corrupted by the fall of man, and that human reason (*logos*) could not function properly in its fallen state. Here it was necessary to maintain a delicate balance between two opposing tendencies in pagan thought. On the one hand, it was essential to reject the idea that a man could know God by a process of deductive reasoning (1 Corinthians 1:21). The gospel was *folly* to the Greeks (1 Corinthians 1:23; Acts 17:32) precisely because it could not be explained by a process relying on logical argument. The intellect of man had to be crucified on the cross and born again.

To many this demand seemed outrageous, and it is not surprising to discover that some theologians tried to evade it. They claimed that the gospel was a secret code which an intellectual could unscramble, provided he had the right key. This type of thinking is called the way of knowledge (*gnosis*) and the different systems which reflect it have been loosely linked together as 'Gnosticism'. It needs to be borne in mind, of course, that the so-called 'Gnostics' were not academic theologians in the modern sense. Their understanding of *gnosis* was essentially mystical, in that knowledge was given to the elect by a spiritual illumination which closely resembled philosophical meditation.

The precise details of 'Gnosticism' vary from system to system, and it must always be remembered that orthodox teachers like Clement of Alexandria (c. AD 200) also advocated this type of enlightenment. Its general effect, though, was to reduce the gospel to an allegorical myth. Potentially offensive ideas like blood sacrifice were reinterpreted in a philosophical way and made more palatable. Historical events were turned into universal principles of spiritual, not physical, life. An event like the baptism of Jesus became the picture-symbol of his illumination by the Divine, since it was obvious that immersion in a muddy stream by an illiterate Jewish prophet could hardly be said to have any spiritual effect!

Gnostic tendencies in the Early Church have received a great deal of attention in modern times. They have been identified as a major cause of doctrinal development, which is supposed to be only a more moderate and balanced appropriation of alien philosophical tendencies. In the understanding of Walter Bauer or James Dunn, the primitive spirituality of the church was rapidly outdistanced and perverted by thinking of this kind, so that even the so-called 'orthodox' party was only the largest and most powerful Gnostic group, which eventually ousted its rivals, including the 'authentic' Christians who remained on the fringes of the Church, and declared them to be heretics.

Liberal theologians have built up a plausible defence of their position, largely by a selective use of the evidence. There are, however, at least two flaws in their argument which must prove fatal to their case. The first is that 'Gnosticism' is not a system but a collective name given to several quite distinct systems. Valentinus, Basilides, Hermogenes and Marcion (though his claim to the description 'Gnostic' is not strong) were not collaborators in any sense, nor were their opponents. Irenaeus, Clement of Alexandria and Tertullian all reacted against them because they sensed that they had deviated from the norm, or Rule of Faith, but they did not mount a sustained or united campaign to exterminate dissenters. Indeed, had they envisaged such a possibility, they might well have turned on each other!

The picture we get of the 'orthodox' about AD 200 is less that of a united ecclesiastical party than of a conservative reaction to innovation which was only starting to grope towards an underlying   rationale for its opposition. Orthodoxy was *felt* before it was articulated, and it is more plausible to attribute the majority consensus to a genuine work of the Holy Spirit than it is to put it down to the machinations of clever individuals in positions of power.

The second objection to the liberal case is that Gnostic tendencies were elitist by nature. In the ancient world, philosophy was the pastime of a minority. It had little influence on general behaviour and philosophers were seldom interfered with by the state. If Christianity had really gone that way it would have become a small, exclusive sect, no more bizarre than the Cynics or the Pythagoreans and equally harmless. The fact that Christianity expanded at the level of the masses, that it was feared and persecuted as a great popular danger and that the philosophical schools, far from recognizing it as a sister, attacked it to the bitter end as an irrational superstition unworthy of a good intellect, is sufficient refutation of the liberal theory.

At the popular level, the early Christians met a different foe altogether: pagan religion. This was almost completely divorced from intellectual life, and philosophers generally despised it. It came in a variety of forms, but in general it was characterized by sensuality and superstition. The former is more prominent in the Old Testament, which frequently warns against the fertility cults of Canaan. The latter appears throughout the Bible, which condemns divination and the exploitation of psychic phenomena as Satanic. The disciples cast out demons more often than they engaged in philosophical debate, and this balance of priorities was certainly present, though partially submerged from our view, in the Early Church as well.

Already in the late second century we learn that the bones of Polycarp, who was martyred in AD 156, were preserved at Smyrna and venerated by believers. By the fourth century, the bone of a martyr could become quite literally a bone of contention in the church, as when the wealthy and wicked Lucilla campaigned for the overthrow of Caecilian, bishop of Carthage. Poor Caecilian had revealed his impiety by refusing to kiss a martyr's bone which Lucilla had held out to him when receiving communion. When Christianity replaced the various pagan cults in the Roman Empire it took over the ancient temples and cults and baptized them as much as possible. The end result was that by the Middle Ages relics were doing a roaring trade and superstition, directed towards the Virgin Mary, the saints and the sacramental elements of the Mass, was once more the religion of the people.

Against this background it needs to be stressed that, in spite of popular pressure, the Church authorities stood firm and refused to allow superstition to affect its official teaching and message. To some extent it even counter-attacked. The Delphic Oracle was shut down and the Olympic Games, held in honour of the gods, were suspended. Thousands of statues were destroyed. Witchcraft and black magic were outlawed and offenders were put to death if caught. Popular devotional practices reached some outlandish extremes, but although many odd things were tolerated, they were not established as points of doctrine. Indeed, strange as it may seem, the elevation of pious practices and beliefs to the level of official dogma is largely a phenomenon of post-Reformation Roman Catholicism. The sacrifice of the Mass, first proposed in the ninth century, did not finally become dogma until 1562. The cult of Mary received dogmatic recognition as late as 1854, and it is worth noting that her main shrines are mostly of recent origin. Lourdes dates only from 1858, Knock from 1879 and Fatima from 1917! It is yet one more sign that the Reformers were closer to the outlook of the Early Church than were the proponents of Counter-Reformation Catholicism.

The beginnings of Christian theology

To understand the general attitude of Christians to both philosophy and popular religion we can hardly do better than look at the writings of Tertullian (*c.* AD 200). Tertullian is unique in that he wrote with equal concern about both the intellectual and the popular levels of pagan thought. He is often accused of having been anti-philosophical, but this is true only to the extent that he regarded the philosophies of his day as manifestations of mankind's rebellion against God. He was certainly not anti-intellectual, as anyone can see from his theological writings.

Tertullian believed that the Scriptures were the source-book of truth, and that only a Christian whose mind had been redeemed from sin could read them. Any kind of Gnosticism was therefore bound to fail, because it assumed that the unaided intellect was able to reach some understanding of God. Tertullian saw very clearly the inner link between intellectual idolatry and the more popular form which prevailed all around him. In his mind, *doctrine* and *discipline* were the same thing. Purity of mind and purity of body went together.

It must be admitted that Tertullian was a sharp-tongued critic who was not above demonstrating his point by accusing his theological adversaries of living immoral lives. The charge is highly unlikely, because philosophy and popular religion kept their distance from each other, but it does make an important point. Despite its pretensions, philosophy could not claim any special moral achievement. In its own way, it was just as immoral and ungodly as a fertility cult.

At the popular level, Tertullian's attentions were focused on the phenomenon of martyrdom. He had no interest in venerating bones, but understood persecution and death for the sake of the Name (of Christ) primarily as a *confession*. Christians were not put to death because of their odd practices – Tertullian points out that Christian worship was restrained and sensible when compared with pagan cults – but because of what they believed. He did not deny the presence of charismatic gifts in the Church, and he showed strong sympathies with the prophetic witness of Montanus, who foretold the imminent end of the world. Many people believe that he actually became a Montanist and left the Church; but however great his sympathies may have been in that direction, they never influenced the content of his confession of faith. To the end, Tertullian remained loyal to the gospel of Scripture, and sought to develop a conceptual framework of thought in which the sanctified mind could express the saving truth of Christ.

The construction of a systematic theology may be said to have begun in earnest with Tertullian, and its evangelistic purpose is nowhere clearer than in his writings. Combating heresy and spreading the gospel to pagans were the main aims of his life, and he used his intellectual gifts fully to that end.

Tertullian began with an assumption about God, or the Supreme Being, which was common to both Jews and philosophers. This was that God was one objective reality responsible for the existence of all things. He had no equals and no rivals. In himself, he was quite different from any creature, though Jews and pagans each understood this difference in their own way. For the Jews, God was 'wholly other'. He could not be seen or depicted, nor was it possible for him to enter into his creation, because his nature was incompatible with anything created. On the other hand, he was a personal being, who had spoken to his chosen people Israel through Moses and the prophets. This made it possible for the Jews to know God's will and by doing it claim a special relationship to him.

Pagans on the other hand tended to believe that each man's soul was a spark of the divine spirit which had been separated from the main centre. A man could be a 'god' if his soul was abnormally large or free from the encumbrance of the body, and salvation of a sort was possible by an eventual re-absorption of this soul into the divine spirit from which it had originally come. Tertullian seems to have inherited this idea in its Stoic form. According to Stoicism, everything, including the divine spirit, was material. This spirit was a very refined form of fire (one of the four elements – earth, air, fire and water – which constituted matter) and was also Reason in the pure sense. The human soul was a spark of the divine fire which united man to God by means of the rational faculty. At the end of the age the world would be consumed by the purifying divine fire and then begin again in an ongoing cyclical pattern.

What could a Christian make of such a theory? Tertullian knew from the Bible that the Stoics were right to think of God as Reason (*Logos*) and Spirit, but wrong to confuse them. In fact, God possessed both Reason and a Spirit which had a distinct identity as well as being part of his nature. When God sent his Reason into the world he did not cease to be rational. Likewise, when he brought forth his Spirit he did not cease to be spiritual. It was, therefore, necessary to conceive of a rational, spiritual God who possessed a Reason and a Spirit which were not merely qualities of his divine nature.

It was at this point that the Jewish conception of God made itself clearly felt. The God of the Bible was an active subject, possessing characteristics analogous to those of human beings, who were created in his image. This God had entered into covenant – a legal transaction – with Israel. In Roman law a party to a legal action was called a *persona* (a word originally borrowed from the theatre, where it meant the distinguishing mask worn by a character in a pantomime), and Tertullian thought that it could be used of God as well.

The Bible, however, revealed that on God's side there were three parties to the covenant, the Father, the Son and the Holy Spirit, each of which was therefore a person in his own right. But although Tertullian got his language from the Roman law-courts, his thought pattern was much closer to Judaism. This is because he saw the three divine persons as sharing the personal nature of God the Father. Like many second-century Christians, he thought of Reason and Spirit as eternally latent within the unity of God. At the moment of creation, God generated his Reason and exhaled his Spirit, endowing each of them with the qualities of his own nature. This is why Reason is called the Son, and why its generation did not leave the Father as an irrational being.

To the modern mind, this may sound somewhat confusing, but Tertullian regarded it as no more than the logical explanation of John 1:1-14. Look at the first verse: 'In the beginning was the Reason (*Logos*) and the Reason was with God and the Reason was God.'

The first clause states that Reason always had some existence of its own, the second distinguishes it from God and the third emphasizes its divinity. Interpreting the second and the third clauses without contradiction meant saying that God had a personal nature. In himself he could be called the Father, but this did not preclude the possibility of other persons sharing his nature. On the contrary, the very name implied the existence of offspring who shared in the same substance as he did.

Acceptance of this, however, destroyed another fundamental tenet of Stoicism. For if Reason and Spirit were God's offspring, then it was clear that mankind could not also claim this distinction. The Son was unique – the only-begotten – and he became a man, something which would hardly have made sense if all men were sparks of the divine. Tertullian was forced to draw a clear line between the Creator and his creatures, even though some people insist that he always thought of God as highly refined matter. Even if this is true, there could be no question of simply passing from God to man without a fundamental change of substance.

Though Tertullian's theological scheme is not without its faults, the fact that he learned to distinguish three persons within the one nature of God makes him the principal founder of Christian systematic theology. But as has been hinted at already, his way of looking at God was by no means the only one which was possible within the bounds of 'orthodoxy'. In fact, Tertullian had hardly put down his pen when Origen, a brilliant scholar who worked quite independently of his great contemporary, came up with a very different explanation of the same underlying reality.

Unlike Tertullian, Origen received his education in the philosophical schools of Alexandria. His chief mentors were Ammonius Saccus, the pagan philosopher who later taught the founder of Neoplatonism, Plotinus, and Clement of Alexandria, a Christian who had absorbed the biblical scholarship of Philo the Jew. As a result, Origen's writings betray a profound interest in the Scriptures which are refracted through the prism of late Middle Platonism. As a scholar, Origen was unsurpassed in ancient times. He managed to master Hebrew, and embarked on textual study of the Old Testament. He was also practically the first Christian to write commentaries on the Bible, and as such he stands at the head of a long tradition.

Yet in spite of his undoubted learning, Origen's writings are handicapped by a fatal flaw which pervaded the whole of his work and compromised its value in the estimation of subsequent generations. This was his commitment to Platonism, which determined the use which he made of his source material. Platonism helped him to see that spiritual realities were more important than material ones, but it also distorted his vision, to the point where material things like the human body were nearly eclipsed in his mind.

In interpreting the Bible, Origen followed Clement and Philo in saying that the text had three levels, or senses, in which it was to be understood. The first of these was the *literal sense*. Origen never denied its importance, as we can see from his efforts at textual criticism, but he admitted that it said a number of things which the pious mind found offensive. The literal sense spoke as if God had a body, with arms, eyes and feet. It referred to the wrath of God, as if a divine being could manifest passions appropriate only to fallen human beings. It was therefore plain to Origen that the literal sense of the Scriptures had a purpose which went beyond itself. This purpose was to make men aware of the spiritual reality of God and point them in the right direction so that they might enjoy communion with him on the spiritual level.

The first stage of this awareness was contained in the *moral sense* of Scripture. The 'arm of God' was meant to signify that God was not indifferent to moral issues, and that he would punish the wicked for their vices. The water used in baptism was a sign of moral cleansing which must accompany conversion and which formed the basis of spiritual growth.

The next stage was found in the *spiritual sense* of Scripture. This sense revealed to men that behind the appearance of human forms there was a spiritual reality in which Christians are privileged to participate. Because of the spiritual sense we can find Christ and the gospel in the most unlikely passages of Scripture. Jacob's ladder, the wilderness journey of Israel and the Song of Solomon all become paradigms of the Christian experience of God. In thinking in this way, Origen came quite close to the teaching of Paul in the New Testament. Paul had said, after all, that the rock which followed Israel in the desert was Christ (1 Corinthians 10:4), and Origen thought he was merely taking statements of this kind to their logical conclusion.

In the fourth century, John Cassian added a fourth level of interpretation, derived from an aspect of Origen's spiritual sense. This was the *anagogical sense*, according to which the revelation of God on earth corresponded as in a mirror to the reality of God in heaven. If the Word became flesh by being born of a virgin, then this fact of birth must have a corresponding reality in heaven. Tertullian and those who had gone before him had not known how to explain the generation of the Son of God outside space-time categories of thought. Because of this, they had tended to say that the Son (and the Spirit) had been latent in God the Father from all eternity and had emerged only when he desired to create the world. They had not meant by this that the Son was the first creature – he was *begotten, not created* – but had only been trying to explain how a divine being could experience something which by definition could happen only in time.

Origen cut across this problem with his use of anagogy. Birth in time on earth reflected birth in eternity in heaven, therefore the Son was eternally begotten of the Father, and it was wrong to suppose that there was ever a time when the Son had not existed. The Son was the exact replica (Hebrews 1:3) of the Father and therefore shared fully in his eternal nature. At the same time, however, Origen also knew that the gospel revelation portrayed Christ as doing the will of his Father, who had sent him. It followed that the Son had always done the Father's will, and that this subordination of obedience was likewise part of the Son's eternal nature. He was equal, but in second place, and therefore dependent on the one who had begotten him.

Origen's use of anagogy to explain the Person of Christ was rooted in his concern to insist that the scriptural revelation offered us a knowledge of God as he really is. It would be easy, but wrong, to dismiss Origen as a fantasizer who used the Bible as a quarry for fashioning his own ideas. He firmly believed that the Scriptures were an accurate record of a God who could be known and experienced by men.

This God had reproduced himself in the Son and then again, through the Son, in the Spirit. Father, Son and Holy Spirit were thus three distinct beings whom the spiritually enlightened believer could perceive. Following the teaching of Plato, Origen believed that it was from the substance of the Spirit that God had created the souls of men. These souls had been detached from the divine spiritual fire and, on growing cold, they had fallen into the material world where they had been trapped in human bodies. The spiritual life was thus the search for a way out of this prison and back to God.

For Origen, the first stage in this process was the contact made with the Holy Spirit. It was he who entered the heart of man and gave him the knowledge that he was a child of God (Romans 8:16). But the Holy Spirit did not come to speak about himself. On the contrary, he came to bear witness to the Son (John 16:14), thereby taking the human soul one step higher into God. The Son in turn was the mediator between God and men (1 Timothy 2:5-6) whose task it was to take the soul back to the Father. In this way, the three Persons of the Trinity represent rungs on the hierarchical ladder back to God. To achieve its salvation the soul must know and be in fellowship with all three.

But what did this knowledge consist of? Who were the Son and the Spirit in the experience of the Christian believer? Here Origen had no hesitation. Both the Son and the Spirit were God, formed from the Father's own nature and sharing fully in it. Because he believed this nature to be immaterial, Origen experienced no difficulty in claiming that it reproduced itself without losing any of its substance. The difficulty which had faced Tertullian, who had spoken of the Son as a portion of the divine nature, therefore did not arise.

What estimation should a student of theological history make of Origen? On the credit side, he was a thorough-going biblical scholar who was concerned to uncover the spiritual meaning of the text. He saw the Scriptures not as a history book, nor as a guide to archaeological discoveries, but as the Word of God addressed to spiritually-minded people in every age. His brilliance at tying doctrine to devotion was a model for his own time, and for one hundred and fifty years the life of the Greek-speaking church revolved around his teaching. Even today he is recognized, if mainly through his disciples, as a leading master of the contemplative life of spirituality which has always been a characteristic feature of monasticism.

On the other hand, there is a debit side which must also be taken into account. Origen was the leading biblical scholar of his day, but he lacked that sense of the Scriptures which is so necessary for putting scholarship in its proper context. Tertullian had his faults in this respect, but his legal emphasis came much nearer to the outlook of the Bible than did the Platonism of Origen. It was this, more than anything, which altered his understanding and made his interpretation of the Bible ultimately unacceptable. Origen felt a close kinship with Paul's typological exegesis of the Old Testament, but in fact he never understood it. Paul used the Old Testament to point to Christ as its fulfilment in historical time. He believed that the same God who had spoken to the prophets had also spoken in his Son, in whom he fulfilled his promises.

Origen, on the other hand, had a Platonic understanding of the Old Testament, which for him was not typology but allegory. The prophets were not so much pointing to a future revelation as concealing, in symbols and images, a particular spiritual experience. Origen did not take the historical progress of linear time seriously, except in so far as later generations had climbed higher up Jacob's ladder into the mystery of God. His emphasis on anagogy, which was designed to secure the validity of the biblical revelation by regarding it all as divine truth 'seen through a glass darkly' (1 Corinthians 13:12), destroyed the movement inherent in God's revealing acts, replacing it with the static vision of Platonism. It also led to trouble on the doctrinal front.

The two centuries which followed Origen's death in AD 254 witnessed a theological ferment which has had lasting consequences, in that out of it came the definitions of faith which are now standards of Christian belief. But it is seldom appreciated just how much Origen himself was responsible for the problems which arose during that time. When Athanasius struggled against Arius over the correct interpretation of Christ's divinity, they were both following Origen as they each understood him. Athanasius began with the equality implied in eternal generation and argued that this ruled out any form of subordinationism. Arius, on the other hand, assumed the eternal subordination of the Son to the Father and argued from that that he must have lacked something of the Father's nature and thus could not have enjoyed the status of equality implied by eternal generation. Either way, it was clear that the Son of God could not be eternally begotten and eternally subordinate at the same time. One or the other had to give, though in Origen's mind the two could be held together on the anagogical model.

In sum, it must be said that if Origen used philosophical concepts to build his theology, it was the inappropriateness of these same concepts which eventually invalidated his system and caused the Church so much anguish. Tertullian's theology, despite its lapses, was fundamentally sound and later orthodoxy did little more than tidy up loose ends in his work. Origen, on the other hand, has been completely reworked. His contribution remains, but it has been given a new context and a different meaning. Although his writings were eventually condemned because of his Platonic view of the soul, it is significant that the issue which forced his system into a crisis was the incarnation of Christ. God's supreme act in history simply could not be reconciled with a philosophy which knew only different levels of awareness in the pursuit of ultimate reality.

Christianity and philosophy

We must now turn our attention to the wider issue of the relationship between Christianity and philosophy, on which so many modern theories have been based. If it can be shown that Origen's commitment to Platonism was a major cause of theological debate in following generations, what is to be said about the wider rapport between the two disciplines? The question faces us on two levels, which are of very unequal importance.

The first is *lexical*. There is no doubt that Plato, the New Testament writers and the majority of theologians and philosophers in ancient times used a common language – Greek. As they were concerned with the same questions about God and man, it will not come as an inordinate surprise to discover that there is a fairly large stock of technical vocabulary common to all schools of thought. How significant is this? Can we seriously maintain that Christians clothed their theology in philosophical garb because they had no choice but to speak the language of their time?

Here we must be very careful. There is no doubt that terms like *logos* (word, reason), *hypostasis* (substance, person) and *ousia* (being, essence) are found in many places outside Christianity. There is also no doubt that they possess a range of possible meanings no narrower than that of their English counterparts. Can we say precisely what we mean by *person* or *being*? Such terms are in common use, but depend for their meaning on the context in which they are employed. The same is true of Greek. It is not the words themselves which matter, since their meaning is never rigidly fixed, but their context which is all-important. At that level, Christianity cannot so easily be pinned down and equated with a particular philosophical system.

Take a word like *hypostasis*. It is used in the New Testament, most obviously in Hebrews 1:3. Origen used it to refer to the three beings who shared the common nature of God. Tertullian had meanwhile translated it into Latin as *substantia* and used it to mean the single divine essence. Great confusion was caused in the Church by the different uses of the same word. Yet each meaning is legitimate in its own context. *Hypostasis* refers in the first instance to an objective reality which can be perceived by the intellect. When Tertullian thought of God, he thought of the One Being, and therefore, for him, this objective reality was singular. When Origen thought of God, he saw three Beings, each of whom shared the same nature. Thus, for him, the objective reality was threefold. One word, with one 'meaning', therefore came to be used in two potentially contradictory senses!

How can a problem of this kind be dealt with? When the Greek-speaking followers of Origen heard about Tertullian's theology, they were scandalized. Matters were made even worse when they discovered that the threefold element in God was designated by the Latin term *persona*, a word whose natural Greek equivalent was *prosopon* (mask). It was possible that such a theology could be understood to mean that Father, Son and Holy Spirit were no more than symbolic names for the one God in his different activities. Instead of three persons, there would be one being who changed masks according to whether he was acting as creator, as redeemer or as sanctifier.

This notion is not a fantasy – it was apparently held by a certain Sabellius, who was accused, among other things, of saying that the Father had died on the cross! Tertullian would certainly never have accepted this; in fact his main work on the Trinity is directed against one Praxeas who said the same thing as Sabellius. But it has not stopped a number of Greek theologians, both ancient and modern, from claiming that the Western theological tradition is fundamentally Sabellian! It took the genius of a Basil the Great (c. AD 329-379) to understand that the Latin word *persona* meant *hypostasis* and not *mask*, and it is thanks to him that the two traditions in theology were reconciled on this point.

Not for long, though. Jerome, who had an ever-ready eye for scandal, complained in a letter to Damasus, bishop of Rome (366-384), that the Greeks spoke of three substances in God! Hilary of Poitiers (d.368) had already said as much in his translation of Basil's theology, though of course he did not use the term in its commonly accepted meaning of *essence* (*ousia*). By making that mistake, Jerome virtually accused the leading Greek theologians of his day of tritheism, or a belief in three gods!

Of course the fallacy of such reasoning has long been recognized. In his *Institutes of the Christian Religion* Calvin says (I, 13, 5):

... how greatly is Jerome perplexed with the word Hypostasis! He suspects some lurking poison, when it is said that there are three Hypostases in God. And he does not disguise his belief that the expression, though used in a pious sense, is improper; if, indeed, he was sincere in saying this, and did not rather designedly endeavour, by an unfounded calumny, to throw odium on the Eastern bishops whom he hated. He certainly shows little candour in asserting that in all heathen schools *ousia* is equivalent to Hypostasis – an assertion completely refuted by ... common use.

What the misunderstanding between Greeks and Latins revealed was the need to distinguish two levels of objective reality in God. The Persons of the Trinity could not be confused with or submerged in the single essence of God, yet they were not on that account any less real. Some means therefore had to be found by which the plurality within the unity could be expressed without losing the underlying validity of either concept. In trying to do this, the Fathers of the Church were forced to define *hypostasis* in a way which is without parallel in ancient philosophy yet does not do violence to the semantic range of the word in the Greek language.

Another aspect of the lexical argument over philosophy is less subtle, but demands our attention because it has been raised in this connection since at least the fourth century. This is simply whether an 'unbiblical' word can be used in Christian theology. *Hypostasis*, as we have seen, is not 'unbiblical', though many scholars would doubt whether its use in dogmatic theology is justified on the basis of Hebrews 1:3. But other terms, like *trinity* (*trias*) and *consubstantial* (*homoousios*) do fall into this category, and were rejected by some Christians like Arius on the ground that they were alien impositions on scriptural thought.

This argument returned at the Reformation and is widespread today among those who try to discredit dogmatics. Once again, Calvin summed up the problem and offered a solution to it (*Institutes*, I,13,3):

The unerring standard both of thinking and speaking must be derived from the Scriptures: by it all the thoughts of our minds, and the words of our mouths, should be tested. But, in regard to those parts of Scripture which, to our capacities, are dark and intricate, what forbids us to explain them in clearer terms – terms, however, kept in reverent and faithful subordination to Scripture truth, used sparingly and modestly, and not without occasion? Of this we are not without many examples. When it has been proved that the Church was impelled by the strongest necessity, to use the words Trinity and Person, will not he who still inveighs against novelty of terms be deservedly suspected of taking offence at the light of truth, and of having no other ground for his invective, than that the truth is made plain and transparent?

More serious than the argument that Christianity borrowed its language from pagan thinkers is the accusation that with this language came an *ideological* content as well. Once again, we may take *hypostasis* as a key concept to illustrate this process. In the Neoplatonic philosophy of Plotinus (204-270), which was subsequently modified and developed by a number of disciples, of whom the most noteworthy are Porphyry (c. 233-c. 304) and Iamblichus (d.c.330), we find a number of surprising parallels to Christian thinking. Plotinus held that there were three basic realities, the One, the Mind and the Soul, which his disciples called *hypostases*. These sound suspiciously like the *autotheos* (God-in-himself), the Logos and the Spirit of Origen. When we discover that Plotinus arranged his realities in a hierarchical order and taught that the Soul had emanated from the Mind which had in turn emanated from the One, we are even more struck by the similarity. Finally when we read that both Origen and Plotinus had studied philosophy with the great Alexandrian teacher of Middle Platonism, Ammonius Saccus, we realize that there must be some connection between the two.

In the fourth and early fifth centuries, there can be no doubt that Neoplatonism exercised a powerful influence in intellectual circles. Marius Victorinus, whose writings influenced the great Augustine, was a converted philosopher who was steeped in the teaching of Porphyry. Augustine himself knew both Plotinus and Porphyry at first hand, and scholars debate their relative influence on him. Finally the Cappadocian Fathers (Basil the Great, Gregory of Nazianzus and Gregory of Nyssa), who among them developed the classical Trinitarianism of the Eastern Church, all studied at Athens in schools where the teaching of Iamblichus was dominant.

No-one can seriously doubt that Christianity and Neoplatonism co-existed and were intimately linked with each other during the period when the Church embarked on its most ambitious work of dogmatic definition. What was the nature of this special relationship? Did it influence and distort the presentation of the gospel which we now confess in the creeds?

To answer this question properly we must go back to the second century. The first intellectual pagan to take notice of Christianity was Pliny the Younger. He had no serious interest in the new religion, which he regarded as mere superstition, but had to deal with it because its popular appeal was upsetting the religious order of Bithynia where he was governor (AD 111-112). Somewhat later Tacitus writes about Christians in connection with the Great Fire of Rome in AD 64, but he is even more contemptuous than Pliny. Later still (about AD 135) Suetonius managed to mention the expulsion of the Jews from Rome in AD 49 because of arguments about 'Chrestus', a figure of whom he professed complete ignorance, and he also has a brief mention of Nero's persecution.

Such condescension would not last much longer though. Before the death of the philosopher-emperor Marcus Aurelius in 180, at least two major works had been addressed to the imperial government in defence of Christianity. One was the *Apology* of Justin Martyr, who was put to death in 156, and the other was the so-called *Embassy* of Athenagoras, which can be dated to 176-177. The authors of these works argue that Christianity was not a vile superstition, as many educated people supposed, but a reasonable religion far loftier than anything devised by Plato or the Stoics. Athenagoras, in particular, gives a brief summary of Christian belief which reads astonishingly like the more developed credal theology of the fifth century. Rather surprisingly, he gives a clear exposition of the Trinity, the first of its kind in Christian literature.

The pagan response to these intiatives was not slow in coming. Marcus Aurelius was not impressed. In 177 he ordered a general persecution of Christians throughout the Empire, which marks the first time that the Roman authorities attempted a systematic repression of the new religion. About the same time, however, an unknown pagan philosopher by the name of Celsus undertook to refute Christianity on intellectual grounds. Celsus' book marks a turning-point in intellectual history, a fact which makes its subsequent loss all the more regrettable. It was the first non-Christian work which sought to take Christianity seriously, which in itself makes it a landmark of importance. But even more significant is the way in which Celsus apparently argued his case.

Our knowledge of this comes from Origen's refutation *Against Celsus*, in which he quotes substantial chunks from his adversary's writings. These were collated and studied by the Danish scholar Carl Andresen, who published his findings in his book *Logos und Nomos*, which appeared in Germany in 1954. Andresen's brilliant study showed that, in order to make his points, Celsus was obliged to adopt the fundamental presuppositions of his opponents. This procedure went beyond the sort of *ad hominem* arguments which are frequently found in apologetic literature of all kinds. What Celsus ended up trying to do was to explain that a basically monotheistic way of salvation could be constructed out of Platonism, a fact which made conversion to Christianity unnecessary.

Celsus did not destroy Christianity. On the contrary, he embraced its main ideas and adjusted his philosophy to cope with them – thereby revealing that the new religion had gained the upper hand intellectually and could introduce major modifications in the accepted philosophical notions of his time. Something of the same may well have been true of Plotinus. It certainly was the case with Porphyry, who attacked Christianity violently whilst at the same time absorbing its main ideas.

It must be remembered that all this was going on at a time when high government officials were Neoplatonists, and Christians were still a despised and persecuted sect. The intellectual battle was in full swing long before the official recognition of Christianity in 312-313, and the Christians were winning from the start. We cannot now reconstruct the course of events in detail, because our evidence is fragmentary; but it looks strongly as if Platonism was refashioned to meet the challenge of Christianity, not the other way round. Christians may well have been influenced by the philosophical schools, but they remained on the offensive and gave far more than they got.

The close similarity of Neoplatonic teaching to that of Christianity may have been due to the former's attempt to caricature the latter. Certainly, the philosophy of Plotinus cannot compare in profundity with the theology of Origen. For while both men acknowledged a divine hierarchy of three *hypostases*, it was the theologian, not the philosopher, who found himself compelled to confess that the three were one – an equation which defeated any attempt at imitation which a Platonic philosophy might care to consider.

Another factor which must be taken into consideration here is the way in which Christianity appealed to the masses – a phenomenon unheard of in pagan antiquity. The philosophical schools were the preserve of an intellectual elite which prided itself on its culture. Their attacks against Christianity were an attempt to preserve this social isolation against the threat of a democratic, intellectual religion. When Gregory of Nazianzus went to Constantinople in 380 he complained that he could hardly get his hair cut, because the barbers of the city were too preoccupied arguing about the consubstantiality of the Son with the Father! Such an experience would have been inconceivable in pagan times, and it shows us just how revolutionary a creed Christianity really was.

What would have happened had things really been the other way round? Do we know what Christianity would have looked like had it succumbed to Neoplatonist influence? Fortunately we do, and the answer to these questions provides the final proof of our case. The philosophical schools were not suppressed in 380 when Christianity became the only legal religion. They were allowed to continue, largely because their influence was so unimportant, until the time of Justinian, when they were finally closed (in 529). The leaders of the schools either retired or fled to Persia, though some later returned to the Roman Empire. What is highly significant though is that there appeared at about the same time a Neoplatonic corpus of writings which claimed primitive Christian authorship, and as such was to exert enormous influence on the medieval Church.

Who wrote these documents is a mystery, but their appearance soon after 500 is generally regarded as far more than a mere coincidence. Their supposed author was none other than Dionysius the Areopagite, who had been converted under Paul's preaching when the apostle visited Athens (Acts 17:34). The forgery was a clever one, in that whoever did it realized that so apostolic a pedigree, if believed, would guarantee the writings a place of the highest honour. They were not immediately accepted by everyone, but in the confused conditions of the seventh century they made steady progress. By the ninth century they were required reading, and they retained their authority unimpaired until the sixteenth century. The Reformers called their authenticity into question and today only a few Eastern Orthodox writers still regard them as genuine. Even so, they are still published and widely read, so that their influence is far from exhausted.

The aim of the pseudo-Dionysius (or Denys) was simple. He wanted to convey Neoplatonism to an audience which would receive it only in Christian dress. He was not hostile to Christianity and probably thought that the two could be reconciled along the lines he proposed. In this respect his sincerity should not be doubted, and his considerable achievement can be seen in the continuing popularity of his works.

What pseudo-Dionysius said was that God could be known only by an ascent up the ladder of the celestial hierarchy. The practice of prayer and meditation would lead the mystic from one experience to another, until at last he would know the transfiguration of uncreated light, which was the ecstatic union with the divine. The scheme of Dionysius had little understanding of sin, which became an inevitable consequence of finitude rather than the fruit of disobedience to the law of God. The passion of Christ lost its atoning significance and became instead a mortification of the flesh which turned the fleeting ecstasy of the transfiguration into the eternal glory of the ascension. Christ was the Saviour in that he opened the gates of heaven to anyone prepared to work his way there by mystical experience.

The way of ascent proposed by Dionysius became the foundation of Christian mysticism and has always been opposed to dogmatic theology. The main reason for this is that the mystical experience of God is apophatic, which means that it rejects all human attempts to explain it as inadequate. Where Dionysian mysticism has thrived, dogmatic theology has withered, and the two forces have usually been at loggerheads in the course of Church history.

Whatever one thinks of the pseudo-Dionysius, there can be no doubt that his writings are a Christianized form of Neoplatonism. There is also no doubt that his followers, whilst they have usually defended the existing credal formulations of the Church, have been generally hostile to theological development. When Neoplatonism invaded the Church its effect was to stifle dogmatics, not to encourage confessional statements of an unbiblical character. Yet even pseudo-Dionysius bears witness in his own way to the triumph of the gospel. Neoplatonism survived in the only way that it could – by being clothed in the garb of an alien religion. The culture which had despised the faith of Christ and then sought to exterminate it ended its days as a pensioner in sheltered housing provided by the followers of the One whom they honoured as the Way, the Truth and the Life.

4

The Rule of Faith

In the last chapter we sketched the progress of evangelism in the early centuries of the Church, and saw how Christians were obliged to confront the main philosophical currents of their time. We also indicated that the formulation of Christian doctrine had more to do with a particular understanding of the teaching role of Scripture than with any desire to absorb an alien philosophical tradition into the life of the Church. Now we must take these assumptions and look at them positively in the light of credal development within the early community.

Who wrote the first Christian confession of faith and where it appeared are unknown. In the New Testament there are signs that expressions like 'Jesus is Lord' (Philippians 2:11) may have had a certain currency in this respect. Some scholars, like James Dunn in his book *Unity and Diversity in the New Testament*, have suggested that this particular formula may have been *the* hallmark of a Christian, long before a more developed, complex and rigid 'orthodoxy' emerged as the norm. There may be some truth in this, but caution is necessary when Dunn suggests that the bare statement, 'Jesus is Lord', united men of very different theological outlook in a common confession. The Early Church was not a confederation of divergent theological positions united by a form of words to which all could assent in good conscience. On the contrary, all the evidence suggests that it was a close-knit community which shared a comprehensive set of beliefs, even if these were not always set down in writing.

The evidence for this comes mainly from the New Testament itself. The phrase 'Jesus is Lord' comes from the famous Christological passage in Philippians 2. Some scholars think Paul may have been quoting a Christian hymn; if so, the testimony is even older than the date of the Epistle, which can hardly be put later than about AD 62. The remarkable feature of this passage, which on any reckoning is very early, is that its teaching about Christ is so highly developed.

Jesus is not only a pre-existent heavenly being, but he is even 'in the form of God,' and did not regard it as out of place to count himself 'equal with God'. This same Jesus then came 'in the form of man' – the parallelism with 'the form of God' is very important, because it indicates that Christ's divinity is on the same logical plane as his humanity – to die on the cross and to rise again for us. The crucifixion was not the unlucky end to a promising career but the fulfilment of the plan of God which was confirmed and completed in the resurrection, ascension and heavenly reign of Christ.

To extract the confession 'Jesus is Lord' from this sequence and emphasize it as if nothing else mattered is clearly impossible. It cannot be squared with Paul's tendency to rebuke his congregations for having forgotten the essence of his teaching. A very early letter like Galatians (written about AD 49) is severe to the point of ferocity on this subject. It is hard to imagine how the poor Galatians could have gone so badly astray and called down even anathemas on their heads if all they had been taught to subscribe to in the first place was 'Jesus is Lord'.

The Pauline Epistles obviously assume far more than that, and other parts of the New Testament concur in Paul's demands. The writer to the Hebrews could rebuke his hearers for their failure to appreciate the priestly significance of Melchizedek, which few would claim is the most lucid part of the Scriptures. He also clearly thought that even the babe's milk of the Word (Hebrews 5:11-14), on which they were being inadequately nourished, contained a fair degree of theological sophistication.

The teaching of Jesus and the Apostles was wide-ranging and comprehensive, as we can see from the New Testament, though even that represents only the tip of an iceberg (John 21:25). The selectivity of the written record is a recognized fact, which is enshrined in the name *canon*. This word corresponds to the Latin *regula* (*rule*) and was used in Roman law to mean a *summary* of a statute. *Regulae* or *canones* were composed by lawyers to provide a quick guide to the statute-book for those who were too busy to read the small print for themselves. They were not arbitrary productions but carefully ordered statements of the main points of the law. As such they were admitted in the courts in lieu of complete statutes, and they quickly became the only form of law a non-specialist would ever come across. Eventually they were written down in a series of learned *Digests*, which culminated in the famous sixth-century Code of Justinian.

Scripture and tradition

It seems probable that the early Christians thought of the New Testament in roughly this way – as the official digest of Christian teaching, handed down by *tradition* (*paradosis*). There has always been argument over the precise relationship between Scripture and tradition. It has centred on whether the latter is to be understood as the *complete teaching* of the Apostles or as the *canonical digest* of it given to us as the New Testament. Those who hold the former view maintain that every practice which can be traced to the Apostles must be accorded a place within the Church as part of its authoritative teaching. Thus for the Eastern Orthodox, tradition in this sense is everything. Its transmission has taken two basic forms, oral and written (Scripture), which have equal weight but do not contradict each other. The Latin mind wanted a neater definition than this, and gradually restricted tradition to that which had come down by oral transmission only. But like the Eastern Church, Rome has always given oral tradition an authority equal to that of the written revelation.

The Reformers differed widely in their attitudes to tradition (which they understood in the Latin sense), but all agreed that it could not have the same authority as Scripture. One of the main reasons for this is that oral transmission is highly unstable and subject to constant modification. Our evidence for it at earlier stages of Church history must depend on written records, many of which are hard to interpret correctly and some of which are mutually contradictory. The most obvious example of 'tradition' is the primacy of the Pope in the Church, but the Reformers knew that this had grown out of all recognition since the days of Peter, even if that apostle had been the leader of the Twelve and the first bishop of Rome.

Since the Reformation, historical and critical studies of Christian origins have shown that the Apostles' Creed, which in the Middle Ages had been ascribed to the Twelve, was not composed by the Apostles. The *Apostolic Tradition* ascribed to Hippolytus (third century) is now thought to have little connection with any apostolic source, though recently it has been widely used as the basis of liturgical revision because it offers us our most complete picture of early Christian worship. Similarly, the claims made by people like Polycarp, Papias, Irenaeus, Tertullian and Origen about various aspects of the Apostles' legacy have frequently been called into question by scholars who doubt their authenticity.

There is every reason to believe that historical scepticism has often gone too far and cast doubt on the origin of practices which undoubtedly do go back to the Apostles themselves. The difficulty is that we cannot be certain what those practices were, or how they were understood. It is fairly certain, for example, that oil was widely used in baptismal and other forms of anointing (James 5:14), but we do not know for sure what its significance was. To derive its meaning in earliest times from later evidence is highly dangerous, since the history of ritual can be written largely in terms of an ever-increasing wealth of allegorical explanations designed to invest a given practice with as much theological significance as possible. The long medieval controversy over the use of unleavened bread at Holy Communion occurred precisely because a theological meaning was attached to a practice which had evidently been a matter of indifference in earlier times.

For all these reasons, therefore, Protestants have seldom had much time for appeals to tradition, although the more theologically acute have generally recognized that in the earliest Christian usage the term referred primarily to the written record. They have therefore claimed that Scripture and tradition are *the same thing, i.e.* that what we have recorded in the New Testament is what was handed down by the Apostles.

Strangely enough, the logic of this position is strengthened if we consider that other, hitherto unknown, apostolic writings may well be found in some future archaeological discovery. What if Paul's letter to Laodicea, for example, were suddenly to turn up and be 'authenticated' by computer analysis? Would we have to add it to the New Testament? Here the answer must be no, because although such a letter might have some claim to inclusion in the canon as an apostolic document, it would not be part of the tradition, of that which was actually *handed down* from apostolic times. A right understanding of *canon* will not have trouble accepting that we no longer have access to the full quantity of apostolic teaching, but it cannot allow that the digest we possess is insufficient to meet the needs of the Church, or that God intends future generations to have more of his Word than that which we now accept as the New Testament.

If we can accept that the New Testament is the received, canonical tradition of the Apostles, we are well placed to understand how the creeds as we know them came into existence. For even the New

Testament, though it was undoubtedly a digest of Christian teaching, was still too large and complex to be easily mastered by new converts. Soon it was being placed on a par with the Old Testament as the Church's *lex* (law), whose study was the preserve of specialists. For the ordinary believer, who may well have been illiterate, it was necessary to prepare a summary of the digest, and it is from this pastoral need that the various creeds emerged.

Baptism and confession

The evidence is, as usual, fragmentary and open to various interpretations; but there is little doubt that the earliest confessions were tied to the administration of baptism. Some inkling of this is given in the Great Commission of Matthew 28:19, in which the risen Christ tells his disciples to teach all nations, 'baptizing them in the name of the Father, and of the Son, and of the Holy Spirit'. This familiar formula is often thought to have been a later insertion, ascribed to Jesus by an evangelist who wished to give later liturgical practice some basis in the teaching of Christ.

This assessment sounds plausible until we ask ourselves where this baptismal formula came from in the first place. We know that it appeared more than a century before any serious theological work on the Trinity was undertaken, so it could not have derived from that. In any case, everyone agrees that baptismal practice preceded theological reflection and dogmatic construction. Where then did the formula come from? Paul is unlikely to have invented it. He speaks of baptism into Christ (Romans 6:3) without mentioning the Father and the Spirit, and his one formulaic reference to the Trinity puts the persons in a different order (2 Corinthians 13:14). Other parts of the New Testament talk about baptism, but without any reference to the Trinity as such. Had Trinitarian baptism developed in the course of time, one would expect to find some explanation for it, but this is conspicuously absent. Even in Matthew we do not have it explained – an odd circumstance if we remember that the doctrine of the Trinity was not fully understood or accepted even among Christians. The conclusion that its presence is due to the direct command of Jesus, while not inescapable, seems to be considerably less unreasonable than is often supposed.

It appears that candidates for baptism were asked a number of questions designed to ascertain whether they had mastered the basic teaching of the faith or not. These questions followed a Trinitarian pattern like this one, which is taken from the *Apostolic Tradition* ascribed to Hippolytus:

1. Do you believe in God the Father Almighty?
2. Do you believe in Christ Jesus, the Son of God,
   who was born by the Holy Spirit from the Virgin Mary,
   who was crucified under Pontius Pilate, and died,
   and rose again on the third day living from the dead,
   and ascended into the heavens, and sat down on
   the right hand of the Father, and will come to judge
   the living and the dead?
3. Do you believe in the Holy Spirit in the holy Church?

Candidates for baptism would be expected to answer each of these questions in turn, a practice which has been reintroduced in some modern baptismal liturgies. Two things stand out here which are worthy of notice. First, the second question is much longer than the other two, and gives a quick summary of the life and work of Jesus. Second, the pattern corresponds closely to that followed in the Apostles' Creed.

It needs to be stressed here that formulations like the one above are typical rather than normative or mandatory. There are many similar examples, none of which is exactly the same as another. In that respect, standardization was a slow process which was not finally complete until the sixteenth century or even later! The Apostles' Creed, for instance, did not appear in its present form until the seventh century, and had to contend for many centuries with other variants; it is one of the ironies of Church history that, when the Church broke apart at the Reformation, concern for orthodoxy led to such standardization that today all branches of the Church use the same text!

In relation to ancient times, therefore, we are talking in the first instance of a pattern of confession, which was fixed only slowly. At the same time, we must distinguish between the baptismal questions and the form of confession taught to baptismal candidates beforehand. There is a close similarity between them of course, but the difference of style makes itself felt from the start. The question and answer pattern was always supplemented by a more declaratory form of confession, which strictly speaking is the proper ancestor of our creeds. In terms of content, the most striking feature of the declaratory confessions is their tendency to tack on additional, non-Trinitarian material. This tendency is by no means universal, but it happened very early on and became a standard feature, as we can see from the Apostles' Creed:

> I believe in the Holy Ghost
> the Holy Catholic Church
> the communion of saints
> the forgiveness of sins
> the resurrection of the body (and)
> the life everlasting.

What we cannot say for certain is what role, if any, declaratory statements of this type may have played in the worshipping life of the Church. Some scholars have held that a newly-baptized person would be expected to recite a summary of faith as part of his profession, but we have no solid evidence for this. On the other hand, we do know that their dual purpose of proclaiming the Gospel and confirming young Christians in it was taken very seriously. The close link between the summaries and baptism is brought out by the use of the word *symbolon* (Latin: *symbolum*) as the name for this type of confession. A *symbolon* was a symbol or sign of faith, and the word could be used to describe the act of baptism itself. Its easy transference to the statement of belief connected with baptism shows how inseparable the two were in practice, even if the precise details of their relationship are now no longer available to us.

The Apostles' Creed

The emergence of the baptismal symbol of faith leads us naturally into a consideration of the earliest credal documents which have come down to us. From the start, it is obvious that there was no fixed form which could be isolated as *the* creed. Different statements of belief appeared in most parts of the Mediterranean world during the course of the second and third centuries. Many attempts have been made to establish links between them, but the more closely the problem is investigated the more difficult the task becomes. There is a broad categorization into Western (Roman, and after about 250, Latin) and Eastern (Greek) types, but this means little more than that the Roman creed of which we have some knowledge has features not found elsewhere. It must be concluded that many different texts were in use without provoking friction or dissent. The main reason for this must be that the Trinitarian pattern and the extended exposition of the life and work of Christ are standard features common to them all. Points of difference are minor and seldom have doctrinal implications of their own. One of the most important of these is a difference in the opening sentence:

I believe in   God (Western)
I believe in one God (Eastern)

This difference has often been explained as theological, on the ground that the Eastern form emphasizes monotheism in a way which is more theoretical. The unity and simplicity of God were philosophical issues which the more pragmatic West had little time for, and therefore did not include in its *symbolum*. Much can be made of this, but, when all is said and done, it can hardly be claimed that the two statements are alien to one another. Indeed, most early Christians probably did notice, and the writings of people like Irenaeus and Tertullian show an eclecticism in such matters which argues against any rigid formula on either side.

At the same time however, standardization of a sort was taking place and had been accomplished at Rome by about 200. Our earliest evidence for a Roman creed comes from Tertullian, who makes a number of references to a *regula fidei* (*rule of faith*) which he then proceeds to quote. At times these references sound remarkably like the Apostles' Creed as we know it. Take the following, from his treatise *On the Veiling of Virgins* (1,3):

The rule of faith which is one everywhere and unalterable ... teaches us to believe in one God almighty, creator of the world, and his son Jesus Christ, born from the Virgin Mary, crucified under Pontius Pilate, raised on the third day from the dead, taken up into heaven, now sitting on the Father's right hand, destined to come to judge the living and the dead through the resurrection of the flesh.

A statement like this is too formulaic in tone to have been invented by Tertullian himself; it must reflect some confessional statement. But which one? Tertullian may have been quoting a local baptismal symbol used at Carthage, or he may have been referring to a creed in use at Rome, from where he believed Carthage had received its Christianity. On the other hand, the 'Eastern' features (note the *one* God) may indicate a more distant source, and it may even be that Tertullian has reconstructed a number of statements and merged them into one. There is certainly no reason to suppose that by *rule of faith* Tertullian meant a fixed form of words. His own usage is inconsistent in this respect, and it must be concluded that *unalterable* refers to the content of the teaching, not to the exact mode of its expression. It is even possible that *rule of faith* still refers in the first instance to Scripture (as the true *canon*), whose teaching is here briefly summarized in a series of recognized formulae embedded in Tertullian's own words.

This early flexibility eventually gave way to greater fixity, however. Some have thought that pressure from Gnosticizing heretics was influential in hardening the Church's arteries, but although theological controversy may have played some part, its effect on a baptismal symbol was more likely to produce greater numbers of variants to the wording. This is because there was a tendency to insert words specifically in order to combat particular deviations. These insertions were rarely standardized, and their identification provides evidence for the date and location of individual aberrations. Thus we find *only-begotten Son* replacing *only Son* in some Eastern documents, in order to counteract the heresy of adoptionism, which claimed that Jesus was just a man, adopted by God to be his Son.

A more important motive than this was the growing need to fix the Church's liturgy, particularly in controversial matters like baptism. What bothered the ancients was not the infants vs. adults controversy of modern times, but the efficacy of baptism in the threefold Name of God. If a man, woman or child were baptized, was he then cleansed from sin in a way which would make rebaptism necessary if he sinned again? Indeed, was rebaptism possible, or did post-baptismal sin destroy one's hope of salvation? Then again, what happened if a heretic performed the rite? Was such a baptism genuine? A matter as serious as this could not be left to chance, and it soon became necessary to establish a recognized form so that people could be sure it had all been done properly.

The fixing of a credal formula was an inevitable part of this process, though there is little evidence that the development was anti-heretical in intention. The threefold Name was what mattered, and baptism by heretics was generally admitted if it met that condition. The form of words was still not precisely settled, and there are minor variations among the different witnesses. Furthermore, there are a number of creeds, clearly derived from the Roman one though not identical with it, which proliferated throughout Western Europe after the fourth century. One of these, probably from Southern Gaul or Catalonia, was taken up by Charlemagne in 813 and made the standard form in his empire. Rome resisted it for several centuries, but adopted it in the end, possibly during the reforms of 1014 or slightly later. This, our Apostles' Creed, may be compared with the version of the Roman creed which was commented on by Rufinus of Aquileia about 404:

Rufinus	**Apostles' Creed**
I believe in God	I believe in God
the Father Almighty	the Father Almighty
	maker of heaven and earth
And in Christ Jesus	and in Jesus Christ
his only Son our Lord	his only Son our Lord
who was born from the Holy Ghost	who was *conceived* by the Holy Ghost
and the Virgin Mary	*born of* the Virgin Mary
Who under Pontius Pilate was crucified and buried	*Suffered* under Pontius Pilate was crucified, *dead* and buried
	He descended into hell
on the third day rose again from the dead	The third day he rose again from the dead
ascended into heaven	He ascended into heaven
sitteth on the right hand of the Father	And sitteth on the right hand of *God* the Father *Almighty*
From thence he shall come to judge the quick and the dead	From thence he shall come to judge the quick and the dead
and in the Holy Ghost	*I believe* in the Holy Ghost
the holy church	the Holy *Catholic* Church
	the communion of saints
the forgiveness of sins	the forgiveness of sins
the resurrection of the flesh	the resurrection of the *body and the life everlasting*

Here the resemblance is obvious, though the differences (italicized in the Apostles' Creed) are numerous and important. A feature of the old Roman creed is its tendency towards inversion – *Christ Jesus* instead of *Jesus Christ*, and *who under Pontius Pilate was crucified*. This is a typically Roman feature, though it is absent in Tertullian, who preferred the 'Eastern' form we now use. Tertullian also has the phrase *maker of heaven and earth*, which Rufinus omits. This reference to the creation may have crept into the Apostles' Creed under Eastern influence; but the obvious quotation from Genesis 1:1 is not especially characteristic of Eastern creeds, and many scholars think that, when it does appear in the East, it is as a result of Western influence! In any case the text of Rufinus is incomplete, so too much should not be made of this 'omission'.

More important are the changes resulting from theological controversy, which are obvious here. The first concerns the Virgin Birth. Rufinus confesses this clearly enough, but without specifying the relationship between the Holy Spirit and Mary. Was Jesus half God and half man? Or was he God who used Mary as a vehicle for his entry into the world?

The Christological controversies of the fourth and fifth centuries made it clear that Jesus was fully God and fully man, but reaffirmed that he did not have a human father. Thus we now confess that his *conception* was the work of the Holy Spirit but that his *birth* was that of a human child from a human mother.

There was also controversy concerning the death of Christ on the cross. Was Jesus God as well as man? If he was God, how could he suffer and die? Did he not simply go through the motions without actually enduring human pain? This idea would have robbed Jesus of his humanity and destroyed the incarnation, so it was ruled out and the creed was expanded to take account of the difficulty. For good measure the descent into hell (Psalm 139:8; 1 Peter 3:18f.) is added, to make the point that no form of human suffering is foreign to Christ's experience.

The change from *flesh* to *body* in the statement on the resurrection dates from 1539 and is apparent only in English translation; but it emphasizes a point to which the ancients were far from insensitive. There had always been a concern among Christians to emphasize that the material world was also the object of redemption in Christ. It was for this reason that the early Christians stressed that the flesh was redeemable, over against a type of Platonism which believed that the soul was divine but that the flesh was irretrievably evil. It was a necessary emphasis, but rather lopsided in its over-reaction to Platonism. The *body*, which links both flesh and soul, corrects this imbalance without distorting the truth which the original statement meant to defend. On the contrary, it affirms another equally important truth, which is that flesh and soul cannot be separated. It is not, and never has been, Christian doctrine to believe that only the soul is saved, or that it can be divorced from the body.

There is also an emphasis on catholicity, the communion of saints and everlasting life which does not appear in Rufinus. This reflects a deeper awareness of the universality of Christ's Church which transcends the obvious but spiritually insignificant barriers of time, space and death. Finally there are the cosmetic adjustments which reflect Eastern influence. *I believe* is added to the third article of the creed to distinguish it more clearly from the second, though it was not thought to be necessary at the head of the second article. *God* and *Almighty* are added to *Father* in the second article to emphasize the link with the first article. They serve no doctrinal purpose, other than being a rather obscure reminder that *Almighty* has not always been linked to *Father*, nor has *Father* in the first article always referred exclusively to the First Person of the Trinity. A more exact translation of the Greek text underlying the first article would give us:

I believe in (one) God, the Father, the Ruler of all.

At first God was thought of, in his Trinitarian fullness, as the Father of creation who upholds everything by his power. But it was inevitable that the universal fatherhood of God would give way to a more Trinitarian conception, in line with the Church's concern to emphasize the full deity of Christ. As long as *Father* remained a term applicable both to the First Person of the Trinity and to the whole Godhead, expressing the equality of the Son to his Father within that Godhead was bound to cause difficulties. *Almighty* remains a curiosity, though. Its position suggests that it applies to the Father *alone*, which is the heresy of Arius. This is not the intention, since the ancient purpose was to affirm the ruling providence of the Trinitarian Godhead. It no longer does this clearly, but it would be unsatisfactory to restore the Greek word *Pantocrator* because this would also suggest Arianism

– the Father as 'Ruler of All' would be ruler over Christ as well! *Almighty* is acceptable because it speaks of the power latent in the Father, though the creed does not explicitly extend it to the other two Persons of the Trinity, to whom it also applies.

This curiosity is a reminder of how subtle Christian doctrine can be, and how important it is to get it just right. It also shows us how hard it is to write a doctrinal statement which covers everything without being too long! Above all, it shows us that the creeds, though definitive in what they affirm, are not a bar to theological investigation but an invitation to press further into the truth of Scripture. For a generation which cries out for fresh study and exploration, the creeds still offer an unsuspected treasure-store of material waiting to be tapped by the adventurous and the creative.

The Creed of Nicaea

When we turn from the Roman creed to the East we enter a different world. Of course, as we have already seen, contacts between the two parts of the Empire were widespread, and Eastern influence was always a factor to be reckoned with at Rome. Whether there was much movement the other way may be doubted, though Harnack believed that the old Roman creed was exported to the East where it became the basis of credal development in much the same way as at Rome. Harnack's thesis was largely discredited by the work of H. Lietzmann, who published his findings in 1922. Lietzmann proposed a parallel credal development in the East on the basis of a common model which was not the old Roman creed but a native product with distinctive features of its own.

This creed did not exist in the manuscripts, but was reconstructed by Lietzmann out of the available material. As such it is a brilliant piece of work, which shows clearly how the Eastern tradition differed from the Roman:

> I believe in one God, the Father, the Ruler of all
>   maker of *all things visible and invisible*
> And in *one Lord* Jesus Christ, the only *begotten* Son of God
>   Who was *begotten from the Father before all worlds*
>   *through whom all things came into being*
>   *Who (for our salvation) became man*, suffered
>   and rose again on the third day and

ascended into heaven
And will come (again) to judge the quick and the dead.
And in the Holy Spirit.

The italicized words represent the main differences between this typical reconstruction and the old Roman creed. They are substantial enough to show that the East had a distinctive outlook which did not derive from a Western model.

First, the creation is expressed in a more philosophical way. The biblical image of *heaven and earth* is replaced by the more 'scientific', though equally correct, *visible and invisible*. The difference no doubt reflects a background of Platonism, according to which the invisible world had a close connection with the divine and was thought to be more 'real' than matter. In the light of that, it was necessary to emphasize that the invisible world was also creaturely.

The Christological article betrays no interest in the Holy Spirit or the Virgin Mary, despite the fact that it is deeply preoccupied with the Son's origin. There is a clear influence from John 1:1-14 and Colossians 1 in this article, and once again it reflects the more philosophical concerns of the East. The Son is begotten in the eternity of the Father and appears to be the agent of his own incarnation. Great emphasis is placed on the divine activity of the Lord Jesus Christ and on his absolute uniqueness, without going to the point of calling him God in his own right. This is an important point, because in it lies the seed of later controversy.

We then skate over the death of Christ with nothing other than the word *suffered*. This supplies an emphasis missing in the West but is totally inadequate from every other point of view. On this slender basis it is not even necessary to confess that Christ actually died! On the other hand, it is undoubtedly characteristic of Eastern theology, in which ideas of sacrifice and atonement were never easily absorbed. Even today, though the credal imbalance has long since been corrected, it cannot be said that Eastern theology has developed a very satisfactory doctrine of the cross, and this lack has affected the whole of Eastern Orthodox thought. To this day a philosophically-minded concentration on the light of glory is more congenial to the East than the starker reality of Christ crucified.

Lietzmann's achievement in isolating the independent origin of

Eastern creeds was very great and substantially faithful to the tradition it was trying to represent. Nevertheless, it has certain weaknesses which need to be recognized. First, he did not uncover an attested creed but composed a hypothetical reconstruction. As such it is *typical*, not historically *real*. J.N.D. Kelly has shown, in his masterly study of *Early Christian Creeds*, that Lietzmann's model cannot be regarded as the archetype of later developments. On the contrary, it seems that the East, much more than the West, possessed a diversity of baptismal symbols which defies scholarly harmonization. Lietzmann's theory supposes that Church life in the East ran parallel to that of the West, but that too is a false assumption. In the West, Rome was always dominant, and it served as a clearing-house for Eastern ideas which never ceased to pour in. In the East, on the other hand, there was no single centre of theological tradition which could impose the same degree of uniformity that obtained in the Latin half of the Empire.

In the circumstances, the existence of a wide variety of attested baptismal formulae, all corresponding in some measure to Lietzmann's broad outline, is not surprising. But whereas the Western credal tradition, despite its underlying unity, took many centuries to achieve complete standardization, things worked out very differently in the East. There it was the sudden eruption of theological controversy which forced credal harmonization against all the odds, and which made orthodoxy a battle-cry so strong that it became the hallmark of the Church's self-awareness.

It all started in 318 when Arius, a priest (presbyter) of Alexandria began to explain his understanding of the Person of Christ. Arius was a bright scholar who had trained at the theological school of Antioch, then one of the greatest centres of Aristotelian philosophy, as well as being the home of the ancient Church. Arius was well read in the Scriptures and deeply traditional in his thinking. He knew that before Origen's time the great theologians of the Church had all believed that the Trinity had come into being when God the Father brought forth his Word and his Spirit. This event had supposedly taken place at the beginning of the creation, when God the Father set out to make the universe with the aid of his two 'hands'. Arius also knew that Origen had taught that Jesus the Son of God was subordinate to his Father in heaven as well as on earth. To believe otherwise would have seemed like a denial of the accuracy of revelation. The earthly Jesus would have had a relationship to the Father different from that of the Son of God in heaven, and therefore he would not have been an accurate representation of the Son.

From Aristotle, Arius learned that a difference of name implied a difference of substance. An apple was not a tree, nor was the Father the Son. If the distinction between an apple and a tree were illusory, they could both be given the same name. On the other hand, if Father and Son had to be distinguished from each other by name, it was obvious that they were not the same thing. To Arius this meant that if the Father was God, the Son could not also be God in the same sense. He could be divine, but his divinity could be only partial and derivative. He could not occupy the same space that monotheism dictated was reserved for God with a capital G.

In support of this, Arius adduced a whole series of biblical texts, culled from any number of unlikely places. The key verse was Proverbs 8:22, which Arius held was a statement about the generation of the Son and which he read as follows, from the Septuagint:

The Lord created me [i.e. the Son] a beginning of his ways, for his works.

To this Arius could add the well-known statement that Jesus was 'the firstborn of all creation' (Colossians 1:15), as well as many other passages which he took to imply that the Son was a creature inferior to the Father.

The result of all this was Arianism, the belief that Jesus was a divine creature who had entered the human race. Its spiritual power lay in the attractiveness of having a saviour who was like us (as a creature) yet more powerful (because he was a divine being). It avoided the crude adoptionism of Paul of Samosata, who had taught that Jesus was a mere man, without so far identifying Jesus with God as to make it impossible for him to experience human suffering and death. Arianism was a subtle heresy which had an answer for everything, and it had a wide popular appeal. It was not stamped out in the Greek-speaking world until after the death of one of its champions, the emperor Valens, in 378.

Ironically, Valens died at the hands of the Goths, a Germanic tribe which had only recently been converted by the Arian missionary Ulfilas (or, Wulfila, in Gothic). The result was that most of the barbarian tribes which poured into the Roman Empire were Arians, who used their distinctive heresy as a kind of 'colour bar' to separate them from the masses and preserve their elitist quality. Only very slowly did this break down, and the last Arians were forcibly converted after the Third Council of Toledo in 589. Even then the situation was far from secure, and an underground Arianizing tendency persisted in Spain until well after the Arab conquest in the early eighth century. We last hear of it in 794, when it was anathematized by Charlemagne at the Council of Frankfurt.

Of course, none of this could have been predicted by the horrified bishop Alexander, to whom Arius was obliged to offer explanations. Before long, Arian ideas were circulating all over the East and causing dissension everywhere they went. Christianity had only recently emerged from hiding, and its fortunes seemed to be tied to the career of the emperor Constantine, who did not finally crush his rivals for the throne until 324. Once that happened, it was clear that the emperor was going to do something about the controversy, which was threatening to split the Church he had done so much to help. To forestall imperial interference, a group of bishops met at Antioch in January 325 and drafted an anti-Arian confession. It was very long, not always clear, and showed that the Church as a whole had not yet got to grips with the heresy. But it is important because it is the first of the synodical confessions which were to become the standard credal forms of the East.

As it turned out, the Synod of Antioch was a trial run for the council which met at Nicaea on 19 June 325 under the joint presidency of Constantine and his ecclesiastical adviser, bishop Ossius (Hosius) of Cordoba. Constantine wanted a compromise solution which would uphold orthodoxy without offending any more Arians than was absolutely necessary. The bishops debated how best to achieve this aim, and eventually they produced the following credal statement:

We believe in one God, the Father, Ruler of All
    maker of all things visible and invisible.
And in one Lord Jesus Christ, the Son of God,
    begotten from the Father, *only-begotten,*
    that is, from the substance of the Father,
    God from God, light from light,
    true God from true God,
    begotten not made,

of one substance with the Father
through whom all things were made
things in heaven and things on earth,
Who for us men and for our salvation
came down and became incarnate;
he became man, suffered and rose again
on the third day, ascended to the heavens
and will come to judge the quick and the dead.
And in the Holy Spirit.

Here the link with Lietzmann's reconstruction is obvious, as are the differences. *Only-begotten* is displaced from its usual position before *Son of God* and given an independent place, both to confound Arius, who could have agreed that Jesus was God's only Son, and to explain the term more fully. All that follows is designed to shore up the Son's deity and to deny that he is a creature. This is why it is said that all things, both in heaven and on earth, were created through the Son. The key phrase, however, is the line *of one substance with the Father*. In Greek the first three words are rendered by the single term *homoousios*, of which the official Latin translation is *consubstantialis*. It was on the meaning of this word that the next theological controversy was to turn.

Arius was defeated and deposed at Nicaea, but his ideas were not. In fact, they had hardly been countered in any serious way. The orthodox had the imperial army, but the Arians had the proof-texts from Scripture and the weight of tradition, as it appeared to them. Moreover, the orthodox advantage was precarious and short-lived. Constantine tried to patch things up with Arius in 332, and swung away from the orthodox die-hards who refused compromise. This position remained the official imperial policy until 361, when Julian the Apostate renounced Christianity altogether. Julian died in battle in 363 and his successor Jovian reverted to orthodoxy for a while, but in 364 his successor Valens leaned once more towards Arianism. It can therefore be said with justice that Arian sympathizers ruled the state for forty-three of the fifty-six years which separated the Council of Nicaea from that of Constantinople in 381, compared with only eleven years in which the orthodox were in the ascendant.

Things got so bad at times that Athanasius, Alexander's successor as bishop of Alexandria, appeared to be the only defender of orthodoxy left. Providentially, he was more than equal to the task, and the defence of the Nicene settlement was largely his work. Athanasius was bishop of Alexandria from 328 to 373, a span of forty-six years, seventeen of which he spent in exile. In 339 he was forced to flee to Rome, but although he was not there long, the journey proved to be highly fruitful. In Rome, he met Western theologians and their ideas, which were re- markably like his own. The West had played little part in Christological debate until then, but after 339 it became Athanasian to a man.

By then, of course, Athanasius had gone far beyond a merely political solution to his difficulties. He had begun the counterattack against Arius in a famous book *On the Incarnation*, which is still in print. This treatise is really the second part of a longer work which deals with the fall of man and his need of a saviour. Arius is nowhere mentioned, and the whole book is cast as an evangelistic tract designed to win over pagans. But although he does not say so explicitly, it is clear that Athanasius was trying to present orthodox Christianity in a way which would make it a convincing alternative to the subtle heresy which was threatening the Church.

The book is distinguished by a clear and forceful use of Scripture, in a way which goes against the allegorizing tendencies usually ascribed to the Alexandrian school. Athanasius' technique was as brilliant as it was simple. Instead of arguing against the proof-texts of Arius, he sought to demonstrate that the logic of the Scriptures as a whole made the incarnation of the Word inevitable. God did not become man because some philosopher thought it would be a good idea, but because he had created man in his own image. It was because man was uniquely related to God – so uniquely that even angels did not share in their relationship – that only God could make good Adam's disobedience and restore the human race to fellowship with himself.

It is true that Athanasius tended to express himself in a way which nowadays would be called 'universalist', but this should not be misunderstood. He was deeply impressed by the death of the Word, which he believed completely changed the destiny of the human race; but at the same time he recognized that not all men entered into the inheritance which Christ had procured for them. Some souls remained invincible to the end, and so they perished in a death from which there was no resurrection.

Athanasius' presentation of the whole history of salvation demonstrated that the incarnation was a logical necessity within the created order and the plan of God. Later, he tackled the Arians on their own ground. His four *Discourses* against them took their favourite texts to pieces, showing that within the framework of the whole Bible these texts could not be interpreted in an Arian sense.

Athanasius was hampered by a faulty Greek translation and his lack of Hebrew; he was also inclined (as a modern exegete is not) to accept a verse like Proverbs 8:22 as Christological, which did not favour his argument. Yet in spite of these disadvantages he was able to show that Arius was wrong. How could the Son be a creature when the text says that he was brought forth 'for his works'? Surely this was the creation, in which the Son was a co-worker with the Father. The text further states that the Son was 'created a beginning of his ways', but God's ways do not have a beginning as men understand that term. Therefore the Son was not created in the human sense, but begotten in an eternal and mysterious way.

Such dexterity in the use of Scripture established Athanasius as the leading theologian of his time, and his name became the hallmark of orthodoxy. Even centuries later, when men sought to discover who had written the greatest Western creed, it was to him that they naturally turned, and so for a thousand years he was hailed as the author of the 'Athanasian' Creed.

But Athanasius was not merely a gifted exegete. He was also skilled in logic and in the use of words, which he controlled with unusual power. He was not disturbed by the many meanings which attached to the term *hypostasis*, and was content to study the point of issue, rather than hang on an empty formula. He did not mind how the unity of the Father and Son in the Godhead was expressed, as long as the principle was guarded. He was a man so conscious of his relationship to God that he could never be side-tracked by a hair-splitting theology.

Yet at the same time he was quick to spot error and denounce it. When Eusebius of Caesarea proposed that the word *homoousios* could be modified to *homoiousios* (of a like, or similar, substance) he immediately sensed the danger latent in this 'minor' alteration. If the two words were used of mankind, they would indeed be interchangeable. I share the same substance as my father; it is also a similar substance, by which I mean that my humanity is an extension of my father's substance, which shares the same properties.

When the terms are applied to God, however, a numerical difficulty occurs. I share humanity with my father, but we are two human beings; Jesus shares divinity with his Father, but they are not two Gods. It is therefore wrong to say that the Son is of a similar substance to his Father. He must be of the same substance, because   numerically speaking there is only one God. It is a subtle point, but it was of great importance in the struggle against a semi-Arian theology which would eventually have cut the link between Jesus and his Father, and destroyed the principle of the incarnation.

There was one point, however, on which Athanasius was less satisfactory. That was the great question of the human soul. Like other Greeks before him, he was deeply influenced by the belief that man was created in the image and likeness of God. Like them, too, he was perplexed to know just what these were. It was commonplace to assume that the image and the likeness were two different things. When man fell, he lost the likeness (spirit) but retained the image (soul). This image was the image of Christ the Word (Logos) because neither of the other persons could be portrayed, and because it possessed the faculty of reason, which had been stranded, though not corrupted by the fall. It was to rescue this reason (*logos*) that Reason himself became flesh.

The difficulty came in describing this incarnation. Did Jesus of Nazareth have a human soul or not? Athanasius was never quite sure. Jesus was a man, so presumably he did have a human soul. On the other hand, the presence in him of the divine Reason was such that this soul was virtually absorbed by it. Certainly it could not have acted independently. But in that case, what did the human soul of Jesus do? Was it not superfluous to his make-up? The problem thus posed was tackled by a disciple of Athanasius who thought he had the answer. Apollinarius maintained that in Jesus the divine Reason took the place of a human soul. As a man, Jesus was a combination of Word (Reason) and flesh, just as John 1:14 proclaimed.

Apollinarianism, as this heresy came to be called, was highly attractive to the Alexandrian mind, which was frequently to be accused of it in the way that the West was accused of Sabellianism (modalism). It was dangerous for two reasons. First, as Gregory of Nazianzus pointed out, 'what was not assumed was not healed'. If Jesus did not have a human soul, then no human soul could claim to be saved. The Saviour would have come to redeem only the flesh! Second, it was well known that it was the soul, not the flesh, which was the seat of sin. Only a Pharisee might have thought otherwise, and Jesus had made it plain to them that evil comes from within a man (Mark 7:20, 21). If that is so, of course, the source of evil in man must be dealt with if salvation is to have any meaning. Third, a Jesus who did not have a human soul could not have been tempted, since temptation works on the soul, not on the flesh (though the flesh might be the *source* of temptation).

For all these reasons, therefore, Apollinarius was condemned and a shadow was cast over the brilliant achievement of Athanasius. But the main thrust of his labours as a defender of Nicaea was not to be blunted, and soon after his death his faithfulness was rewarded by an overwhelming victory for his theology.

The First Council of Constantinople

The fourth century was a time of theological ferment at every level, and it is not to be thought that the voice of Athanasius was the only one to be heard in defence of orthodoxy. Others of equal force and ability took up the cry and launched themselves into territory which up to then had remained largely unexplored.

Before Nicaea (and for some time after it among semi-Arians and the like), most Christians had thought of the Trinity as a hierarchy of three divine beings. When the Son was declared to be the equal of the Father in every respect, this neat scheme was upset. Father and Son were now on the same level, but what about the Holy Spirit? What happened was that many minds now moved from the picture on the left to the one on the right:

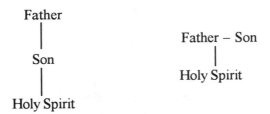

The views of these people were expressed in different ways by Eunomius and by Macedonius. Both men insisted on the subordination of the Holy Spirit; but while Eunomius apparently tried to hang on to the former model because it accorded better with Platonism, Macedonius was prepared to think of the Spirit as subordinate to both Father and Son equally. On the basis of Scripture it seemed as if they had a strong case. The Holy Spirit was not personal in the same sense as the other two Persons. He did not fit the family analogy which the names Father and Son suggested. There were scriptural texts in which it was not clear whether 'the Spirit' meant the Holy Spirit or the essence of God. In many places, Father and Son were mentioned together without the Spirit. All these things seemed to point to a subordinate role for the third member of the Trinity.

Once more, as with Arius two generations before, the Church was caught with an inadequate theology. The Creed of Nicaea was no more enlightening than the Roman creed in the West. 'I believe in the Holy Spirit' was so vague it could mean anything! But it is significant that the best minds of the time sensed the danger and set out to combat it. Basil of Caesarea started the counter-argument, but in a way which was unusual for his time. Basil wanted to reconcile as many Eunomians and Macedonians as he could to the orthodox faith, so he determined not to say anything which might offend them before they had heard his argument. In fact, in all his writings, Basil never quite said, in so many words, that the Holy Spirit was God!

Instead, he attacked his enemy from the rear and worked his way forward. In the Scriptures the Holy Spirit was the Giver of life, a prerogative which belonged to God. He was worshipped and honoured alongside the Father and the Son. He had inspired the prophets to write what everyone acknowledged was the Word of God. He was even called the Lord, a title reserved for God the Father and the Son. All these evidences pointed in a single direction. Basil also pointed out that the Holy Spirit proceeded from the Father (John 15:26), an expression also used of Jesus (John 8:42).

At this point Basil encountered a difficulty which was to cause great embarrassment later on. For him, as for Origen and the entire Eastern tradition, the Father was the fountainhead of deity, the personification of the nature of God. To proceed from the Father, therefore, meant that the being in question shared in the divine essence. But how? Unlike Macedonius, Basil ended up with a scheme rather like this:

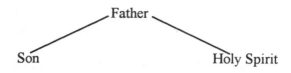

The Father was the source of the Godhead in which both the Son and the Holy Spirit participated. It was a very traditional scheme, reminiscent of the 'two hands' of God which had been widely held before Origen's time. But in the theological context of the fourth century, it was bound to raise awkward questions. If the Son and the Spirit came equally from the Father, were they twins? Could a man go to the Father through the Spirit without the mediation of the Son? These questions sound odd to us, but they were real enough to people who were puzzled by Jesus' teaching. Why had he called the Holy Spirit *another* Comforter? Why had he told his disciples that they would do greater things than he had done when the Holy Spirit had come?

These questions were tackled, in a preliminary way, by Gregory of Nazianzus, a close friend of Basil's and an exponent of his thought. Gregory said that the Son was begotten (generated), whereas the Holy Spirit proceeded from the Father. There was a difference between the two, but nobody could say what it was. God had revealed the fact, but the explanation of it was hidden in mystery. So it would remain, until, as always, a new controversy would make further exploration of this mystery a pressing necessity.

Meanwhile, there were more immediate problems to face. The death of the Emperor Valens in 378 finished Arianism in the East. The orthodox were now in the ascendant, and there were other heresies to denounce. A council was called to meet at Constantinople in 381, principally in order to restate the faith of Nicaea. One hundred and eighty-six bishops, all of them from the East, gathered in the capital where one hunrdred and fifty of them reaffirmed their orthodoxy, fortified now by the teaching of Athanasius, Basil and Gregory, who was actually present at the opening session.

What happened next is a matter of dispute. For centuries it was believed that the Creed of Nicaea was modified by the inclusion of these new insights and then reaffirmed as the 'Nicene' Creed. This version of events was first mentioned at the Council of Chalcedon in 451, where the longer creed was produced and read out as the 'Faith of the 150 Fathers'. It is recorded, though, that many of the delegates at Chalcedon expressed surprise at this; they had never heard of it before. Between 381 and 451, years of intense controversy, the creed in this form never appeared once! The fact that it carried some conviction at Chalcedon indicates that it was not a forgery, but where it came from is a mystery. Scholarly study has shown that it is not derived from the Creed of Nicaea, despite many resemblances, and it is probable that it originated as yet another baptismal creed, augmented to include the theology of Constantinople I some time after the Council had completed its work.

Our Nicene Creed closely resembles this document, though it is expressed in the singular form *I believe*. The points of difference are mostly unimportant, and reflect the fact that the official Latin text differs in odd particulars from the Greek, which is reproduced in translation below. There is the usual rendering of *Pantocrator* as *almighty*, the inclusion of *God from God* in the second article, and a change from *and* to *of the Virgin Mary*. The only alteration of any consequence is the Western addition of *and the Son* after *proceedeth from the Father* in the third article. This occurred in the sixth century and eventually led to a controversy which helped split the Eastern and Western churches apart.

Rightly or wrongly, this Creed is now included in the proceedings of the Council of 381, a place which is confirmed in the decrees of the fifth and sixth sessions of the Council of Chalcedon (22 and 25 October 451, respectively). But although its exact pedigree is a matter of speculation, its theology is clearly the same as the orthodoxy proclaimed by the 150 Fathers. It reads:

> We believe in one God, the Father, ruler of all
>   maker of heaven and earth
>   of all things visible and invisible.
> And in one Lord Jesus Christ, the only-begotten Son of God
>   begotten from the Father before all ages
>   light from light
>   true God from true God
>   begotten not made
>   of one substance with the Father
>   by whom all things were made
>   Who for us men and for our salvation

came down from heaven
and was incarnate by the Holy Ghost
and the Virgin Mary
and became man
and was crucified for us under Pontius Pilate
and suffered and was buried,
and rose again on the third day
according to the Scriptures
and ascended into heaven
and sitteth on the right hand of the Father,
and will come again with glory
to judge the quick and the dead
Whose kingdom shall have no end.
And in the Holy Spirit
the Lord and giver of life
Who proceedeth from the Father
Who with the Father and Son together is worshipped
and glorified
Who spake through the prophets
In one holy Catholic and Apostolic Church
We acknowledge one baptism for the remission of sins
We look for the resurrection of the dead
And the life of the world to come.

When we compare this Creed to the one of Nicaea, we notice the highly developed third article on the Holy Spirit, the explicit recognition of a resurrection of the *dead* (not of the *flesh*) and the strong Western influence throughout.

The first article combines *heaven and earth* with *visible and invisible*, thereby linking West and East, biblical imagery and philosophical accuracy. The second article makes specific reference to the suffering of Jesus on the cross, tying it literally to the witness of Scripture. This makes a considerable advance on the earlier creed, and is not typical of the Eastern tradition. The only oddity is the omission of *died* between *suffered* and *was buried*, which preserves the Eastern reluctance to mention the fact of Christ's death too openly. Lastly, the final article contains a non-Trinitarian appendix which also reflects a Western, rather than an Eastern, model.

After 451 this Creed, slightly adapted for personal and liturgical use, was accepted as authoritative by East and West alike. It is the only credal statement to be recognized by all branches of the Christian Church. At first it was recited mainly at baptisms, but gradually it began to be said (not sung) during the Communion service as well. This practice began among the heretical Monophysites in 476, as an attempt on their part to be more orthodox than the orthodox. The Creed was introduced into the liturgy at Constantinople in 511 and after 589 it was used in Spain, though only as a preparation before the Communion service began.

Charlemagne eventually put it in after the Gospel, sometime around the year 798. This custom had reached him from England via Alcuin of York, and had originated in Ireland. It seems that the Irish monks had got the Creed from Spain and treated it with their characteristic originality! Eventually, about 1014, even Rome gave way and admitted it to the liturgy, where it has remained ever since. For some unknown reason the English Reformers dropped the word *holy* before *catholic and apostolic Church*, and this curious form is preserved in the Book of Common Prayer; otherwise, they did not amend it.

Non-liturgical churches have not made much use of this Creed, to their great loss, but all of them accept its doctrine. More than any other document, the 'Nicene' Creed remains for all Christians the touchstone and guarantee of orthodox, biblical belief.

5

The City of God

In studying the doctrinal struggles of the fourth century, one thing stands out in contrast both to the earlier period of the Church and to the situation which obtains in our own time. That is the prominent role played by the state. At times imperial involvement in Church affairs may have been ambiguous or ineffective, and it was certainly opposed by bishops like Athanasius, who believed that the emperor was supporting a policy injurious to the interests of the orthodox. But there it always was, convoking councils, promulgating decrees and repressing dissent.

The modern mind, accustomed to freedom of religion and separation, for all practical purposes, of Church and state, finds this difficult to understand. Did the state hijack the Church and make it conform to the wishes of secular rulers whose own faith was at best highly suspect? Are the statements of orthodoxy transmitted to us products of an age which is now behind us, and is their binding character no longer applicable as a result? The demand for doctrinal pluralism in the name of religious freedom is a hallmark of liberalism so sacred that virtually no denomination today would dare embark on a heresy trial, or excommunicate a member for doctrinal aberrations. The spectre of the Inquisition, of the stake, and of a thousand crimes committed by the state in the name of Christian orthodoxy, hangs like a heavy cloud over the Church and causes many people to dismiss the centuries of 'Christendom' as a departure from the gospel of Christ.

If we are to examine the justice of these claims, we must look carefully at the situation which obtained during the formative period of Church-state relations. Christianity is unique among the great monotheistic religions in that it never associated a state apparatus with its inner essence. 'My kingdom is not of this world' said Jesus (John 18:36), in marked contrast to the Jews who expected the Messiah to restore the Israel of King David, and to the Muslims, who followed Muhammed's command to spread the word of Allah by the sword. The followers of Jesus betrayed no such tendencies. The Apostles taught that the existing state was appointed by God, and enjoined civil obedience on their congregations (Romans 13:1-7; 1 Peter 2:13-17). This did not preclude them from identifying this same state with the Satanic forces of evil which would eventually be overthrown (Revelation 18); but as this destruction was part of the eschatological fulfilment of the gospel, it cannot be regarded as a call to revolution.

Whether the Apostles thought that Christians should have some form of political involvement is unclear. Jesus said that Caesar's subjects should give him his due (Matthew 22:21), but that is not quite the same thing. For most Jews of his time, political involvement meant paying taxes and they had a dim view of tax-collectors. This was not just because they were collaborators with a foreign power, but because they lived off a corrupt system. Every tax-collector was appointed to raise a certain amount of money for the government, but he was not paid a salary for this. His own earnings were entirely in the form of commission, which meant that he could get rich by being as extortionate as possible. The authorities approved the system because it was the most effective way of ensuring a constant source of revenue, but it was bound to cause unrest among subject peoples. When the Roman Empire eventually fell, the relief from taxation was so great that the provinces, despite a lingering loyalty to the imperial idea, were hardly more than lukewarm towards the attempts made to restore it.

Apart from tax collection, the other form of political involvement was military service. During the first century AD there was a visible shift of power away from the civilian administration to the army, whose commander-in-chief was the emperor. Rome never established a hereditary monarchy, and the forms of republican rule survived intact for centuries. The emperor himself was only the first citizen (*princeps*), a position which he retained until the reform of Diocletian in AD 285. Diocletian then made it plain that it was the emperor who was head of state, not the two consuls who had been elected annually since 509 BC. Even so, the dual consulate survived until AD 542, and the senate retained a shadowy existence even longer, dying out only with the final collapse of the Empire in 1453.

The form of democracy remained intact, but the reality was rather different. When an emperor died he would be succeeded either by his son or by another strong man specially adopted for the purpose. This second system worked very well at the height of the Empire's glory, from AD 96 to 180, but it broke down when Marcus Aurelius (161-180) allowed his natural son Commodus (180-192) to succeed him. Commodus was incompetent and was eventually murdered. The senate exercised its residual right to appoint an emperor, as it had done in AD 68 and 96, but the army did not support it. Rival commanders fought for supremacy. The result was civil war. There had of course been civil wars before, most notably after the murder of Nero in AD 68, but after 193 they became more or less endemic. It was not until after the eighth century, in very different circumstances, that any ruler was to establish a dynasty which would last more than a hundred years or so.

Such a situation gave the career soldier a degree of political importance which no ordinary citizen had. By supporting or deserting a commander in the field, he could decide the choice of ruler in a way which enabled a good man with a loyal following to seize power with relative ease. The instability of such a system was compensated by the way in which it could dispose of an unpopular or incompetent sovereign. The method seems strange to us, but it was generally quite effective and the state retained its underlying cohesion for many centuries.

Within this set-up, the place of a Christian was ambiguous. There were soldiers in the New Testament Church, perhaps including the one who had professed faith at the foot of the cross itself (Matthew 27:54). On the other hand, soldiers were the agents of persecution, and many early Christians believed that the oath of loyalty to the emperor was contrary to Christian principles. Army religion was pagan, so a Christian had little choice but to compromise his beliefs, at least on parade duty.

Opposition to military service had nothing to do with pacifism though. Christians very quickly came to see themselves as spiritual warriors, doing battle for the faith. Paul's well-known call in Ephesians 6 became the rallying-cry of believers – put on the whole armour of God! It was a cry which touched the deepest chords when the Church began to feel the persecuting power of the state being used against it. The first major persecution came after the great fire of Rome in 64, when Nero needed a scapegoat to shift the blame from himself. It is generally believed that the leading apostles lost their lives in the purge that followed this event, but the New Testament reminds us that Christians had already fallen foul of the state.

Why? Fingers were frequently pointed at the Jews, and they certainly took a leading part at the beginning. The crucifixion of Jesus was in this sense archetypal. The Jewish leaders wanted to get rid of Jesus for theological reasons, and the Romans complied, somewhat uncomprehendingly. The stoning of Stephen, the execution of James and the many trials of Paul fit into a similar pattern. It took a generation for the Romans to realize that Christians were not Jews, but by then the prejudice against them was firmly entrenched. During the second century they were occasionally hunted down and put to death, but the method was somewhat erratic. It is probable that only the lower classes were affected, since after about 180 there is little sign that the church leadership, which by that time was being drawn increasingly from the higher classes, was seriously affected.

In our discussion of ancient philosophy we mentioned the apologies, or defences of Christianity, which were a feature of this period. These writings tell us a good deal about persecution and the attitude of the authorities towards the Christians. The legal basis for persecution was slender, being based on precedent rather than law. Tertullian thought that Nero's decree was still in force in his day, but this is now widely disputed. Pliny the Younger treated Christians as undesirables, but apparently knew of no law against them. Later on, the irrationality of persecuting a harmless, law-abiding sect was to be a major ingredient in Christian protests against the attitude of the imperial government.

Organized persecution on a universal scale broke out in 177, but it was short-lived. There was a longer period of suffering in the decade after 251, during which Bishop Cyprian of Carthage lost his life. Finally there was the Great Persecution of 303, in which Diocletian tried to rid the Empire, once and for all, of the Christian menace. Of these persecutions we have vivid records. Frenzied mobs attacked known believers and accused them of causing earthquakes, famine and disease. Christians were supposed to be atheists because they rejected the pagan pantheon, and cannibals because they ate the 'body and blood of Christ' at secret gatherings. Natural disasters quickly mobilized a superstitious populace and the feeding of the lions began.

Christians defended themselves in the only ways they could. Some ran away and others recanted temporarily. Such behaviour was always regarded as cowardly and disapproved of, but the weaker brethren were usually readmitted after an act of contrition (penance). Within the fellowship, spiritual warfare became the order of the day. The government was only a visible scourge of the devil, who attacked the flesh in many guises. The true warrior had to become an ascetic, preparing himself against the day when he might be called to become a witness (*martyr* in Greek) in the public arena.

The demands of asceticism grew more stringent as time went on. Occasional fasting turned into semi-permanent starvation. Bathing and shaving, luxuries of Roman civilization, were forbidden. Continence within marriage became absolute celibacy, and separation from the world led in the end to retreat into the desert. Elijah, John the Baptist, Paul in Arabia and the wilderness temptations of Jesus became the models for the life of the typical ascetic or hermit (from the Greek word *eremos*, meaning desert). The desert regions of Syria and Egypt blossomed with cells, or *scetae* as they were known from the chief centre in the wilderness near Alexandria. Under the inspiration of Antony, who was born in 251 and died in 356 at the age of 105, this new way of life became a standard feature of the quest for union with God through spiritual warfare in the soul. When Christianity finally acquired legal recognition, it was this type of devotion which captured the imagination and allegiance of those who would sacrifice everything for the sake of Christ.

Official recognition

Crisis hit the Church under the reforming zeal of Diocletian, who not only revamped the administration but tried to restore a sense of pride in the spiritual legacy of Rome and its civilizing mission. Romans, even Christians, were intensely patriotic and this appeal did not go unheeded. What Diocletian failed to see was that the old myths had lost their power. Constant calamity and civil war had destroyed the old confidence, and Diocletian himself had found it expedient to bury the Republic. What he did not understand was that the vacuum thus created had been filled to a large extent by Christianity, which was now widespread in the civil service and in the army.

The persecution of 303 tore apart the fabric of society in a way which had not happened before. Soldiers were put to death, among them Alban, the first British martyr. Local officials recanted by the hundred, turning in their Bibles in order to save their skins. Later these people were branded as *traditores* ('handers-over', a word which has now become *traitor* in English) and attempts were made to put them out of the Church. Many ordinary people were put to death, whilst others were tortured or had their property confiscated. Those who endured to the end emerged with battle-scars which later made them the leaders of the newly-legalized Church.

Diocletian failed, and after his retirement on 1 May 305 his policies were relaxed. He had divided the Empire into four parts, but his successors soon upset his plans. Constantius, who became Emperor of the West, died the following year at York, and was succeeded by his son Constantine. This succession was disputed, and Constantine had to spend eighteen years in constant warfare in order to secure his throne and the Empire.

The key to victory was the capture of Rome, which Constantine achieved at the battle of the Milvian Bridge, on 28 October 312. The day before this battle, he saw in the noonday sun a flaming cross, with the legend *By this conquer* written underneath it. Constantine promptly ordered the *chi-ro* monogram of the Christians to be painted on the shields of his men, who then defeated superior forces and entered the capital in triumph. Early the following year he issued the Edict of Milan which granted toleration to the Christians and brought the Church into the light of day.

The Edict of Milan gained Christian support for Constantine's cause and it was supported somewhat reluctantly by Licinius, Constantine's rival and co-emperor in the East. How far the move was political, and how far it was spiritual is impossible to say. Constantine's vision bears all the marks of a superstitious religiosity which affects many people in times of crisis, only to fade later on. On the other hand, the emperor never forgot the experience. It determined his policies for the rest of his life, making him in later years the revered founder of a Christian Empire. His own contemporary, Eusebius of Caesarea, wrote a biography of the emperor and a number of panegyrical works praising him.

Modern historians have been considerably less deferential than Eusebius, and the question of Constantine's conversion is far from settled. One recent attempt to explain it is that of Alastair Kee, whose book, *Constantine versus Christ*, gives us his assessment of the situation. According to him, Constantine believed in a wonder-working

Old Testament type of God. He was the first of a long line of military Christians, who like Winston Churchill were not so much pillars of the Church as flying buttresses – supporting it from the outside. The book dissects Eusebius' great biography of Constantine to show that even he could not pretend that the emperor had an articulate Christian faith. Right up until his baptism on his deathbed, he remained *fidei defensor*, defender of the faith, without really entering into it himself.

There is obviously a good deal of truth in this judgement, but its significance can be easily exaggerated. Eusebius portrayed Constantine as the Peer of the Apostles, the Regent of God on earth and the source of all virtue. On the other hand, he was a semi-Arian whose beliefs found favour at court towards the end of Constantine's life. Athanasius never sank to such flattery, nor did his followers, who were at odds with the state for nearly half a century. For him the emperor was a fact of life to be solicited if he were orthodox and shunned if he were not. Spiritual battles were to be won by spiritual means, or at least by spiritual people. Instead of the imperial army, Athanasisus relied for support on the solitaries (*monachoi*, or monks) of the Egyptian desert. These men banded together in defence of the truth, and returned in large numbers to the big cities, where they functioned as agitators among the people.

Imperial interventions in Church affairs were sporadic, as was their success. As early as 313, a delegation from Carthage reached Milan with an appeal to Constantine to settle a dispute. The election of Caecilian to the bishopric was being contested by a fanatical group of hard-liners who accused him of having been a *traditor*. They had elected a rival bishop, Majorinus, and seceded from the rest of the Church. The case was tried at Rome, where Caecilian's election was upheld. The following year Constantine called a synod of bishops to meet at Arles, and once more Caecilian was vindicated. Majorinus died soon after this, and was succeeded by Donatus, who had been the mastermind of the affair from the beginning. The Donatists, as the rebels were called, split the North African church from top to bottom by their uncompromising attitude towards *traditores*. Their defeat in the courts merely hardened their opposition, and soon they were courting persecution on the ground that only a martyr could be sure of his salvation.

Constantine sent troops to quell Donatism, but he was unsuccessful. Various attempts were made to achieve some kind of reconciliation, and many Donatists were won back at the Council of Carthage in 411. The rigorist theology of its adherents gave Donatism considerable resilience, however, and the sect did not finally disappear until after the Muslim conquest in 698. Its effect on the Church was divisive and probably disastrous, as zeal without knowledge or love so often is. The main Church was driven into dependence on the state for its survival, since the Donatists resorted to banditry in defence of their claims, and its witness was slowly strangled. When the Arabs arrived, the will to resist had gone and most of the remaining Christians emigrated or converted to Islam. Of all the Mediterranean lands, North Africa was the only one in which Christianity was totally wiped out, a phenomenon which many have attributed in large measure to the evil effects of the Donatist schism on the morale and outlook of the Church.

In the East, Constantine's achievement was greater and more fruitful in the long term. He decided for both strategic and spiritual reasons that the Empire needed a new capital, and after some deliberation chose the ancient Greek city of Byzantium at the entrance of the Bosporus. This magnificent site commanded the gateways to Europe and Asia, and on 11 May 330 it was rededicated in a Christian ceremony as the New Rome, the City of Constantine. For centuries Constantinople would be the chief city of Christendom and the bulwark of the orthodox East, but its cultural significance is greater still.

The New Rome was founded as a Latin city in the Greek-speaking world, but it could not remain like that for long. Soon it became a symbol of the duality of the Empire – Latin in the West, Greek in the East. This duality was confirmed in 395 when the Empire was formally split in two, and it persisted after the collapse of the West in 476. The new capital stood for the fusion of Greek civilization, Roman law and the Christian religion, that unique combination which has so marked European culture. It gave the Greek world a new lease on life, and made the City (*Polis*) the centre of the universe. So strong did this tradition become that even the Muslim Turks have had to recognize it. When they abolished the imperial name in 1928 they could do no more than replace it with the pseudo-Turkish *Istanbul* – in reality a corruption of the Greek words *eis ten Polin* ('in the City').

The founding of the new capital brought into sharp focus another problem which the Church had not previously faced, that of legal status and recognition. After 313 the bishops of each local church received state recognition, and their responsibilities were gradually defined in terms of law. The Empire was divided into provinces and regions known as *dioceses*, and bishops came to be appointed in each major town. They had responsibility for the surrounding area which, in imitation of the state system, was called a diocese as well. Each of these bishops was accorded a rank in line with the importance of his city in the Empire.

In practice, this meant that the top three bishoprics were those of Rome, Alexandria and Antioch. This arrangement had existed long before 313, in fact, though not on a formal basis. The creation of Constantinople, however, provoked a crisis in this familiar system. As the capital and New Rome, it deserved an important place, but before 330 it had been subordinate even to the nearby town of Heraclea. This embarrassment was overcome by giving Constantinople second place, after Rome but before Alexandria. Rome was put out by this, because the political origin of the move was so blatantly obvious. If the time were to come when Rome would cease to be recognized even as the honorary capital of the Empire, its position as the chief bishopric would be lost. Alexandria was equally put out, since it had itself been founded by a great emperor to be the capital of the Greek world, and was now losing that position.

The result of all this was the emergence of a spiritual justification for the ancient priority of the churches. Rome was to be first because Peter, the chief apostle, had been its first bishop and because both he and Paul had been martyred there. Alexandria owed its position to its apostolic foundation by St Mark the Evangelist – not really an apostle, but Peter's disciple and therefore a guarantee of Alexandria's link with, and dependence on Rome. Antioch was clearly beyond doubt. The 'spiritual' argument naturally brought Jerusalem into the picture, since it was there that the Church had started. Jerusalem was accordingly added to the list as the fifth chief city. Constantinople remained among the five, though it lacked an apostolic foundation. Eventually this was compensated for by suggesting that Andrew, Peter's younger brother (just as Constantinople was Rome's younger sister) had founded the see, but this view could never be taken very seriously. Officially the bishops were to be called Patriarchs, but often the more familiar term *papa* ('father') was used instead, whence is derived the English word *pope*.

The place of Constantinople had been recognized at the Council of Constantinople in 381 and its privileges were set out in detail in the twenty-eighth canon of the Council of Chalcedon in 451. Alexandria walked out of Chalcedon, though for other reasons, and Rome refused to recognize this particular canon until 1215! Nevertheless the basic line-up of the Churches was now clear. Rome and Alexandria were united against Constantinople and Antioch. After 451 the balance changed, when Rome disowned Alexandria and Constantinople distanced itself from Antioch. From then until the Arab invasion of Egypt in 641 Constantinople, allied with Jerusalem, tried to balance itself between Rome and Alexandria. Antioch, formerly Alexandria's great rival, lost its main theologians, who emigrated to the safety of Persia after their defeat at Chalcedon, and succumbed in the end to Alexandrian pressure. The sequence of events is important because it was in the context of these wider rivalries that the theological disputes of the fifth century and later were to be hammered out.

The official recognition of Christianity as the only state religion did not take place until a generation after Constantine's death. His grandson Julian (361-363) reverted to paganism and tried to suppress Christianity, but his measures were half-hearted and had no hope of success. The trend was quickly reversed, and Christianity was given exclusive recognition by the emperor Theodosius on 27 February 380. Theodosius was the last man to rule the whole Empire, and during his reign the pagan temples were converted into churches and pagan customs were abolished. By the time he died, in 395, Christianity was the universal, or catholic religion, embracing in its grip the whole of the civilized world.

Augustine

Theodosius may have believed that his support of the Church would pay political dividends, but if so he was to be disappointed. The power of the emperor had declined dramatically after the Gothic invasion of 378, and the Western Empire's days were clearly numbered. The Church now had lands, an organization not susceptible to military coups d'etat, and the loyalty of the urban masses. When Theodosius massacred the inhabitants of Thessalonica for daring to oppose him, Ambrose, bishop of Milan, made him do penance by walking barefoot in sackcloth and ashes through the streets of his city.

Ambrose was typical of a new generation of Church leaders. He had started off as a civil servant and had risen to be prefect of Milan. In 374 the city needed a new bishop, and the populace cried out for Ambrose. He consented, and in the space of a day was ordained deacon, priest and bishop. So dubious a pedigree might have made him the archetypal career ecclesiastic, interested only in administration, but it did not work out that way. He took his new duties with extreme seriousness and used his many gifts to build up the power and influence of the Church. He also became a noted preacher and evangelist, whose hymns gave the gospel to people in a form easy for them to absorb. He died in 397, but his example was widely followed by the aristocracy. As the Empire collapsed they gave their talents to the Church, whose organization survived the barbarian invasions at least partly with their help.

One of the people who came under the influence of Ambrose was a young university lecturer from Carthage. Aurelius Augustinus was the son of a mixed marriage. His Christian mother hoped he would embrace her faith, but he did not. Instead he took a mistress by whom he had a son, and lived as wild a life as Carthage and the study of philosophy would allow. He was well educated in Latin, but knew little Greek – a sign of the times which boded ill for the future unity of the Church. He was attracted to Manichaeism, a Persian cult which claimed that Good and Evil were equal forces doing battle with each other. He was also deeply influenced by Neoplatonism, though the exact source of his knowledge remains a matter of controversy. It would appear that he was mainly attached to the school of Porphyry, but that he also had some independent knowledge of Plotinus, and borrowed ideas from him as well.

In 386 Augustine, who was then 32, went to hear Ambrose preach in Milan. What he heard so impressed him that it provoked a spiritual crisis which sent him back to the Scriptures. Reading them again he came under conviction of sin and began to weep for forgiveness. His conversion was sudden, but it was deep and enduring. The rest of his life was to be dedicated to Christ, first as a humble monk, then as bishop of Hippo in North Africa, where he died in 430.

Augustine's decision to take monastic vows followed a pattern which was becoming increasingly common among the well-to-do, many of whom were perturbed by their riches and by the laxity which these encouraged in spiritual things. There had always been plenty of nominal Christians, of course, but the rise of Christianity to the status of sole official religion made an old problem incomparably worse. The monastic life came to be seen as the last refuge of pure New Testament Christianity, in which sacrifice and endurance played their part in forming the spiritual life.

It was no longer simply an affair of the desert, however. Monasticism had spread across the Roman Empire and branched out from its primitive eremitic style. Basil of Caesarea had pioneered a communal, or cenobitic, type of monasticism which stood in sharp contrast to the independent, or idiorhythmic, type. He had even composed a *Rule* by which these communities were to be governed.

It was this cenobitic type of life which caught on in the West and which appealed to Augustine. He did not leave the world to go to the desert, but used his consecrated life of poverty, chastity and obedience in the service of the wider Church. This was just as well, because there was much to do. He threw himself wholeheartedly into parish life in North Africa, and fought hard for the unity of the Church there. He also raised the standard of Christian learning immeasurably. No ancient writer has left us more material, and few have so stamped their own personality on it. Augustine's was a very human genius which has never ceased to appeal to Christians of every nation, age and culture.

It was whilst he was busily engaged in these tasks that the second crisis in his life occurred. Ever since 378 a tribe of Goths had been wandering around the Balkans, looking for pasture and plunder. Eventually they decided to move westwards, and under their leader, Alaric, they reached Italy in 410. They found the country open and undefended. Encountering little resistance they reached Rome and looted it – the first time the city had fallen to a foreign army in 800 years. The whole world was stunned. Suddenly the reality of Roman decline was brought home. Overnight, as it seemed, the legions left Britain, Gaul was overrun, Spain fell to a group of illiterate tribes on the make.

The shock which these events caused cannot now be imagined. To the Romans, who had ruled the world for hundreds of years, it was like the last judgement. Some pagans muttered that Christianity was to blame for the defeat, since the old gods had deserted the Empire. Many Christians were perplexed that Arian and heathen barbarians could overwhelm a Christian civilization. Whose side was God on? Augustine felt these doubts as much as any patriotic citizen. He too sought an answer, and his mind turned from immediate calamities to wider and deeper issues. What was the nature of evil? How did God control the world? Was there a plan or a purpose in human history?

The answers to these questions form the substance of his great work, *On the City of God*, which he wrote in stages between 413 and 426. It is a cosmological work of unparalleled dimensions, and it has become the most influential study of political theory ever written. Augustine set out to write the history of the world in the light of Scripture, by which he intended to demonstrate that the plan of God could not be set aside by any human sin or disaster. On the contrary, as Paul had said, 'all things work together for good to those who love God, to those who are called according to his purpose' (Romans 8:28).

This encyclopaedic work is written in twenty-two books, which are divided into five parts. In the first part (Books 1-5) he argues that the pagan gods were powerless to protect cities, as the fate of Troy and other ancient towns had long ago demonstrated. Only moral virtue could protect a nation and guarantee success. In its early days Rome had possessed this virtue but corruption had crept in through overweening ambition. The Christian faith, far from ruining the state, had in fact rescued it from an irretrievable slide into depravity.

The second part (Books 6-10) takes up the philosophical problems of polytheism and Platonism. He demonstrates the internal inconsistencies of each, and shows that neither can offer the universal way of salvation found only in Christ. Modern readers of this section are often puzzled at the length to which Augustine goes to refute the absurdities of paganism and are apt to wonder how anyone could have disagreed with his 'obvious' arguments. That this should be so, however, is tribute to the lasting power of his genius. Augustine so thoroughly and forcefully condemned the cult of the gods that paganism has never since been a serious religious option in European society.

In the third part (Books 11-14), Augustine turns from attack to defence. He begins with the Scriptures, claiming that they are the basis of all Christian thought. His approach is clearly philosophical, not exegetical, and his use of texts is sometimes open to question, but the general argument is clear enough. The Bible teaches that the world is a created thing which is essentially good, not evil as the Platonists maintained. He denies the cyclical view of history, according to which the world would keep repeating itself, and argued for linear time, with a specific goal in the second coming of Christ. He explains the origin of sin as disobedience, and says that only the Creator has the power to undo its effects. Finally he argues that human history must be understood as the struggle between good and evil, not in the abstract, but as the two cities (we would say kingdoms) which belonged respectively to God and to Satan.

Part four (Books 15-18) is the history of the world as recounted in the Bible. Augustine speculates on the 'giants' of Genesis, the great age of the early patriarchs and so on. His solutions to the difficulties caused by such stories are always reverent and exalt the inspired text over against possible detractors, though it must be admitted that many of his ideas would not be widely accepted today. He was a strong believer in Old Testament typology, and treated the whole text as a prophecy of Christ. In Book 18 he develops the themes of the two cities much further. Jerusalem and Babylon are their symbolic representations, and references to them in Scripture are usually typological in intent. It is important to note that Augustine does not identify the city of God with the visible Church. The Church contains wheat and chaff together, and they will not be separated until the last judgement. He also leaves open the possibility that men outside the covenant may be saved, and cites Job as an obvious example. Later generations were to interpret the two cities as Church and state, but so crude a conception was never Augustine's teaching.

Part five (Books 19-22) concludes the work with a lengthy discussion of man's destiny. Augustine interprets all human striving as a desire of Peace, which can be found only in Christ. He discusses the last judgement and defends the concept of eternal punishment in hell. He then goes on to talk of the resurrection and eternal life, pointing to the mystical vision of God as the supreme fulfilment of the Christian's spiritual pilgrimage.

Augustine's treatment of his subject can only be described as exhaustive, and it remained for centuries the chief source of practical information on every imaginable topic. So vast is the erudition displayed and so authoritative the treatment, that huge sections of the work were accepted without question as orthodox doctrine, even though the subjects they treated had scarcely been mentioned before and certainly do not appear in the creeds.

This is particularly true of the teaching on predestination and on the after-life. Augustine was the first major theologian who fully understood why the saving purpose of God made a doctrine of predestination necessary. God's plans could not be defeated by the puny will of man, nor could the issue of the conflict between the two cities be in any doubt. The salvation of the elect was neither an accident nor a side-issue in the larger drama of the creation. On the contrary, everything was made for it and was tending towards it. The Christian Church, far from being a disruptive influence, was the true revelation of the eternal purposes of God which would achieve their fulfilment at the second coming of Christ.

Allied to all this was a doctrine of God's grace which Augustine was thrashing out at the same time. It is nowhere mentioned in the *City of God*, but it ties in neatly with the philosophical theology outlined above. The occasion was provided by a British monk called Pelagius, who was active at Rome from about 400 to 418. We cannot be certain what it was that he taught, but both Augustine and Jerome accused him of holding a doctrine of original sin weak enough to allow for the possibility that a man could make an active contribution towards furthering his own salvation. It is quite likely that Pelagius was doing little more than express a view which at that time was widely held in the Church. Certainly it is true that Vincent of Lérins subsequently attacked Augustine's teaching on grace as a novelty which went against the canon of catholic orthodoxy, which was the sum of that believed 'at all times, everywhere and by all'.

Vincent's own semi-Pelagianism, and the common Greek view that man was an active participant in his own redemption, bears out this accusation and makes us see Pelagius in a more sympathetic light. At the same time, it can hardly be denied that Augustine's was the deeper insight into the truth of the gospel. He knew from his own experience that we are saved by grace, not by works (Ephesians 2:8-9) and never ceased to praise God for his mercy shown towards us, miserable sinners. Augustine's cosmic predestinarianism has often been attacked as unbiblical, as a survival from his Neoplatonist days, and even as a sign of a lingering Manichaean tendency. Such accusations are understandable in psychological terms, and nobody would claim that Augustine represented a balanced scriptural view on every issue all the time. After all, that is rather a lot to expect of one individual!

Nevertheless it would be doing the bishop of Hippo an unpardonable injustice not to say that at the heart of all his teaching lay the supreme virtue of Love. For Augustine this was in no sense a sentimental emotion, but the motivating power of the universe. The atoms held together by the mutual attraction of Love, and this same force, working at the highest level of spiritual awareness, linked the soul of the believer to God. Indeed, Augustine went further, and explained the co-inherence of the Trinity as the perfect manifestation of that Love which in Scripture is the essence of God (1 John 4:16). It was for this reason above all that every human action should be rooted in the principle of Love, and that even the government of the state could do no more than seek to attain to the same vision.

The parting of the ways

Augustine died in 430, just before his beloved city of Hippo fell to the barbarian Vandals. He left behind him a monumental achievement which would not be equalled for eight hundred years, and which is still the inspiration of many sections of the Church, both Catholic and Protestant. On the other hand, his writings were not translated into Greek until the late thirteenth century, and the Eastern Church has never really absorbed his teaching. Here more than anywhere we begin to sense a parting of the ways which would eventually split the Church into rival Eastern and Western traditions, mutually exclusive and hostile to each other.

Things might have turned out differently had the Empire held together, but the political events which led to the collapse of the West in the generation following Augustine's death had fateful consequences for the Church. When the last Western emperor was pensioned off in 476, the Empire itself was not dissolved. On the contrary, the imperial insignia were sent to Constantinople, whose emperor was recognized as titular sovereign by the barbarian rulers of the Western provinces. This vassal status did not mean much in practice, but the emperor did what he could to make it work. He had no army to reconquer the lost territory, so he relied on the Church, with its hierarchy of Roman aristocrats, to protect his interests. The bishop of Rome became by default the main imperial official in the West, charged with the duty of receiving the homage of the barbarian chieftains in the emperor's name.

This odd system suited everyone rather well. The emperor could assert his rights without it costing him a penny. The barbarians could rule unmolested, yet at the same time claim a certain legitimacy as the appointed servants of the Empire. The bishop of Rome, now more obviously Pope in the later sense of the word, could rule his own church in freedom and use his position to influence the Eastern churches in a direction which he approved. When, in 483, the emperor moved away from Roman ideas of orthodoxy in order to conciliate the Alexandrians, who were under his direct rule, the Pope excommunicated his opposite number at Constantinople and announced that the Eastern churches were in schism.

The dispute dragged on for over thirty years, and was not healed until after a palace revolution at Constantinople. The remarkable thing about the reconciliation of 519 is that Rome won its case because the emperor felt that it was more important to retain his influence in the West than to conciliate his own subjects. He even went so far as to decree that the Roman church was the supreme arbiter in matters of orthodoxy, a decision which effectively removed the Church from his control. This remarkable decree is not merely of historical interest; it was trotted out as recently as 1870 as evidence for the proclamation of papal infallibility!

Things might have continued in this way indefinitely, had not the young emperor Justinian (527-565) decided to embark on the reconquest of the West. His armies overran North Africa and southern Spain, and in 536 they entered Rome. Italy proved a tough nut to crack, and it was not finally reduced until 554. By then it had been devastated in a way not even the barbarians had managed, and the reimposition of imperial rule was regarded with extremely mixed feelings. An imperial exarch established his capital at Ravenna and set out to rule the Roman church in much the same way as the emperor ruled the church at Constantinople.

There the relationship between Church and state was governed by legal principles which were to remain in force until the fall of the Empire in 1453. The state was a Christian commonwealth ruled by the emperor, whose duty it was to uphold the orthodox faith. He could not establish doctrine on his own (emperors who tried this were always defeated) but he was responsible for calling the general, or ecumenical, councils, which determined the limits of orthodoxy. He was also responsible for enforcing conciliar decrees within his dominions, a task which caused him unending headaches.

The various patriarchs were imperial officials who held office at the emperor's pleasure, though public opinion made it difficult for the emperor to act without the Church's consent in spiritual matters. When Arcadius (395-408) wanted to depose John Chrysostom, who as patriarch of Constantinople had condemned the luxurious living of the court, he had to call in the patriarch of Alexandria to make the deposition canonical. In the end it was a Pyrrhic victory, because Chrysostom became and has remained a great saint of the Church, whilst Arcadius and his henchman of Alexandria are largely forgotten; but it revealed both the dangers and the limits of imperial power.

The next emperor, Theodosius II (408-450), was inept in ecclesiastical affairs. In 428 he appointed the Antiochene professor of theology, Nestorius, patriarch of Constantinople, only to see him deposed three years later at the Council of Ephesus. Theodosius then shifted to the Alexandrian side, so much so that he faced incipient revolt in the churches of Contantinople and even Rome. This was averted by a timely fall from his horse (28 July 450) but his successor Marcian inherited an impossible situation. Taking the side of Constantinople, he called a council which met at Chalcedon on 8 October 451. This council pronounced against the Alexandrians, who promptly led Egypt into what was to become the Monophysite schism. Alexandria would never accept third place behind both Rome and Constantinople, especially when the latter appeared to be leaning towards Antioch, and it could not afford the loss of prestige which would follow on any admission that its theological tradition was less than fully orthodox.

Succeeding emperors did all they could to heal the breach, but Rome and the monks of Constantinople (called the *akoimetai*, or Sleepless-ones, because of their eternal vigilance) prevented any workable compromise. By Justinian's time the schism had spread into Syria and threatened to split the Empire. He pursued a pro-Roman policy at first, but his wife Theodora was a strong supporter of the Alexandrians. When Justinian sent an embassy to evangelize Ethiopia, Theodora countered him with a delegation of her own which succeeded in getting there first. The result is that today the Ethiopian church is in communion with the Alexandrian dissidents but not with Constantinople.

After the capture of Rome, Justinian modified his policy somewhat, though never to the point where he saw eye-to-eye with his wife. After her death in 548, he called a council at Constantinople (553) which went as far as it could to meet the Alexandrian demands. It was too late. Alexandria wanted victory, not compromise, and this it could not have. Schismatic priests were ordained and bishops appointed as rivals to the imperial (in Syriac, Melkite) nominees. Only a handful of expatriate Greeks in the main cities remained loyal to the emperor, who was now almost at war with his subjects in Egypt and Syria. Later emperors tried various expedients to heal this impossible situation, but to no avail. A third council of Constantinople, held there in 680-681, finally confirmed the breach which remains to this day.

By then, however, it hardly mattered. Arab tribes, wielding the sword of the new religion of Islam, had conquered the rebellious provinces in a series of lightning campaigns between 636 and 641. There was little resistance, and the persecuted people welcomed the Muslims as liberators. Time would reveal that they had done little more than jump out of the frying-pan into the fire, but at least one principle was clear. The armies of a Christian emperor were powerless against the spiritual forces of the Church when these were united against him in opposition.

The break between Rome and Constantinople came more slowly but had far greater repercussions. When Italy was restored to imperial rule, the Roman church was treated in the same way as the churches of the East. Its pretensions were never totally denied, but its position was steadily undermined.

In 595 the patriarch of Constantinople assumed the title Ecumenical, a move which was probably designed to upgrade his rank in the hierarchy. Rome protested on the ground that all five patriarchs were equal to one another, but this had no effect. In 653 Pope Martin I was deposed and taken to Constaninople for having dared to contradict the emperor's ecclesiastical policy. There he was convicted of treason and condemned to death, but on the intercession of the patriarch his sentence was commuted to exile and he was banished to the Crimea. An even greater humiliation followed in 681, when Rome was forced to accept the condemnation of Pope Honorius I (625-638) for heresy, the only time a Roman bishop was ever successfully accused of such a crime.

Shortly after this, however, the situation changed dramatically. In 691 or 692 there was held at Constantinople a council which decreed 102 canons, governing the administration and ritual of the Church. It was promptly accepted in the East but rejected at Rome, largely because it enjoined practices which were unknown in the West, such as the use of leavened bread at communion. (The West used unleavened bread in imitation of the Passover, but this was regarded as a Judaizing practice in the East.) The emperor tried to force the Pope to sign the council's decrees, but this time the army supported the church, and the Pope was able to resist without penalty. This surprising change was probably due to the fact that the army in Italy was increasingly made up of local recruits, whose loyalty to a distant emperor was less than their attachment to a fellow Italian. In any case, Rome never again had to bow to an imperial decree from Constantinople.

By this time also, the situation in the West had altered considerably. In 496 Clovis, king of the Franks, had been converted to Catholic Christianity. He used this fact to play on the feelings of the Roman population of Gaul, who resented the Arian rule of the Visigoths. In 511 he destroyed Visigothic power north of the Pyrenees, and almost the whole of France became a Catholic kingdom. Soon afterwards the Arian kingdoms of North Africa and Italy were destroyed by imperial forces and only Spain was left. There the royal prince Hermenegild was converted from Arianism in 585, a crime for which his father King Reccared had him put to death.

The public outcry at this was so great that Reccared quickly repented and went over to the Catholic side himself. This paved the way for the conversion of the whole nation and the new Catholic order was officially launched at the Third Council of Toledo in 589. The Spanish church which came out of this enjoyed a remarkable degree of autonomy, and the many subsequent Councils of Toledo were great national occasions at which matters of church government were regulated without reference to Rome. This organization was eclipsed by the Arab conquest of 711-718, but the church's foundations were solid enough to ensure survival. Spain was to be the only country conquered by the Arabs in which Christianity was never reduced to a minority religion on the fringe of society.

Meanwhile the imperial position in Italy had been weakened by the Lombard invasion of 568. Most of the country fell to these new invaders, who were Arians, and the Empire barely managed to hold on to a few coastal areas, plus Rome, Ravenna and a strip of land running across the centre of the peninsula. This gave the Roman church additional reason to cling to its imperial ties, since the Lombards, even after their conversion to Catholic Christianity during the reign of Aripert (653-661), were a threat to the independence and security of the papacy.

Matters came to a head in the eighth century, when the emperor Leo III tried to impose his policy of iconoclasm. This was a puritan drive to rid the Church of images and pictorial representations of spiritual things, and it was vigorously opposed at Rome. When the Lombards captured Ravenna in 751 and extinguished imperial rule in Italy, there was little incentive for the Pope to look to Constantinople any more.

It is true that he sent an embassy to the Lombards, asking them to restore Ravenna to the emperor, but nothing much came of this. The following year a Frankish messenger reached Rome, asking the Pope whether it was right for one man, Pippin, to rule as 'mayor of the palace' whilst the incompetent king enjoyed the trappings of authority. Seeing his opportunity, the Pope agreed to sanction a palace revolution which would put Pippin on the throne in return for protection against the Lombards. The bargain was struck, the Lombards were destroyed, and in 754 Pippin gave Ravenna and the former imperial territories to the Pope as a guarantee of his independence. Thus were born the Papal States, which continued in existence until the unification of Italy in 1870. The process was complete when Pippin's grandson Charlemagne had himself crowned in Rome on 25 December 800 as emperor of the West.

The restored empire of Charlemagne, which in various guises was to survive until 1806, was not at all like the Eastern empire or the old Roman state. Its legitimacy rested on recognition by the papacy, and the Church never ceased to press its claims to overrule the secular power. It was not the state which took over the Church, but the other way round. The corrupting influence of temporal power was to undermine the spiritual authority of the Church more effectively than any imperial decree could have done, but that is a story which belongs to another, later age. During the formative period of the Church's doctrine it cannot be claimed that the state exercised a decisive influence on its development.

The earthly heaven

The rise of the papacy to temporal power is an important ingredient in the history of the early medieval church, but its obvious prominence is liable to obscure a development which in the long term was just as influential. New Testament scholars have frequently asserted that the Early Church quickly lost any expectation of an imminent Parousia, or second coming of Christ. It is even said that the Apostles themselves revised their beliefs as they grew older, and left behind a Church more concerned with survival in this world than with the coming of the next.

A student of Church history cannot accept this judgement, however. Far from dying out, the Parousia hope intensified as time went on, and it became an integral and fundamental element of the gospel message. During the centuries of persecution, martyrdom was exalted as the sign of the antichrist, whose coming spelt the end of the age. Later on, monasticism integrated this perspective into its own form of Christian discipline. Later still, it sought to erect a social structure in which the conditions of life in the Parousia would be practised in anticipation of the imminent revelation of the sons of God.

The process was given a considerable boost by the collapse of the Western Empire. Only the Church had the resources to carry on functioning more or less normally, and it alone had the spiritual power to rally the flagging remnants of Roman civilization. In the imperial twilight of the early sixth century, two figures stand out who were to take this development and mould it along specifically Western lines.

The first of these was Benedict of Nursia (c. 480-547) who established a monastery at Monte Cassino in Southern Italy. There he gathered a community and placed them under a *Rule* of poverty, chastity and obedience. The *Rule* of St Benedict was not dissimilar to the *Rule* of St Basil, from which it was partially derived, but it had a much broader scope. Basil had been concerned primarily with the cultivation of the spiritual life, but Benedict went much further. He envisaged nothing less than a holy city which would be a microcosm of the kingdom of heaven.

In pursuit of this ideal he was joined by Cassiodorus (c. 477-c.570), a learned Roman aristocrat who thought of the monastery as a centre of learning. The Eastern monks had never been scholars and regarded secular pursuits with suspicion. In the West it would not be so. All the practical wisdom of antiquity was collected and deposited in the monastic libraries, there to be studied and copied until at last secular learning began to flourish once more.

The religious and social ideals of these men spread across Europe, but not so quickly as to absorb all previous development. By 500 monasticism of the Eastern type was well-entrenched in Gaul, especially in the south, and had penetrated right to the remote fastnesses of Britain. Even before the Empire fell, there were hermits like Ninian of Whithorn who had established themselves in remote caves beyond its frontiers. When the imperial organization collapsed, these hermits were joined by refugees from the barbarian invasions. In Britain the hold of Roman civilization had never been strong, and the urban church structure, which continued on the continent, ceased to function. Christianity was soon reduced to a monastic affair almost exclusively, and this pattern was to be the distinctive feature of the Celtic church which emerged at this time.

Its leading figure was Patrick, a Romanized Briton who went to Ireland as an evangelist about 432. We know little of his life or work, which is shrouded in pious legend, but it appears that he tried to convert the Irish through the influence of local chieftains. This practice proved reasonably successful on the Continent, but Irish society was too unstable for tribal conversions to have much lasting effect. As there were no towns of any kind, Patrick had to create his own centres of stability around which the Church could gather and develop. These centres were the monasteries founded by him and his followers.

Irish monasticism embraced the social and cultural aims of the continental monasteries, but it had a decidedly evangelistic purpose as well. After consolidating the home base, its advance was rapid. Columba sailed from Derry to Iona in 568 and began the evangelization of Scotland. By 600 Irish monks were penetrating into England.

There they met another monastic mission, that of Augustine (who, of course, is not be confused with his illustrious namesake of two centuries earlier, the author of *The City of God*). He had been sent from Rome in 597 and had established himself at Canterbury. A century and a half of separation from the Continent had given the Irish church a backward look, despite its learning. For example, Rome had twice altered the method by which it calculated the date of Easter (in 457 and again in 525), but the Celts knew nothing of this. Their monks also wore different habits and shaved their heads differently.

Details like these seem trivial to us: but in an age when few people could read, visual signs tended to take on theological meaning. It soon became apparent, of course, that there was no real difference between Rome and the Celts, and eventually the latter agreed to adopt the more Catholic practices of the Roman church. The first submission came after the Synod of Whitby in 664, and the process was completed when Wales fell into line in 768. The Celtic Church was defeated, but it did not die. On the contrary, its zeal for learning and for evangelism continued to animate the English Church for another two centuries. In 718 Wynfrith of Crediton, better known to us as Boniface, obtained permission from the Pope to begin the evangelization of Germany. From there Anglo-Saxon missionaries spread out across Europe, evangelizing Scandinavia and touching the borders of Russia. The crowning achievement came in 782 when Charlemagne, anxious to restore learning in his empire, sent for Alcuin of York to come and be his adviser in educational and ecclesiastical matters.

Alcuin brought with him the monastic zeal of the English and their passion for correct Latin. He raised standards at Charlemagne's court immeasurably, and began a long tradition of ecclesiastical involvement in secular government which did not die out until the seventeenth century. The earthly heaven of the monasteries now opened its doors to embrace the whole world. Paradoxically, it was Alcuin's reforming zeal which led to another development which, more surely than any, marked the end of the ancient world. In 812 Charlemagne conducted a survey of the Frankish church, and found that people could no longer follow the Latin used in preaching and worship. Accordingly he ordered that the spoken language of the people was to be used in sermons, though not in the liturgy. The curious phenomenon of Latin as a sacred language, no longer 'understanded of the people', was given an official recognition which was not to be successfully challenged until the Reformation.

While these developments foreshadowed the institution of Christian society in Western Europe, the pattern in the East was markedly different. There the continuity of society with pre-Christian times was more obvious, and the Church was never able to secure the same dominance as in the West. Secular law courts and schools continued to function as they always had, and the emperor looked to the 'people' (which in practice meant the army) for his right to rule, not to the patriarch, whom he appointed. Monasticism never grew beyond the primitive stages, and the monasteries did not develop any interest in secular learning.

Nevertheless, it would be a great mistake to suppose that the Parousia hope was any less vital in the East than in the West. The Christian empire was held to be the model of the heavenly kingdom, the emperor was widely honoured as the Peer of the Apostles and the Church was treated as the universal and only gateway to heaven. No-one was more embued with this spirit than the emperor Justinian, who conceived the building of a Great Church at Constantinople which would express the religious ideal of Christianity in stone. The building was begun in 532 and dedicated to the Holy Wisdom (Hagia Sophia) on 26 December 537.

As an architectural monument, Hagia Sophia was, and still is, one of the wonders of the world. It was the first building to be totally enclosed by a dome, and only two churches, St Peter's in Rome and St Paul's in London, both of which date from the seventeenth century, contain a larger free space inside. Despite an earthquake in 1346 and its conversion into a mosque in 1453, the edifice has stood up remarkably well. It was secularized in 1935 and is now a museum in which the mosaics, which had been whitewashed by the Turks, are once again on display.

But Hagia Sophia is far more than a cultural monument. In Justinian's empire it represented the fullest expression of the idea that a microcosm of heaven existed in the Church on earth. Inside its dome was portrayed Christ Pantocrator, the triumphant king on his heavenly throne. Along the walls were the saints and angels, set against a backdrop of gold which spoke of the glory, the splendour and the majesty of heaven. The worshipper in such a place felt himself to be somewhere between heaven and earth, caught up in a spiritual vision which has fired the Christian East to this day. What this can mean, even to a modern believer, is well expressed by the Russian Orthodox priest, Sergei Bulgakov, who saw it in 1923:

> Yesterday for the first time in my life I had the happiness of seeing Hagia Sophia. God bestowed this favour upon me and has not let me die without a vision of St Sophia, and I thank my God for this. I experienced such heavenly bliss that it submerged – if only for a moment – all my present sorrows and troubles and made them insignificant. St Sophia was revealed to my mind as something absolute, self-evident and irrefutable. Of all the

wonderful churches I have seen, this is the most absolute, the universal church. The words of the Easter anthem ring in my mind: Lift up thine eyes, O Zion, and behold; thy children have come to thee from the west and the north and the sea and the east shining with the divine light.

But there was another, more secret meaning in all this as well, which Bulgakov also understood. He goes on:

This is indeed Sophia, the real unity of the world in the Logos, the co-inherence of all with all, the world of divine ideas. It is Plato baptized by the Hellenic genius of Byzantium – it is his world, his lofty realm to which souls ascend for the contemplation of ideas. The pagan Sophia of Plato beholds herself mirrored in the Christian Sophia, the divine Wisdom .... Here one understands anew the whole force and convincing self-evidence of the testimony of St Justin Martyr, the full meaning of which he himself did not know, that Socrates and Plato were Christians before Christ; for Plato was the prophet of Sophia in paganism.

Hagia Sophia became the symbol of Byzantium, that unique blend of pseudo-Dionysian Neoplatonism and Christianity which survived to the dawn of modern times, when its fleeing scholars brought the Renaissance to Italy and the West. Its shape was copied by every church in the East; its liturgy was celebrated unchanged in every town and village.

But what of Justinian, the second Constantine, whose patronage and vision had brought the whole enterprise into being? One might have thought that such a man would have received the undying gratitude of the nation for his magnificent achievement. Alas, it was not to be so. Justinian dabbled in theology and, like many amateurs, managed to fall into heresy. To the Church, this was an unforgivable sin. No amount of money or power could buy the orthodox faith. When he died, he was refused burial in consecrated ground and later generations claimed they could hear his soul at night in the palace, seeking the rest which it was denied. We cannot understand the ancient Church unless we realize that it was the true faith which counted for it above all things. There can be no surer sign than the fate of Justinian as to where its heart and its priorities lay.

6

God was in Christ

Few people would dispute that the fourth century was a period of central importance in the development of the Christian Church and of Western civilization. During that brief span of time the Roman Empire went through a transformation which heralded the coming of the Middle Ages, and the Church emerged from persecution to take over the mainstream of society.

It was a period of transition in less obvious ways too. The baptismal formulae, which had served the Church well in its early days, were inadequate in the face of the philosophical challenges which followed hard on Christianity's success. Questions which had been tackled by Origen and others suddenly acquired new importance, as men sought to construct a complete world-and-life view – what the Germans call a *Weltanschauung* – around their understanding of Christ. The revelation of God to man now became the focus around which the age-old arguments of the philosophical schools converged.

If Jesus was truly the answer to men's needs and the key to understanding universal reality, then a number of problems had to be faced and answered. How could a man plausibly claim to be God? How could an infinite, omnipotent and omnipresent being limit himself to the restrictions imposed by human nature? Did it make sense to say that the eternal God died on a cross in order to redeem mankind? The magnitude of the Christian claim can be appreciated only when we realize that these were the questions to which the church addressed itself with the proclamation that Jesus and his gospel were the answer to the strivings of mankind. It was an astonishing claim to make, and the fact that it was accepted so readily by the masses of the people is one of the most remarkable phenomena of human history.

Accepted it was, but not fully understood. The history of doctrinal development in the fourth century shows that there was a subtle change of emphasis which was designed to get to grips with this new situation.

The stark call for commitment which had led to a kind of an oath-taking (*sacramentum* in Latin has this meaning) at baptism gave way to a maturer phase of growth, in which the faith implanted by that commitment sought the understanding needed to cope with the manifold realities of the surrounding world.

The First Council of Constantinople which was held in 381, only a year after Christianity was proclaimed the sole legal religion of the Empire, marks the end of the 'baptismal' phase of Christian credal development and the beginning of a new 'philosophical' phase, in which the problems outlined above would be tackled and ironed out.

Person and nature

Christians who sought to explain the philosophical foundations of their faith inevitably began with the basic terms which were then being used by philosophers of all schools of thought. As we have already seen, many of the more prominent bishops of the fourth century had themselves received a philosophical education, but this does not mean that their theology was somehow corrupted as a result. As we demonstrated from the history of the term *hypostasis*, Christianity acted as a transforming agent on the philosophical vocabulary, altering the context in which words were employed and thereby giving them new meanings. We must never underestimate the ability of a word to accommodate new ideas, especially when the frame of reference is completely different.

As the process of cultural evangelization continued and deepened, the new social context became increasingly dominant. Words and concepts which had been borrowed from philosophical sources lost their earlier associations, and became embedded in the proclamation of the gospel. In the two generations between the Council of Constantinople and the Council of Chalcedon, this process effected a revolution in ancient thought which dethroned the ancient schools of philosophy and crowned theology the Queen of the Sciences in its stead.

To understand how this process worked and what its impact was on Christian doctrine, we must begin with the philosophical concepts of *being* and *nature*. Technically, these terms can be distinguished as follows:

Being = what a thing *is*
Nature = what a thing *is like*

When Christians thought of God, it was clear to them that in philosophical terms he was the supreme Being. In Platonic thought, he was the only Being in the true sense, because he alone depended on nothing else for his existence. Christians could not go along with this belief in its pure form, because it would have meant denying reality to the material world. On the other hand, they saw the importance of this concept for Christian theology, and generally used the word *being* (Greek: *ousia*) to refer to the One God of the Bible.

This One God had a nature (*physis*) which Christians could only describe as infinite, immutable, impassible and ineffable. These terms are grammatical negatives in order to emphasize the point that God cannot be contained within human limits, but they are not negations in the strict sense. It was also possible to express the same truths in a positive way, by using words like omnipresent, almighty and omniscient, which Christians did too.

In the history of Christian theology, the terms *being* and *nature* have frequently suffered one of two fates. On the one hand, they have often been *confused* with each other. In the case of God this is particularly easy since his nature, as the sum of his attributes, must be totally consistent with his being. It causes difficulty, though, when we consider whether or not God is a person. If we say that we worship a personal God, do we mean that personality (or personhood) is an attribute of his divine nature, rather like omnipotence? Is it a way (mode) by which God expresses himself, but which is something less than the fulness of his being? Or, does *person* describe God's being in a way which goes beyond the attributes of his nature?

Christians who have asked this question have always felt it necessary to distinguish *person* from *nature* in God. Moreover, God is not one person, but three. Each person possesses in himself an objective reality which puts him on a par with the One Being of God. This belief became the most important theological issue in fourth and fifth century debates, and during the course of them the subtleties which had distinguished *nature* from *being* practically disappeared. To say that three persons shared one being meant the same thing as saying that they had one nature. This view was common in the Middle Ages, and was not challenged until Calvin said that God's nature was unknowable, and that we perceive his unity in each of the persons. In saying this, Calvin was harking back to the fourth century belief in the *coinherence* of the persons; but, instead of thinking of this as three persons occupying the same Being (=Nature), he interpreted it to mean that each person reveals the others, and thereby presents in himself the fullness of the Godhead.

Nevertheless, a confusion between *being* and *nature* still persists in theology. We sense it for example in the Prayer of Humble Access, as it is printed in the Communion Service of the *Alternative Service Book 1980*. Here we are called to pray to a God 'whose nature is always to have mercy'. Nature replaces the older word *property* (in the sense of *attribute*), but it is inappropriate because it conveys something more than just a single quality or a characteristic. The revised prayer suggests that God must always show mercy because he cannot act in a way which is contrary to his nature. But if that were true, for God to withhold mercy would be an impossibility, and that is clearly contrary to the teaching of Scripture. 'Mercifulness' cannot be put on the same level as omnipresence, for example.

A similar confusion occurs when we talk of humans. We sense a difference between human *being* and human *nature*, where the original distinction still functions as a living reality, but this is lost when we start to speak of the *natural man*. (In 1 Corinthians 2:14, Paul did not write 'natural man', *physikos*, but 'animal' or 'soul man', *psychikos*.) Yet in this well-worn and often misunderstood phrase, the word *nature* has acquired an objectivity which in the strict sense is more appropriate to *being*. These examples are taken from contemporary usage, but they are useful illustrations of the kind of ambiguity which meets us throughout the history of Western thought, and not least in the late fourth century.

On the other hand, the confusion of these terms has often been matched by an outright *denial* of their applicability to God. In the mystical tradition of the pseudo-Dionysius, which we have already mentioned, any attempt to equate God with Being is regarded as idolatrous. Being and Nature are concepts of the mind, but God-in-himself transcends all human conceptions. To know him, the theologian must go beyond any kind of verbal statement about God and enter by an ecstatic experience into the realm of Non-Being. This kind of thinking, which is sometimes called the Way of Negation (*apophasis*), or Unknowing, has been very widespread through the centuries; but it is important to notice that even the apophatic approach needs the affirmative (or cataphatic) dimension as a starting-point. The philosophical dimension can be transcended, but it cannot be ignored in theological discourse and religious experience.

The second philosophical category which Christians found essential was that of *hypostasis*. We have already seen how elastic a word this was, and its precise meaning was a source of constant confusion. Sometimes it meant much the same thing as *being*; at other times it appeared to mean almost the opposite, something like *appearance* or *existence*. The development of the word *hypostasis* reflects quite well the kind of thinking that was going on in the years after Nicaea. It was gradually detached from its philosophical roots and elevated into what was practically a new idea, whose shape can be explained only as a result of a profound wrestling with the God of the Bible.

To understand how this happened we must begin with the basic formula which since Origen's time maintained that there were three *hypostases* in the one *ousia* of God. Looked at from a philosophical angle, the use of *hypostasis* suggested the following:

Existence = how a thing appears to be
Substance = what I perceive a thing to be

In this scheme, *substance* (=*hypostasis*) is used in a sense closer to *subsistence*, a word which was later coined to represent this concept when *substance* could no longer be distinguished from *being*. Everyone agreed that a *hypostasis* was the thing perceived by the thinker; on that score even Origen and Tertullian could be said to be in agreement, as we have already seen. What was not clear was how this related to its opposite number in philosophy, the concept of existence (in Greek, *hyparxis*). Was it true to say that in seeing the three divine *hypostases*, a believer was seeing God as he presented himself in the world of existence? Could the Father, the Son and the Holy Spirit be regarded as *tropoi hyparxeos*, modes of existence, of the divine Being?

This explanation had a certain appeal to Christians with a Platonic background, because the concepts of Being and Existence were especially familiar to them. In Platonism, Existence referred to the appearance of things in the middle world between Being and Matter (= Non-Being). A human soul achieved its Existence by separating itself from Being and entering human flesh. The difficulty, from the

Christian point of view, was that Platonic Existence was a transitory state which was doomed to disappear. The soul of the righteous philosopher would be spared destruction, but only in the sense that it would be reabsorbed into the divine Being, thereby losing its separate identity. Christians could not accept such a view of eternal life, and therefore they were obliged to work out a formula by which a created being could share an attribute of God's nature (in this case, eternity) without being absorbed into the divine.

The answer was provided by saying that the three *hypostases* in God were not modes of existence, but ultimate realities in their own right. A doctrine of God which imagined him as a single Being appearing in three forms was false and inadequate. Either it would have made any real distinction between the persons impossible, or it would have made each person no more than a part of the divine Being. In the former case, the Son could not have prayed to the Father – quite literally, he would have been praying to himself in a different form. In the second case, God would not have become man in Christ. Only a part of him, his Logos probably, would have undergone this experience, making Jesus less than fully divine. But Colossians 2:9 says that 'in Christ all the fullness of the Godhead lives in bodily form', an assertion which rules out this possibility.

The only solution was to detach *hypostasis* from the kind of dependence on *ousia* which was latent in a word like *hyparxis* and give it a life of its own. This was the achievement of fourth century theology which was crowned by Basil of Caesarea, when he realized for the first time that *hypostasis* and *persona* meant the same thing. Basil probably did not understand the full importance of this equation, which was not formally ratified until the Council of Chalcedon. But the combination of these terms was just the formula needed to liberate each from its earlier limitations and give the common term its special power.

A *hypostasis* had always been understood as an objective reality, though in a somewhat passive sense in that it was primarily an object of contemplation. A *persona* on the other hand was an active subject, though lacking in the substantive quality which attached to *hypostasis*. The third century Roman writer Novatian had seen this and had supplied the necessary undergirding to the Latin *persona*, but he lacked the theological subtlety of his successors and could not follow his discovery through. Only when Leo the Great wrote down his understanding of Christology, an interpretation which was accepted at Chalcedon, did the Western theological tradition join forces with the East in a common confession of orthodoxy. Since that time *person* (= *hypostasis*) and *nature* (= *substance, being*) have been the cardinal terms of Christian theology, the orthodoxy of which may be gauged by the way in which each term is defined and balanced against the other.

The Chalcedonian Christ

With these terms and their meanings firmly in mind, we can examine the formulation of the Council of Chalcedon, according to which Jesus Christ is one divine Person in two Natures. Despite its many detractors, this formula remains the touchstone of Christological orthodoxy to this day.

The process which led to the Chalcedonian Definition began in 381. At the First Council of Constantinople, the theology of Athanasius was upheld, but the Christological interpretation of it made by his disciple Apollinarius was condemned. As we have already seen, the difficulty which both men faced concerned the place of the human soul in Jesus. Athanasius admitted its existence but found little for it to do, whereas Apollinarius believed it could be dispensed with altogether. As far as he was concerned the Word had taken on inert flesh, and merely appeared to be a man.

Alexandrian Christology, of which Apollinarianism was an extreme aberration, had other difficulties too, besides this one. It was a cardinal axiom of this school of thought that the Logos was the active subject of the incarnation, who had assumed humanity and united it to himself. Unfortunately, though, the classical distinction between *person* and *nature* was not yet completely clear. Most Alexandrians thought of God as a *personal nature*, thereby attributing the linking process between God and man to the *nature* of the Logos as much as to his *person* which was only the manifestation of that nature. This position was summed up in the catch-phrase *one nature* (*mia physis*), using nature to mean 'a self-determining being'. This being assumed manhood and united it to himself, without in any way changing as a result.

The process of union in one nature through incarnation did not destroy the divinity or the humanity of Jesus, which were held together

GOD WAS IN CHRIST

by a *transfer of properties* (known also by its Latin name, *communicatio idiomatum*) from the former to the latter. This device was used to explain the miracles of Jesus, which appeared to attribute superhuman powers to his body. Jesus walked on water because his divine nature expressed itself in his flesh. Likewise when he spat on the ground, the mud which he formed was empowered by the divine saliva to heal a blind man's eyes.

These explanations of the miracles sound plausible enough, and are still quite common today. But there is a rub. With a divine nature to rely on for support, how could Jesus have been thirsty on the cross? How could he not have known when the Last Judgment would come (Matthew 24:36)? To questions like these Athanasius and his followers had no real answer. They simply said that the weakness and ignorance of Jesus seen in the Gospels was feigned by the Logos who wished to accommodate himself to the limitations of the human mind.

Such an explanation outraged the theological school of Antioch. The Antiochenes saw in this inadequate explanation the opportunity to get back at Alexandria, which in the struggle against Arius had captured the orthodox label and tarred Antioch with the semi-Arian brush. The great Antiochene masters, Diodore of Tarsus (d. *c.* 394) and his pupil Theodore of Mopsuestia (d. 428), undertook a detailed analysis of the Alexandrian position in order to pinpoint its weaknesses and provide an alternative which would not force theologians to suggest that God was somehow deceiving the disciples in the manhood of Jesus.

Diodore began as a theologian in the Alexandrian mould, but the ideas of Apollinarius made him uneasy with this position. He declared himself against it and developed his own understanding of the human soul of Jesus. Rather like Athanasius, Diodore said that the soul in Jesus was a 'physical factor' but not a 'theological' one. By this he meant that Jesus had a human soul as part of his flesh, though at first he accepted the Alexandrian belief that the Logos had transferred its properties to it. However, he insisted that this transfer took place within the natural limits imposed by the flesh. In other words, the child Jesus had only the wisdom of a child, even though it was a wisdom fully penetrated by the Divine.

Diodore also believed that the Logos as a *personal nature* was fully present in Jesus and, like the Alexandrians, he denied that it could suffer or die. But whereas Apollinarius was able to say that the

Logos had experienced suffering and death, not in itself but by virtue of the complete transfer of properties to the human side of Jesus' one 'nature', Diodore denied this. He insisted that Jesus had *two natures*, only one of which died on the cross. The dead body in the tomb was that of a man whose soul had expired, not that of the Logos, which remained untouched. In the end, Diodore denied any transfer of properties at all, on the ground that this compromised the integrity of the two natures. In this form, it became the standard teaching of Antioch. It may help to compare it with Apollinarius' teaching as follows:

Apollinarius	Diodore
1. The Logos dwells in Jesus and takes the place of a human soul.	1. The Logos dwells in Jesus but does not take the place of a human soul.
2. The transfer of properties is total.	2. There is no transfer of properties.
3. Jesus had one nature.	3. Jesus had two natures.
4. The Logos suffered and died on the cross, not in itself but by the transfer of its properties to the flesh.	4. The Logos did not suffer or die on the cross, but only the human soul and flesh of Jesus.

Before passing on to Theodore of Mopsuestia, it is worth recording that at least one Alexandrian saw the difficulty in Apollinarius' position and tried to put it right. This was Didymus the Blind (c. 313-398). He tried to provide the Athanasian Christ not merely with a soul but with a psychology, while at the same time safeguarding the unity of his nature in the Logos.

Didymus said that the soul of Jesus could experience anguish and temptation, which were the beginnings of suffering (*propatheia*), but was prevented from actual suffering (*pathos*) itself by its union with the Logos. He also admitted that there was a twofold reality in Christ, but he would not call them natures in the Antiochene fashion. Instead, he preferred to borrow other terms like *forms* (*morphai*) from Philippians 2:7 or characters (*characteres*) from Hebrews 1:3. He did not define these terms, and the fact that he also used the word *persons* (*prosopa*) for this dual reality was to cause confusion in the West. Of course, Didymus recognized only one *hypostasis* in Christ, that of the Logos, but he identified this with the *one nature* of Apollinarius, much to the consternation of later generations.

Theodore of Mopsuestia did not follow Didymus, but took up where Diodore had left off. He fully supported the teaching that there were two separate natures in Christ and sought to explain their connection by means of the word *synapheia* (*conjunction*). According to him, each nature had its own identity or *hypostasis*, before the incarnation, as well as its own appearance (*prosopon*). After the incarnation nothing changed but the appearance, which was now one instead of two. The effect of the incarnation can be tabulated as follows:

		before	after
Alexandria	Nature	2	1
	Hypostasis	1	1
	(Person)	1	1
Antioch	Nature	2	2
	Hypostasis	2	2
	Person	2	1

It was on this basis that Theodore was able to say that in the Incarnate Christ there were two natures in one person, a formula which in inverted form was approved at Chalcedon. As Theodore expressed it, the formula is very weak indeed. The union of God and man is not real, but merely an appearance which is the result of a conjunction. The Alexandrians immediately labelled it heretical and were never reconciled to it, even when the Chalcedonian inversion managed to produce a very different Christology using the same words.

Matters came to a head shortly after the death of Theodore in 428. In that year the emperor Theodosius II appointed the Antiochene professor Nestorius to the patriarchate of Constantinople. Politically, this move was resented at Alexandria, which saw its influence being diminished in the capital. Resentment turned to fear when Nestorius began a vigorous persecution of heretics who had taken refuge in the relative anonymity of Constantinople. He was particularly severe on the Apollinarians, a term which at Antioch could include almost any Alexandrian. The patriarch of Alexandria, a rather unscrupulous man called Cyril, bided his time, waiting for an opportunity to get rid of this impending menace. As a young man, Cyril had gone to Constantinople to witness the deposition of the patriarch John Chrysostom, another Antiochene, by his predecessor. Perhaps an opportunity would come for history to repeat itself.

Cyril did not have long to wait. Before long somebody – we do not know whether in innocence or in malice – asked Nestorius whether it was proper to refer to Mary as *Theotokos*, a Greek word meaning 'God-bearer' (usually rendered in English, somewhat unhappily, as 'Mother of God'). This question sounds rather obscure, but it was important for two reasons. At the theological level, it asked the question: was the foetus in the womb the Son of God or was Mary no more than the mother of an ordinary man? At the popular level, it called into question a long tradition of popular devotion, which had grown used to this term as a description of Mary.

Nestorius sensed the pitfall awaiting him and gave an evasive answer. *Theotokos* was all right, but only if it were accompanied by *anthropotokos*, 'man-bearer', since Mary carried a baby with two natures. Such terms were awkward and misleading, however. It was better to emphasize the unity of Jesus by using the term *Christotokos*, 'Christ-bearer'. This word emphasized the conjunction of the two Natures in the one Person of Christ. Nestorius thought that he had found the answer, and published it in his Easter letter of 429. When Cyril read it, he realized that he had found the scandal he was looking for.

Without fully realizing it, Nestorius had raised two vitally important questions:

1. Did *theos* in *theotokos* refer to the divine nature or to the person of the Logos?
2. Who or what caused the incarnation in the first place?

Before 429 neither of these questions had emerged clearly. Now they confronted Cyril with blinding clarity. *Theos* obviously meant the person of the Logos; but although Cyril understood this, he was never able to free himself from the Apollinarian belief in 'one nature after the union'. As a result he was unable to answer the first question in a completely unambiguous way.

The second question was much easier though. Alexandria had always maintained that the Logos was the subject of the incarnation, that God had taken on human flesh. It was, therefore, essential to maintain that God himself had entered the womb of Mary – she was *Theotokos* without qualification. Here Cyril had used the strong card of Alexandria against the main weakness of Antioch. The Antiochenes were so preoccupied with analysis that they could never find an adequate basis for the unity of Christ. For them the person of the Saviour was the result of the incarnation, not its cause. But in that case, what *was* its cause? Were the two natures equal before the union? If so, whatever was it that attracted them to each other? The Antiochenes had no answer to these questions, and so their theology was bound to fail in the end.

Cyril lost no time denouncing Nestorius, and before long both men were appealing to Rome for judgment. This turn of events must have come as a welcome surprise to the Romans, who had never before participated in the Eastern Christological debate. Rome was not particularly neutral though. Ever since the days of Athanasius it had been pro-Alexandrian and against the Eastern emperor, whose nominee Nestorius of course was. A Roman Synod considered the arguments on both sides, but nobody can have been too surprised when it plumped for Alexandria. Pope Celestine sent a letter to Cyril supporting him, and asked him to convey the decision to Nestorius.

Cyril lost no time in making the most of this extraordinary request. He forwarded the Pope's letter, but attached to it Twelve Anathemas, in which he denounced virtually every major point of Antiochene theology. Nestorius was duly outraged, and asked the emperor to call a council to decide the issue.

Theodosius obliged, and ordered a council to assemble at Ephesus on 7 June 431. When the day arrived, only Cyril had turned up in force, though 68 supporters of Nestorius were also there. They waited until 22 June when Cyril, fearing that events might not go his way if anyone else showed up, defied protests and opened the council on his own initiative. Needless to say, Nestorius was quickly deposed and his teaching condemned.

Four days later, though, the Antiochene delegation turned up and the situation was reversed. Cyril was deposed, and Nestorius was reinstated. Finally, on 10 July, the Roman delegation appeared and overturned the verdict a second time. Nestorius was again deposed, this time for good, and Cyril was able to celebrate a complete triumph.

The Council of Ephesus was a shambles, but its final decrees managed to survive all opposition. In one respect, it even brought debate to a final close – or so it seemed. On 22 July it decreed that the Creed of Nicaea should never be changed, but should remain for ever as the standard of the Church's faith. The precise meaning of the decree has been disputed, and it is not agreed whether the ban can be applied to the Niceno-Constantinopolitan creed as well as to the ancient Creed of Nicaea. On this point the Eastern Churches take the stricter line, while the West has preferred a somewhat looser interpretation. But at least one thing was perfectly clear – the age of creed-writing, in the strict sense, was now officially over.

Reactions to Ephesus came thick and fast. Once Nestorius was out of the way, Cyril was more accommodating, and the emperor, whose sympathies were Antiochene, wanted a reconciliation to preserve the unity of his Empire. In a remarkably short time peace was restored when Cyril despatched to Antioch a letter, dated 23 April 433, in which he included the *Formulary of Reunion* which had been drawn up as early as August 431. This document grants Cyril's points, but avoids any reference to the 'one nature' and treads warily on the subject of the transfer of properties. It reads:

We confess our Lord Jesus Christ, the only-begotten Son of God, perfect God and perfect man, consisting of a rational soul and body, begotten of the Father before the ages as to his Godhead, and in the last days the Same, for us and for our salvation, of Mary the Virgin as to his manhood; the Same consubstantial (*homoousios*) with the Father as to his Godhead, and consubstantial with us as to his manhood. For there has been a union of two natures; wherefore we confess one Christ, one Son, one Lord.

In accordance with this thought of the unconfused union,

we confess the holy Virgin to be *Theotokos*, because the divine Logos was incarnate and made man, and from the very conception united to himself the temple that was taken from her.

And with regard to the sayings about the Lord in the Gospels ..., we know that theologians take some as common because they relate to one Person, and others they divide according to the two natures, explaining acts befitting God in reference to the Godhead of Christ, and lowly acts in reference to his manhood.

Cyril's prestige meant that this *Formulary* remained in force until his death in 444, though many of his followers regarded it as a sell-out to the Nestorians. The absence of a 'one nature' clause, which Cyril had made a badge of orthodoxy in spite of its Apollinarian provenance, gave this element its main excuse to cause trouble later.

It was not long in coming. In 448 the attention of the Home Synod of Constantinople was drawn to the teachings of a 'muddle-headed archimandrite' (as he was later to be called), by the name of Eutyches. Eutyches was a rather simple-minded disciple of the great Cyril, addicted like his master to the 'one-nature' formula. Unlike Cyril, however, Eutyches was not sure what this was supposed to mean in practice. He accepted that the Logos was incarnate, but was he made *man*, as the Antiochenes claimed?

Here he exposed the terminological confusion which had always dogged Cyril. Cyril had said, and Eutyches agreed, that the incarnation was best described as 'out of two natures, one nature'. But what was this nature? It could not be *ousia*, because that would mean that two beings had merged into one being, which by definition would be neither God nor man. Nor could *nature* be *hypostasis*, since that would mean that before the incarnation there had been a human embryo with the potential to become a human being without divine intervention – a clear denial of the virginal conception of Jesus, and Nestorianism of the worst sort. Eutyches eventually got to the point where he almost denied any real humanity in Christ, saying that this had been absorbed by God at the incarnation; but his views were never taken very seriously. It was his political importance which mattered. When he was condemned on 22 November 448, Alexandria hailed him as a hero, even though its wiser heads distanced themselves from his theology.

Events now moved quickly. Dioscorus, Cyril's successor at Alexandria and a plotter of the first order, petitioned the emperor for a council. A decree to that effect was published on 30 March 449 and the council was called to meet at Ephesus on 8 August. The intervening months were filled with diplomatic activity. The position of Rome was uncertain, but it was thought that it would support Alexandria as usual. Flavian, the patriarch of Constantinople who had presided at the condemnation of Eutyches, was in disgrace at court, where Dioscorus obviously had the emperor's ear. No doubt fearing the worst, Flavian wrote a letter to Pope Leo in Rome, setting out his teaching and asking for Leo's support.

Flavian approached the problem raised by Eutyches in the following way. First, he identified *nature* with *ousia*, or *being* – the confusion already noted. Then he said that out of two natures, the incarnation had produced one *prosopon* (the Nestorian formula) and one *hypostasis* (a concession to the Alexandrians). *Prosopon* and *hypostasis* were thus thrown together for the first time, a fact which was to make it easier for the Greeks to accept an equation of the Latin *persona* (= *prosopon*) with *hypostasis*. Flavian had hit upon the right formula, in that he saw the need for two distinct levels of Christological inquiry: one emphasizing unity, other duality. But he still saw the unity of person as the product of a coming together of two separate natures, an Antiochene trait which failed to grasp the activity of the Logos with sufficient clarity.

Flavian's letter reached Rome on 21 May 449. Leo replied immediately, offering Flavian his support, and promising a more detailed explanation later on. This was despatched on 13 June and has gone down in history as the most succinct product of ancient Christology to have come out of the Latin-speaking world. Generally known as the *Tome*, this document gives a neat answer to the problems which were dividing the East. Leo's intervention in a dispute of which he had no first-hand knowledge was not universally welcomed, and there are still critics today who blame him for the subsequent disruption in the Eastern Church. On the other hand, as we have seen, the dissensions in the East were deep and serious long before Leo entered the fray, and it is hard to think that he can be blamed for an outcome which could have been foreseen long before.

That being said, it remains true that Leo's *Tome* did in fact provoke a realignment of forces in the East which was to have lasting consequences. For a start, he broke the traditional alliance between Rome and Alexandria by agreeing to support Flavian. He also insisted that the primacy of his own see, which had been agreed upon in 381, gave him the right to make definitive pronouncements in doctrinal disputes. This point was not accepted in the East, but the reception give to the *Tome* strengthened Leo's prestige and enabled him to stake out a claim on which his successors would not be slow to build.

Leo's *Tome* contains two basic principles on which any biblical Christology must be based. First, he agreed with Alexandria that the Logos was the subject of the incarnation, and he tied this specifically to the Person of the Son. Second, he agreed with Antioch that Jesus was a man in the fullest sense. The right formula to express this was the Antiochene statement that Jesus was a manifestation of two natures in a single person.

This was sufficient to condemn the *Tome* in the eyes of Dioscorus, and it has often been taken as evidence that Leo favoured the Antiochene position. Certainly many Antiochene theologians at the time regarded Leo's *Tome* as a victory for their cause. Even Nestorius, who was still alive and in exile, claimed that it represented his position fully.

Closer inspection yields a rather different result though. Leo used the Antiochene formula and received support from that quarter; he also alienated the Alexandrians. But in fact, the content of his Christology was more Alexandrian than Antiochene, at least at the level of fundamental principle. The fact that Leo made the Person of the Son the *cause* of the incarnation and not its *result* gave the Antiochene formula a completely different meaning. No longer could a person be regarded merely as an aspect of a nature, as it generally was in the East. Person was now to be a concept in its own right, detached from Nature and set up in contrast to it. What had been worked out in Trinitarian theology was now to be applied directly to Christology, a process which ironed out the philosophical difficulties into which Christological enquiry had fallen, and which achieved a new integration of theology generally.

The *Tome* of Leo reached the East in time to be brought to the council at Ephesus; but when the bishops assembled for their deliberations, Dioscorus, who acted as chairman, would not allow it to be read out. Leo's delegates were arrested and thrown into prison, whilst many leading Antiochene representatives were beaten up or harassed. Flavian himself was probably treated in this way, and it seems that he died of his wounds not long after the council ended. In the circumstances, it is hardly surprising that the Alexandrians won the day. Eutyches was reinstated and most of his opponents were deposed. The 'one nature' doctrine of Cyril was proclaimed to be orthodox, and all other views were anathematized.

Those who fell victim to the machinations of Dioscorus were quick to react. Flavian himself managed to get a letter off to Rome, and he was followed by others of the Antiochene school. When Leo heard what had happened he was furious, and began to campaign for another council to undo the work of the 'Robber Synod' of Ephesus. He managed to get the support of the Western emperor and his court, and made moves to influence those close to Theodosius II, especially his sister Pulcheria. He wanted a new council to be held in Italy, where Rome would be properly represented, and sent envoys to Constaninople to bargain for this.

When the envoys arrived, they discovered that Theodosius had just fallen from his horse and died. His appointed successor was the general Marcian, who promptly consolidated his position by marrying Pulcheria. It was the situation Leo wanted. The new imperial couple would not hear of a council in Italy, but instead convened one to meet opposite the capital, in the residential suburb of Chalcedon, where the government could keep a close watch on any unruly behaviour.

The council met on 8 October 451, and the atmosphere could not have been more different from that of Ephesus two years before. Leo's *Tome* was read out and hailed as the expression of the purest orthodoxy. The decisions of earlier councils were reviewed and upheld, including the condemnation of Nestorius in 431. The council was most anxious to affirm the orthodoxy of Cyril, and its defenders claimed that Cyril's 'one nature' Christology, properly understood, did not contradict the orthodox formula. Cyril may have suffered from terminological imprecision, but his teaching was perfectly sound.

The positive teaching of the council reflected Leo's *Tome* in the light of the wider Christological controversy. The council made it clear that *person* and *hypostasis* were the same thing, not different as Nestorius had said. It also stated that the *person/hypostasis* was a principle in its own right, not to be deduced from the nature. It further maintained that in Christ there was only one *person/hypostasis*, that of the divine Son of God. The human nature of Jesus did not have a *hypostasis* of its own, which in simple language means that Jesus would not have existed had the Son not entered the womb of Mary. There was no 'man' apart from this divine action. Lastly the council rejected any union of the natures which might obscure the integrity of either. Jesus was fully God and fully man, without interference by one nature on the other.

The council did not deny that there was a transfer of properties in some sense, but this could not be understood in terms of the effect the divine nature had on the human nature. The principle of union was the divine *person/hypostasis* which could take attributes of Jesus' divinity and use them in his humanity, without compromising the latter's integrity. Just as important, the transfer of properties became something partial and variable, rather than a necessity following on the incarnation itself. This was a major advance in thinking because it allowed for the possibility of special miracles associated with the man Jesus of Nazareth without making it impossible for him to suffer and die on the cross. The two sides of Jesus, divine and human, were each preserved and protected in a way which did justice to the teaching of Scripture, while at the same time providing an explanation of Jesus' freedom to perform miracles.

On 22 October 451 the council published the *Definition of Faith*, of which the most significant paragraph reads:

In agreement, therefore, with the holy fathers we all unanimously teach that we should confess that our Lord Jesus Christ is one and the same Son; the same perfect in Godhead and the same perfect in manhood, truly God and truly man, the same of a rational soul and body; consubstantial with the Father in Godhead and the same consubstantial with us in manhood; like us in all things except sin; begotten of the Father before all ages as regards his Godhead and in the last days the same, for us and for our salvation, begotten of the Virgin Mary the *Theotokos* as regards his manhood; one and the same Christ, Son, Lord, only-begotten, made known in two natures without confusion, without change, without division, without separation; the difference of the natures being by no means removed because of the union but the property of each nature being

preserved and coalescing in one person (*prosopon*) and one
hypostasis, not parted or divided into two persons but one and
the same Son, only-begotten, divine Word, the Lord Jesus
Christ; as the prophets of old and Jesus Christ himself have
taught us about him, and the creed of our fathers has handed
down.

The close link between the working of this paragraph and the
Nicene Creed is obvious, as is the concern to emphasize, by the
constant repetition of 'the same', that the Person of Christ is one in
every aspect of his incarnation. Within this essentially Alexandrian
framework, allowance is made for the teaching of Antioch, particularly
in the use of the word *coalescing* to describe the union of the two
natures. The principle of unity in diversity could hardly have received
clearer expression, and it is no accident that the Chalcedonian
Definition remains to this day the supreme expression of an orthodox,
biblical faith.

This is not to say, of course, that the Definition has not had its
detractors. The Alexandrians walked out of the council, and despite
many attempts to persuade them to change their minds, were never to
abandon the 'one nature' Christology of Cyril.

In modern times scholarly sympathy has lain more with Nestorius,
and Chalcedon has been denounced as 'docetist' on the ground that it
denied the existence of a human hypostasis in Jesus. Docetism (from
the Greek word *dokei*, 'it seems') is the belief that Jesus appeared in
human flesh without becoming a man, and orthodox Christology is
accused of it almost as a matter of course among liberal theologians
today. Taken by itself, the Definition may be open to this charge
because it says nothing about the human nature of Jesus having an
identity of its own.

But what modern liberals do not realize is that the difficulty is not
new. It was perceived very clearly in the century after Chalcedon and
answered in a most original way. The council's work cannot be
understood in isolation. It provided a resolution of outstanding disputes
but did not close the door to further Christological enquiry. On the
contrary, it made such enquiry both possible and necessary, by
providing the basic guidelines along which a more complete
theological construction could be built. To understand the full impact

of the council's work, we must take a brief look at the fall-out from it and examine the general lines along which future doctrinal development would proceed.

Aftermath

The Council of Chalcedon marks a turning-point in the history of theological thought. It welded Western and Eastern traditions into a unity which would not be seen again, though the price paid for this in the East was to be very high.

The Nestorians were finally discredited, despite Nestorius' plea that he subscribed to the teaching of Leo. Life in the Empire became very difficult for them, and many of their leading figures emigrated to Persia. There they were rewarded by the Shah, who in 484 gave Nestorianism legal recognition as the only form of Christianity tolerated in his dominions. The Nestorians developed great missionary zeal, and their churches spread from Babylonia to China. Unfortunately they were never able to consolidate their gains, and after the eleventh century decline set in. Today they are a tiny community, known as Assyrians or Chaldeans. About half live in Iraq and the rest are dispersed across the world, with the largest number in the United States.

The Nestorian church has had a sad history, but it has not waned without bequeathing at least one legacy of lasting importance. The school of Antioch was Aristotelian in its philosophical method, in contrast to the Platonism of Alexandria. After the rise of Islam, Nestorians were influential in bringing Aristotle to the notice of the Arab world. There he was cherished, studied and improved, until in the twelfth century Spanish scholars translated his works from Arabic into Latin. The rediscovery of Aristotle in the West provoked a theological revolution which challenged the whole basis of classical orthodoxy and eventually resulted in the new synthesis of Thomas Aquinas (1226-1274).

Today the Aristotelian tradition in philosophy still leans in the Nestorian direction. That explains why so many modern theologians, embued with the spirit of scientific pragmatism, have attempted to rehabilitate Nestorius as a truer exponent of the Gospel picture of Christ than the one provided by the Council of Chalcedon.

The church of Alexandria met a different fate. The followers of

Dioscorus were too numerous to be exiled, suppressed or even controlled. They murdered or disregarded imperial envoys almost at will, and before long they had extended their influence into Syria as well. Their theologians were the most able in Christendom, and for a long time it seemed as it they might be able to overturn the decisions of Chalcedon. The emperor Zeno was so impressed by their tenacity that in 482 he issued a decree, now known as the *Henotikon*, which praised the orthodoxy of Cyril, laid great stress on the Virgin Mary the *Theotokos* and repeatedly emphasized the unity of Christ's natures. To these affirmations Zeno added the following denunciation:

> Everyone who has held or holds any other opinion, either at the present or another time, *whether at Chalcedon* or in any synod whatever, we anathematize.

This clause did not quite condemn Chalcedon outright, but made it clear that its decisions could be at least partly wrong. Rome broke with Constantinople over it, but the way towards a reconciliation with Alexandria seemed open.

Had the Alexandrian church been content to abide by the teaching of Cyril, which everyone accepted as orthodox, there might have been no problem. But by 482 the discussion about Christ's nature was moving into a new and more delicate phase. Most of the Orientals clung to the 'one nature' formula, which became their badge of distinction. These Monophysites, as we now call them, pursued the logic of this belief as it applied to the human flesh of Jesus. If the Logos had united this flesh to himself in a single nature, could we infer that Jesus' flesh was incapable of sin?

Severus of Antioch (c. 465–c.540), who represented moderate Monophysitism, said that this was the case, not because the flesh of Jesus was different from ours, but because it was in indissoluble association with the Logos. This position was close to the orthodox one, except that it maintained that Jesus *could* not have succumbed to temptation, rather than simply that he *did* not. This is a subtle difference, but it is essential in considering whether Jesus was truly a man, subject to the same pressures and temptations as the rest of us (Hebrews 4:15). The situation was further complicated by more extreme elements, represented by Julian of Halicarnassus (early sixth century), who maintained that the flesh of Jesus was incapable of sin even *before* it was united with the Logos. This broke any link between his flesh and ours, and opened Julian to the charge of Docetism.

Another characteristic of Monophysite Christology was the emphasis it placed on the *operations* or *energies* (*energeiai*) in Christ. This teaching insisted that there was a distinction between what a being, or nature, was, and what it could do. In Christ, the human nature had no operations of its own. In simple language that means that Jesus did not think and act in the same way as other people. In him there was only one centre of operation, which lay in the nature of the Logos. As a result Jesus had only one consciousness and one will, both of them divine and not human. The acts of the human body were the manifestations of decisions taken by the divine will, a belief which, like the question of exposure to sin, brought the reality of Jesus' manhood into question.

To our Western minds, these ideas appear to be a denial of the gospel witness, but they struck a powerful chord in the East at that time. It is quite probable that Athanasius, had he been alive about 500, would have felt more at home with Severus than with anybody at Rome, and it was the knowledge of this that fired so much Monophysite polemic. 'We are the true orthodox,' said the Monophysites, 'because we follow the tradition of Athanasius and Cyril, uncontaminated by the heresies of Nestorius and Leo.' Certainly it is true that many people at Constantinople felt themselves spiritually more akin to the Monophysites than they did to the West, and this gave their teaching a better reception at court than it might have had.

This sympathy manifested itself more clearly at the Second Council of Constantinople in 553. The council did not repudiate Chalcedon or affirm the 'one nature', but it did agree to condemn the leading Antiochene theologians who had expressed opinions contrary to those of Dioscorus. There was some reluctance to pronounce anathemas on men who had died in orthodoxy over a century before, but this objection was overcome. The Western church was the most reluctant to agree, and parts of it went into schism for the next 150 years, but on the whole the condemnations were allowed to stand. Theodore of Mopsuestia's works were banned *in toto*, in belated recognition of the fact that Nestorius had done little more than repeat his main ideas.

Sadly, the events of 553 were not enough to satisfy the more extreme Monophysites, whose hold over their flock was total. One of these, Jacob Baradaeus, was already setting up a rival church organization in Syria, and the dispute acquired a new look of permanence. A further attempt at conciliation was made by the emperor Heraclius in 638. In his *Ecthesis* of that year, he decreed that the incarnate Christ had only one will, though he maintained the 'two natures' doctrine of Chalcedon. This compromise had no effect in the East, which at that very moment was being overrun by the Arabs. It was accepted at first by Rome, but soon repudiated. Monotheletism, as this teaching is called (from the Greek word *thelema*, will), died a fairly speedy death and was condemned along with Monophysitism at the Third Council of Constantinople in 680.

This council decreed that Christ had two wills, a fact which could be verified from his words in Gethsemane: 'Not my will, but thy will be done' (Matthew 26:39). Earlier generations had used this verse as evidence that Jesus was not God, but now there was a more sophisticated approach. In his divinity, the will of the Son was one with the will of the Father, an important point because it emphasized the voluntary nature of Christ's sacrifice. His reluctance was the normal human fear of suffering and death which anyone in similar circumstances would feel. As the council of 680 saw, these two factors had to be kept in balance in order to do justice to the biblical picture of Christ.

By 680, the Monophysites were a separate church, living under Muslim rule. Indeed, it was their brand of Christianity which in a popular form had influenced the Prophet Muhammed. Muhammed rejected the divinity of Christ, but he retained the Monophysite emphasis on the Virgin Birth and a belief that Jesus did not really suffer and die on the cross – a misunderstanding of the Monophysite Logos doctrine. Despite persecution the Monophysites were remarkably resilient and embarked on a number of missionary ventures. The Egyptians, or Copts, reached Ethiopia and won it over, whilst the Syrian Jacobites founded the so-called church of St Thomas in South India, both of which are still thriving. Today the majority of Christians in the Middle East belong to this church, and there have even been attempts in recent years to heal the breach caused by the Council of Chalcedon.

Monophysites and Nestorians are only part of the picture of course. Constantinople and Jerusalem remained loyal to Chalcedon and tried to counter anti-Chalcedonian Christology with explanations of the 'one person in two natures' doctrine put forward by the council. Their orthodox theologians had to solve three basic problems. They had to explain how the human nature of Christ could exist without a human person, or 'identity'. They had to distinguish clearly what belonged to the Person of Christ and what belonged to his two natures. They also had to say how a divine person could function in a human nature without compromising either the divinity or the humanity.

A first attempt to answer this was made by a Constantinopolitan who is known to us as Leontius of Byzantium (c. 485-c.543). Leontius asked himself why the human soul of Jesus was not a person as other human souls were. To answer this he fell back on Origen's Platonic idea of the soul. He said that the soul of Jesus had detached itself from the Godhead at the beginning of time, but that instead of falling into the material world it clung to the Logos, not only by nature (as Origen had said) but in hypostasis as well. As a result it lost its distinctive identity and did not suffer with the flesh on the cross. This sounds like Apollinarianism, but it is not. Apollinarius had allowed for the suffering of the Logos by the transfer of properties, an idea which Leontius denied.

Leontius was condemned in 553, but he left behind two important principles which were to be extraordinarily fruitful. First, he said that every nature must have a hypostasis in order to exist. It was, therefore, necessary for the human nature of Jesus to have a person, or identity of its own. Second, he said that a nature could exist *within* a hypostasis, without exhausting its capacity. As a person, the Son of God could give an identity to the human nature of Jesus without losing or compromising his divine nature. This doctrine, Leontius called *enhypostasia*.

It was taken up and elaborated by his contemporary and namesake, Leontius of Jerusalem. The two men have been hopelessly confused in the manuscript tradition, so that we cannot know exactly who said what. But it seems that it was Leontius of Jerusalem who tied the doctrine of *enhypostasia* to the formula of Chalcedon.

He maintained that the hypostasis of the incarnation was the Logos, the Son of God. This Logos gave an identity to the human nature of Jesus, and in this capacity he suffered and died on the cross. In this way it was made clear that the divine person (*hypostasis*) and the divine nature were separate principles, which could not be fused with one another. In his human nature the divine person lived a normal human life, not abandoning the attributes of his divine nature, but not allowing them to distort the human nature by removing its limitations. Put in the most simple language, Jesus could be fully God without knowing, as a man, the secrets of nuclear physics or even how to use a telephone. His omniscience as God did not automatically carry over into his life on earth as a man.

The doctrine of Leontius became the standard orthodoxy of East and West, and so it remains to this day. Detractors of Chalcedon, who claim that the council never got to grips with the true manhood of Jesus, are apt to overlook this later development, and as a result their perspective is distorted. We cannot understand Chalcedon unless we are prepared to get to grips with the way it was explained and defended in the East after 451.

By 680 the boundaries of Christological orthodoxy had been fairly carefully delineated, but there was to be one more controversy before peace was finally to be secured. In 726 the emperor Leo III published a decree ordering the destruction of images of Christ, on the ground that the Second Commandment forbade any pictorial representation of God. This decree was probably no more than a puritanical reaction against pictures, but it quickly developed into a theological controversy. God could not be depicted. But Jesus had been a fully visible man, and in this capacity could be painted (or photographed!). But was the painting a representation of the divine person, or merely of the human nature?

Here the doctrine of Leontius of Jerusalem made itself felt very clearly. The human nature of Jesus had a divine identity, or hypostasis. It was, therefore, axiomatic that any portrayal of Jesus was a portrayal of God, a belief supported by the words of Jesus: 'he who has seen me has seen the Father' (John 14:9). Furthermore, it was necessary to make pictures of Christ, not only for the instruction of illiterate believers, but to do justice to the reality of the incarnation. These points were made by John of Damascus (c.675-c.749), a Greek Christian who was in the service of the Arab Caliph and, therefore, beyond the reach of the emperor's persecuting agents (though, ironically, Leo's teaching about the destruction of images is closely paralleled in Islam).

John compiled a summary of the teaching of all the orthodox councils and bishops, a labour which makes him the first systematic, historical theologian. His writings were so well received that even today they are the basic textbook for Eastern Orthodox students of theology. Iconoclasm, as the destruction of images is called, was condemned at the Second Council of Nicaea in 787. This council decreed a veneration of images which was later to assume fantastic proportions. Strangely enough, the Latin text of the council's decree used the word *salutare*, which need mean no more than *greet* or *acknowledge*, but the Greek word is *aspazein*, kiss – which is much more explicit.

The council was rejected by Charlemagne and his theologians at the Synod of Frankfurt in 794, though for reasons which were largely political. It was later received in the West, though the veneration of icons (as opposed to statues) never established itself as a normal practice. In the East, however, a renewed outbreak of iconoclasm in the ninth century reinforced this tendency among the Orthodox. When iconoclasm was finally crushed in 843, the year of the so-called Triumph of Orthodoxy, the veneration of icons became the obligatory practice which it remains today. By that time, however, no-one in the West was taking much notice of developments at Constantinople. The two halves of Christendom had entered into a medieval isolation which before long would turn to indifference, then hostility and finally schism.

The Western reaction to the Council of Chalcedon was, as always, much simpler than anything found in the East. Apart from Canon 28, which confirmed the privileges of the see of Constantinople, Rome saw nothing amiss with the council and defended it against all attack. Leo's *Tome* was not thought to need any improvement, and it was incorporated without further ado as one of the doctrinal standards approved by the council. This attitude did not encourage further speculation, and Chalcedon acquired an air of finality in Christological matters which it has retained ever since. On the other hand, theological discussion could not be stopped, and an explanation of the council's doctrine was particularly necessary in view of the threat posed by Arianism.

This explanation was given in its classical form by Boethius (c.480-c.524). Boethius was trained in classical philosophy and the tone of his work may be gauged by the fact that some people have doubted whether he was ever really converted to Christianity at all! Like Ambrose before him, he was a cultivated aristocrat who used his talents for the benefit of the Church. In a treatise officially directed against Eutyches (who by then had been dead for at least half a century),

Boethius attempted to define the meaning of *person* and *nature*. He knew that *nature* was a broader category than *person*, because whilst both a stone and a man had a nature, only the latter could be called a person. *Person* was obviously not an aspect of nature, however, like colour or size. So it seemed clear to Boethius that, like nature, it was also a substance. But it was not a universal substance, like man, only an individual substance, like Cicero or Plato.

From this Boethius deduced that *a person is the individual substance of a rational nature*. This definition contains elements of the orthodox definition, but it lacks the refining fire provided by Leontius of Byzantium. As a result, the medieval West came to think of persons as individual manifestations of the higher forms of nature. As such, persons were conscious of receiving God's grace, which was also thought of as a supernatural substance given by God to perfect created nature. The end-product of all this was the doctrine of transubstantiation, according to which the natural elements of bread and wine used at Communion were transformed by grace into the body and blood of Christ. This grace was consciously perceived by the believer, who could participate in the spiritual fellowship of Christ simply by eating the consecrated bread!

For many centuries the definition of Boethius was accepted without question on the strength of its great antiquity and apparent authority. The revival of learning in the twelfth century brought the question to the fore again, and in the later Middle Ages scholars and theologians struggled to make sense of what Boethius was saying.

The breakthrough eventually came when Martin Luther discovered the doctrine of justification by grace through faith (Ephesians 2:8; Romans 1:16-17). Suddenly it became blindingly clear that the believer in Christ had a relationship with him which was personal in a way which did not rely on the consecration of natural elements like bread and wine.

The revolution which this discovery initiated opened the way to a rediscovery of the spiritual character of grace, which has been such a strong feature of Protestantism; but the Reformers were slower to see its implications for the Trinity and for the Person of Christ. Like their Catholic opponents, they read the ancient Fathers through medieval eyes, which dulled their appreciation of certain aspects of classical orthodoxy. They did not reject it, of course, but they were not as sensitive as they might have been to the systematic correspondences between *grace* and *person* which, if pursued, would have anchored their own theological systems much more firmly in the orthodoxy of the creeds.

Today we have both the opportunity and the need to fill this gap. Modern challenges to the Christian faith no longer focus on the question of grace, because the theological framework in which grace operates is widely rejected. We have returned in our own time to the basic questions of person and nature which are now being put to us by psychology as much as by liberal theology. Consciousness, the sub-conscious, the pre-natal state and the development of the 'personality' are issues which now confront us more often than the old problems of meritorious works, free grace and saving faith.

The creeds of Christendom are basic statements of belief which take up these questions and answer them in the context of the Person of Christ. There is a great need today to return to these foundations of our faith and probe just how they can help us to answer the doubts of our time and bring the gospel of Christ to bear once again on the affairs of men.

The Theological Synthesis

The Council of Chalcedon did not bring peace to the Church, but like the First Council of Constantinople 70 years earlier, it ushered in a new stage in the process of doctrinal definition. Where the generation of Cyril and Nestorius had been concerned with formulation and definition, the post-Chalcedonian theologians were more preoccupied with explanation and consolidation. Systematic theology in the true sense now became a pressing need, as men sought to discover the wider implications of their particular doctrinal positions and to relate their beliefs to each other in a logical and consistent way.

It was during this period that orthodoxy acquired its final shape. One aspect of this was the increasing deference which was paid to past masters of theology, whose teaching was claimed to be the model for all future generations. The fourth-century writers had honoured Tertullian, Origen and Justin Martyr, but they had also criticized their positions and did not feel bound to copy what they had done. By the sixth century attitudes had hardened. Tertullian and Origen were both condemned as heretics, though the ban imposed on their works was never very effective. On the other hand, Cyril of Alexandria, Augustine, and above all Athanasius, were held up to the Church as the saints whose doctrine was beyond reproach and beyond question.

Creative theology was now concerned mainly to advance or develop their positions, although the careful reader will not be slow to detect subtle shifts which indicate that the teaching attributed to the great masters would not necessarily have received their full approval. This situation may sound odd, but it has a ready parallel in the Protestant world, where it is a well-known fact that Lutherans and Calvinists have developed theological positions which are not always identical with the teaching of Luther or Calvin!

The process of sorting out the wheat from the chaff is a necessary one, and it follows any major period of intellectual activity. The sixth, seventh and eighth centuries were not as brilliantly creative as the two hundred years which preceded them; but they are important, both for the work of editing and collation which they did and for the stamp which they put on the developments which had occurred. It was at the popular level that the beliefs worked out by theologians were to have their lasting impact. Without this popularization, the genius of the creative period would have been lost to posterity.

Popularization

Already in the fourth century, popularization was becoming a fine art. Arius had apparently written hymns to convey his message, and the idea soon caught on. The Church had had psalms and hymns before, but congregational singing on a large scale was the result of fourth-century efforts. Ambrose was a prolific composer, and the Latin West generally took the lead, though it was in the East that the great festal Liturgies were written and used as the focal point of worship. The Liturgy was developed as a form of musical drama, in which hymns were incorporated along with large stretches of spoken and chanted prose. From the start, congregational participation must have been minimal, since only a trained choir could really master the technique. Today the Eastern Churches pride themselves on what they see as lay participation in these services, though to a Western onlooker the 'laity' look more like a male voice choir!

In this, the Western tradition was somewhat different, and although there was a considerable development of the Liturgy, hymns retained their separate existence much longer. They disappeared for a time in the Middle Ages and were only partly reintroduced at the Reformation, but since the eighteenth century they have largely regained the position they held in late antiquity. Indeed this development has now gone so far that hymn singing is presented on television as a religious service in its own right.

The main difference between ancient and modern is in the emphasis. Modern hymns tend to stress subjective religious experience, whereas their ancient counterparts are more like expositions of doctrine. This difference was noticed in the nineteenth century by scholars who had read the Fathers of the Early Church, and they began to translate and imitate the style of the ancients. As a result ancient hymnody is now once more available to us, and it is

well-known even to people who know nothing about the theological
climate in which the hymns were written.

One of the best and most prolific authors was Prudentius (348-
405), much of whose work was beautifully Englished by John Mason
Neale. A particularly well-known processional hymn of his is *Corde
natus ex parentis*, which puts across to us the doctrine of the
incarnation:

> Of the Father's love begotten
> Ere the worlds began to be
> He, the Alpha and Omega
> He the source, the ending He
> Of the things that are, that have been,
> And that future years shall see,
> Evermore and evermore.
>
> He is here whom seers aforetime
> Chanted while the ages ran
> Whom the faithful word of prophets
> Promised since the world began
> Long foretold, at length appearing.
> Praise Him every child of man,
> Evermore and evermore.
>
> Blessed was the day for ever,
> When by God the Spirit's grace
> From the womb of Virgin Mother
> Came the Saviour of our race,
> When the child, the world's Redeemer,
> First displayed His sacred face.
> Evermore and evermore.

This is the Nicene Creed set to music, not intentionally, but in
spirit and feeling. The devotion to Christ is overwhelming. Although
it is the story of the incarnation, there is none of the mawkish
sentimentality of the average Christmas carol. Here was the world's
Redeemer, actively displaying his sacred face, and when we grasp
the power of these words we can begin to understand why the
iconoclasts were to have such a hard time. Prudentius was not a great
theologian as intellects go, but he has probably touched more people
with the message of the orthodox gospel than any of the bishops who

argued such fine points of doctrine at Nicaea or Chalcedon.

As time went on, the need to popularize grew, though styles and standards rose as the Church became more obviously the chief guardian of our culture. Hymnody, which had started with popular tunes and easy rhymes, became a polished art, eventually producing its own characteristic plainsong, or Gregorian Chant, named after its chief sponsor, Pope Gregory II (715-731). The Creeds were also set to music and sung, though their style was not very suitable for it. Before long, though, the hymn tradition was making itself felt in the confessional parts of worship, and a new type of creed, not quite a hymn but much more rhythmic and repetitive than the earlier sort, made its appearance.

Perhaps the best known of these is the great *Te Deum Laudamus*, which is usually ascribed to Nicetas, bishop of Remesiana, who lived at the time of Ambrose and Augustine. It is a canticle modelled on the psalms and it rapidly became a favourite hymn of praise and thanksgiving. Columbus had it sung when he discovered America, and it was standard fare after victory in battle. It is still widely sung today, and appears as part of Morning Prayer in the Book of Common Prayer.

The Athanasian Creed

More sophisticated, and about a century later in date, is the *Quicunque Vult*, an anonymous 'creed' which may or may not have been written for singing. This work appeared in Southern Gaul about 500, and it was soon attributed to Athanasius, despite the fact that it was composed in Latin and was unknown in the Greek East. It spread rapidly, and for many people became the touchstone of orthodoxy. The so-called Athanasian Creed retained its exalted position until the eighteenth century, when it was attacked as unchristian by liberal elements influenced by Deism and the Enlightenment. Attempts were made to have it excised from the Book of Common Prayer, but fortunately these were unsuccessful. On the other hand its use declined considerably, and today few Christians in any church have heard of it or used it. This is a pity, because despite its length and repetitiveness, which are not to our modern taste, the Creed remains the most readily accessible summary of classical orthodoxy. A student finds it too long to grasp at one go, so we must set it out and comment upon it here in stages.

The creed opens with the famous 'damnatory' clauses, which have been the object of repeated attack:

> Whosoever will be saved, before all things it is necessary
>   that he uphold the Catholic Faith.
> Which Faith except everyone do keep whole and undefiled,
>   without doubt he shall perish everlastingly.

The rather negative tone does not commend itself to an age which engages in interfaith dialogue, but there can be no doubt that it is a faithful reflection of the beliefs held by convinced Christians, both in ancient times and today. Note first that the emphasis is put on the need for right belief as the guarantee of salvation. Many people have criticized this on the ground that it appears to make salvation the fruit of intellectual argument, but that misrepresents the creed's purpose and feel. It does not speak of *believing* the Catholic Faith but of *holding* it, an image which has grown stale with use but which introduces an important dimension which is not purely mental. In modern terms the question it puts to us is not 'Do you accept it?' but 'Does it grab you?' 'Are you clinging to it for dear life?' The Catholic Faith is something to *keep*, a treasure to be loved and guarded with one's life.

Then note the careful balance between the Church and the believer within it. The Faith is an objective reality, true in itself at all times and in all places. It is catholic because it is both universal and all-embracing, *the* answer to the needs and aspirations of all men everywhere. At the same time, it cannot be taken for granted. Every Christian, in so far as he is able, must hold and keep it in its entirety, without spot or blemish. To be Christian means to be born again into a new life which calls forth total commitment. To ignore or compromise even a small part of it is a betrayal of God's trust, and a sign that the new life in Christ has not taken firm root in the soul. Having made this simple but fundamental point, the unknown author goes on:

> And the Catholic Faith is this, that we worship one God in
>   Trinity, and Trinity in Unity
> Neither confounding the Persons, nor dividing the
>   Substance.

Once more we find an explanation of the Faith which is not merely intellectual. We are not just to *believe* in the Trinity but to *worship* one God in Trinity, which is not at all the same thing. There is a direct personal relationship at the heart of the Faith, and its supreme expression can only come in praise and worship. Only in the context of knowing God do we know the Trinity, yet to know the Trinity is the sum of Christian wisdom and experience. Note how the writer guards against abstraction by stressing that we worship *one God* in Trinity. Only later does he make reference to *Unity*, an understanding of God which does not make sense until we have known and confessed the Persons of the Trinity.

Next we find, in one short line, the whole theological controversy of the fourth and fifth centuries neatly summarized. We are not to confuse the Persons in the manner of the Sabellians, because each has his own distinctiveness which can neither be merged nor swopped with another. At the same time, we must not divide the Substance (Nature) as Jerome feared the Greeks were doing. There is no place in the Church for any who say that the Logos or the Spirit are merely parts of God the Father. The basic point having been thus laid down, the author elaborates as follows:

For there is one Person of the Father, another of the Son and another of the Holy Ghost.
But the Godhead of the Father, of the Son and of the Holy Ghost is all one; the Glory equal, the Majesty co-eternal.

Here the concept of *Person* is put in its proper perspective. It is not a common category of abstract thought into which the different Persons fit. On the contrary, Father, Son and Holy Spirit are each individually described as Persons, making it clear that it is they who have determined the category, not the other way round. Furthermore each Person possesses the Godhead, which is the same for all not merely in quality but in quantity. There are not three equal gods but there is only one God, whose three Persons each share the divinity fully. The light with which they shine is equal, so that it cannot be said that one Person leaves the others in the shade. The power by which they rule is co-eternal, so that none can claim superiority over the others by virtue of priority. All forms of Arianism or subordinationism are firmly set aside. We read on:

Such as the Father is, such is the Son, and such is the Holy Ghost.
The Father uncreate, the Son uncreate and the Holy Ghost uncreate.
The Father incomprehensible, the Son incomprehensible and the
    Holy Ghost incomprehensible.
The Father eternal, the Son eternal and the Holy Ghost eternal.
And yet they are not three eternals but one eternal.
As also there are not three incomprehensibles, nor three uncreated,
    but one uncreated and one incomprehensible.

The primacy of Father, Son and Holy Spirit over the common term Person is now reinforced at the level of Nature. The characteristics of God are attributes held in common by each of the three together. They are not aspects of a divine Substance which are parcelled out to the Persons or which the Persons merely manifest. Each of the three is uncreated in his own right, and it is in knowing them that we perceive this truth about them. The concept of creation has no place in the Godhead, an affirmation which counters both Arianism and Platonism, which thought of the Son and the Spirit as emanations from the One, who was identified with the Father.

All three are equally beyond our control, which is perhaps the best way to interpret *incomprehensible*. It does not simply mean that they are beyond our understanding, nor does it mean that we cannot know them or see the logic of their operations. This verse has frequently been ridiculed along these lines by liberal theologians trying to prove that the creed is nonsensical, but such an attitude reveals no more than arid intellectualism typical of post-Enlightenment thought. *Incomprehensible* means that the Persons cannot be grasped or pinned down. They cannot be contained or limited by human beings, either mentally or in religious observances. God in the splendour of his majesty remains free, and it is in his freedom that he has chosen to enter into a relationship with men.

The three Persons are also *eternal*, a concept which is implicit in their being *uncreated*, but which adds a further dimension. Who they are and what they do have a permanence about them which no other being can match. Unlike angels, or men who have received the gift of eternal life, their permanence is a fixed part of their unchanging nature. It is a guarantee that our salvation can never wear off or cease to operate. God's will does not shift according to circumstances, but works out his plan in the context of his eternal being.

The section concludes with a reminder that these attributes are not shared by the three in the way that human beings might share characteristics with each other. God is one, and in discerning his attributes we discern the unity which the three Persons manifest to perfection.

From the attributes to God we move on to the titles by which he is known, and once more we discover that they are common to all three Persons:

> So likewise the Father is Almighty, the Son Almighty, and the Holy Ghost Almighty.
> And yet they are not three Almighties but one Almighty.
> So the Father is God, the Son is God, and the Holy Ghost is God.
> And yet they are not three Gods but one God.
> So likewise the Father is Lord, the Son Lord and the Holy Ghost Lord.
> And yet not three Lords but one Lord.

The three names of God are paraded in review for our assent. We have already discussed the term *Almighty* in the other creeds, and seen how its application to the Father as *Pantocrator*, Ruler of All, had to be reinterpreted in the light of subsequent Christological controversies. Here the underlying force of *Pantocrator* is retained in that *Almighty* appears as a title, not as an attribute, but the imbalance of the earlier creeds is corrected so that there will be no misunderstanding.

God and *Lord* are familiar terms and need no explanation, except to say that they reflect the double aspect of the Trinity to which reference was made in an earlier section. The Trinity is God in his Glory and Lord in his Majesty, his Being and his Kingdom being united in the one object of our worship. This sounds perfectly obvious, but it contains an important point in that it affirms that what God *does* in his Kingdom will always be in perfect harmony with what God *is* in his Being. We need not fear that he will ever act in a way which is contrary to his nature, though we must be careful not to suggest that God is *bound* by this fact. To act in accordance with his nature is not a bondage but a complete liberation, since only God has the freedom to realize the full potential of his own Being.

The writer goes on to sum up:

> For like as we are compelled by the Christian verity to acknowl-
>   edge every Person by himself to be God and Lord;
> So we are forbidden by the Catholic religion to say, There be three
>   Gods or three Lords.

Here there is a parallel emphasis which highlights the role of the
two 'opposing' forces, which between them have created the balance
by which orthodoxy is affirmed and protected. The 'Christian verity'
is the revelation of God in Scripture, especially in the New Testament.
It is because of its witness that we are forced to abandon a simplistic
monotheism and confess a Trinity of Persons. This Trinity is not a
philosophical construction invented by clever men but a direct
unfolding of God, given and witnessed to by God himself.

At the same time, this revelation must be held in tension with
what is already known. The hermeneutical principle which must
govern our understanding of the Trinity is the 'Catholic religion' of
the covenant people of God. The Early Church saw no difficulty in
assuming to itself the place of Israel in God's plan, and before that
the uncomplicated faith of Adam and Eve in the garden. The
particularity of the gospel was matched by its universality, so that no
man could be excused if he rejected it. Protestants have sometimes
reacted against the phrase 'Catholic religion' because of the association
of this expression with Rome, but there is no mention here of a Pope
or an ecclesiastical hierarchy. It is not so much the Church as an
institution, but rather the religion as a way of life, which is the object
in view here. This is a covenant faith, whose norms and boundaries
serve to guard against false interpretations of the revelation.

We now proceed to a consideration of the Persons in their
individuality:

> The Father is made of none, neither created nor begotten.
> The Son is of the Father alone, not made, nor created, but begotten.
> The Holy Ghost is of the Father and of the Son, neither made, nor
>   created nor begotten, but proceeding.

Here the distinctions are set out in order, with an explanation of
what is not to be understood by them. None of the Persons may be
described as *made* or *created*. Originally there was little difference
between these terms, but here they are intended to mean two kinds of

origin which are not really the same. *Made* refers to an origin out of an existing substance, as one might say that a chair is made out of wood. It is wrong to say that any of the Persons is made out of a divine substance, a statement which has particular relevance to the Holy Spirit, who is not merely the personification of the spiritual nature of God. *Created*, on the other hand, refers to an origin from nothing (*ex nihilo*). This too is impossible, since there was never a time when the Creator did not exist.

The Father is not begotten, which means that there is no point of reference to which his Person must be related. Some theologians have assumed that the name 'Father' requires the co-existence of the 'Son' since otherwise there would be no meaning in the term, but the creed does not accept this. Without denying the co-eternity of the Son, it manages to affirm that there is an order, which in theology is called an *economy*, within the Godhead. At the same time the creed presents the matter as a statement of fact, not as a quality or an attribute of the Father's Person. Neither the creed nor the Bible speaks of *unbegottenness* as an attribute in the way that Gregory of Nazianzus was tempted to do and which later became a standard feature of Eastern theology.

The Son, in contrast to the Father, is *begotten*. This means that his Person must be related to the Father in order for us to understand him. It does not imply subordination of any kind, but merely expresses that relationship whereby the Son does his Father's will and inherits his Father's kingdom and promises. It also makes him peculiarly suited to be our mediator, because in being united to the Son we can enter by grace into the relationship with the Father which he possesses by nature. As the firstborn of many brethren (Romans 8:29) he makes it possible for us to know the Trinity in spirit and in truth. Furthermore, the Son is uniquely begotten and relates in this respect to the Father *alone*. We need have no fear that by participating in Christ we might be led into a relationship with some other being or deity.

The Holy Spirit is not begotten like the Son, but *proceeds*. Some have interpreted the present tense to mean that this action of proceeding is an eternal process which is never completed; but if there is any truth in this, it should not be interpreted in a way which would make the procession imperfect or compromise the reality of his Person. The term, as we have seen, comes from John 15:26 and invites two comments. First, it is definitely not the same as *begotten*. Theologians have always found it difficult to explain *how* the generation of the Son differs from the procession of the Spirit; but *that* it differs is clear from Scripture. The Holy Spirit is another Comforter without being another Saviour, and the work of Christ cannot simply be transferred to him. The procession testifies to his role as God's witness and agent in the world, making the work and the mutual love of the other two Persons real in the heart of the believer. It is in the Spirit that we share the Sonship of Christ, a principle which is fundamental to the New Testament (Galatians 4:6; Romans 8:16).

The other point made here is that the Spirit proceeds from the Father and *from the Son*, an addition which is not found in the original text of the Nicene Creed or in John 15:26. What are we to make of this? The doctrine of the double procession of the Holy Spirit can be traced back to Augustine, who regarded him as the expression of mutual love which bound the Father to the Son and vice versa. Furthermore, a careful reading of John 14:15-31 shows that Augustine was not making this up. In verse 17 Jesus says that the Spirit will dwell in the disciples, and then in the next verse says that he himself will do the same. In verse 23 he says that both he and the Father will come together, and then in verse 26 adds that the Holy Spirit will be sent by the Father *in the name* of the Son, an expression which implies that the Son also has authority in the matter of the Spirit's mission in time, and therefore also in the matter of the Spirit's procession in eternity.

The doctrine was current at Rome in the fifth century, and Pope Leo I, author of the famous *Tome*, regarded it as orthodox. In a letter to the Spanish bishop Turibius of Asturica (Astorga), dated 21 July 447, Leo included the double procession as part of the orthodox faith which he wanted to see affirmed at a council to be held in Toledo. We do not know whether this Second Council of Toledo (the First had been held in 400) ever took place, but the doctrine was certainly proclaimed at the Third Council of Toledo in 589, which may have had it inserted into the Nicene Creed. At any rate, the Creed with its expanded article, which is known as the *Filioque* clause from the Latin text of the addition, spread across Western Europe and was introduced into the Liturgy by Charlemagne. It was not formally adopted at Rome until 1014, but by then it had already figured in a schism between Rome and Constantinople which broke out in 867 and lasted for a few years.

The *Filioque* clause was never accepted in the East, and although it did not provoke the great schism of 1054, it helped to prevent a reunion of the churches in 1274 and again in 1439. Today it is a major difference between the Eastern and Western Churches. The ecumenical movement has put pressure on the West to drop the offending article from the creeds, on the ground that it was not in the original text of the Nicene Creed and was added uncanonically. It is too early to say what the outcome will be, but the presence of the *Filioque* clause (*'et Filio'*) in the Athanasian Creed is certainly authentic enough, and the doctrine can claim scriptural support. However great the desire may be for a reunion of the churches, this cannot take place at the expense of truth, or in ignorance of the fact that the presence (or absence) of this doctrine has produced very different theological traditions out of otherwise common material. The full story lies outside the scope of this book, but the *Filioque* clause can fairly be said to be a piece of unfinished business which the ancient Church has bequeathed to its medieval and modern successors.

In blissful ignorance of this tempestuous future, the author of the Athanasian Creed carries on:

So there is one Father, not three Fathers; one Son, not three Sons; one Holy Ghost, not three Holy Ghosts.
And in this Trinity none is afore, or after other; none is greater or less than another,
But the whole three Persons are co-eternal together and co-equal.
So that in all things, as is aforesaid, the Unity in the Trinity and the Trinity in the Unity is to be worshipped.
He therefore that will be saved must thus think of the Trinity.

The whole teaching of the preceding sections is summed up at the end, and we are taken back to the Trinity in Unity which we were called to worship at the beginning. It is a pity that the text succumbs to the attractions of parallelism to the point that it replaces the *one God* by the *Unity* in Trinity; but if this is a blemish, it is a minor one. In view of what has gone before, it cannot really be used as evidence to say that the God of this creed is no more than a philosopher's abstraction.

The Trinity having been discussed at great length, it is now time for the author to move on to Christology:

> Furthermore it is necessary to everlasting salvation that he also believe rightly the Incarnation of our Lord Jesus Christ.

This transitional verse seems at first sight to be unexceptional, and for many centuries its significance quite probably went unnoticed. Today, however, this is no longer possible, thanks to the work of Karl Barth (1886-1968). Barth almost singlehandedly rescued the doctrine of the Trinity from theological oblivion. He sought to give it meaning and relevance in a Church which had so emphasized the humanity of Christ as to have made Christianity over into a religion of good works performed in imitation of Jesus.

Barth saw the inadequacy of liberalism in this form, and insisted that Jesus was far more than a moral example for us to follow. He was nothing less than the Revelation of God, the one source of our knowledge of the divine. In Christ we meet God, and in Christ we discover the three modes of being in which God manifests himself. Barth did not like the term 'person', which to him sounded too much like a human image and was therefore idolatrous; and this dislike has naturally opened him to the standard charge of Sabellianism, which is constantly made against Western Trinitarianism. It is perhaps unfair to accuse Barth of this, but he comes very near to something else, which is Christomonism. This is the belief that God is revealed not only fully, but exclusively (and maybe exhaustively), in Christ.

In terms of theological method, Barth has started with Christology and related the Trinity to it. This is perfectly understandable in the light of nineteenth-century thought, but classical orthodoxy looks at the matter the other way round. In the Athanasian Creed, Christology is discussed *furthermore*, i.e. in addition to the exposition of the Trinity and in dependence on it. This difference may not seem to be very important, but it makes for quite a different understanding of God. In Scripture, as in the Creed, the Person and work of Christ are presented within a wider context. The Bible speaks of Jesus as the final, full and complete revelation of God's purpose for mankind, but it never says that Jesus is the *only* manifestation of God. In a peculiar way Barth has focused the unity of God in the revelation of Jesus Christ, and has fallen into the trap of 'confounding the Persons' by reducing them to mere modes of being.

Many of Barth's followers have gone even further, and have so overloaded the figure of Jesus Christ that his suffering and death on the cross have become, virtually without qualification, the suffering and death of *God*. The subtlety of the classical distinctions is completely gone, with the result that it has recently been possible to speak of the 'death of God' as if this were a theological necessity in the outworking of man's salvation!

The Athanasian Creed goes on to expand the mystery:

> For the right Faith is, that we believe and confess that our Lord
>   Jesus Christ, the Son of God, is God and Man;
> God, of the Substance of the Father, begotten before the worlds,
>   and Man, of the Substance of his Mother, born in the world;
> Perfect God, and perfect Man, of a reasonable soul and human
>   flesh subsisting;
> Equal to the Father, as touching his Godhead, and inferior to the
>   Father, as touching his Manhood.

The fine balance which is such a beautiful feature of this creed is now brought to a crescendo of perfection in the most difficult task of all. First, the objectivity of the Faith is stressed. It exists and is true, whatever our attitude toward it might be. But it goes beyond just being there. The right Faith is a call to commitment, urging us not merely to believe its truth but to confess and proclaim it to the world. There is no such thing as 'dead orthodoxy' in the eyes of the Athanasian Creed!

Now we meet the object of our confession, the Lord Jesus Christ, face to face. We must know him, says the Creed, before we attempt to understand him. Christianity is not a pastiche of different religious and philosophical ideas thrown together around the name of Jesus of Nazareth. What a fallacy it is to suppose that the gospel can be pieced together by logical argument! It can be studied and analysed of course, and the creed proceeds to do that, but only when Christ has been believed and confessed as Lord. It is here, at the point of conversion, that the stumbling-block for so many has come. It is not merely conservative Christians today who think that liberal theology would not exist if its practioners were truly converted people; the Athanasian Creed says as much in a single sentence.

The first element in a true confession of Christ must be the recognition of his place in the Godhead. He is the Son of God, not in some adoptionist sense but within the Trinity. It is the Second Person who has become man in Christ, and the full force of John 1:1-14, as well as the insistence of Alexandrian Christology, is brought out in this line. Yet the incarnation is not a change of state, or even of status. It is a union of two elements, God and Man (not the abstractions of Divinity and Humanity), which each retains its substance and its attributes without compromise on either side. Jesus is not a part-God or a part-Man, but perfect in each nature, and the concern of Antiochene Christology receives in turn its proper recognition.

In his divine nature, Jesus is God, sharing the Substance of his Father but not begotten of it – an important distinction. The Son is begotten of the Father's Person, not of his Nature, since that would imply that the nature of God was not simple but complex and in some way divided. *Before all worlds* means simply outside time, with the added assurance that the Son was fully existent at the moment of creation. In his human nature, the Son is born of a Virgin, from whom he acquires his manhood. Mary is not the mother of the divine Substance, but only of the human, though the child in her womb was truly the Son of God. It is interesting to note the absence of the word *Theotokos*, of which so much was being made in the East at the same period. This may be because Nestorianism was not perceived as a threat, but it may also simply be that *Theotokos* was a technical theological term for which there was no ready equivalent in Latin. It should be noted that *begotten* (*genitus*) is paired with *born* (*natus*) to bring out both the similarity and the difference between the heavenly generation and the earthly one; it is one of those neat distinctions which is easily missed, although it contains a point worth bearing in mind.

Perfect God can stand on its own, but because of Apollinarianism and Monophysitism, *perfect Man* cannot. The manhood of Christ must be explained as 'bipartite'. Man has a reasonable soul, in contrast to animals which have a soul (*anima* means 'soul' in Latin) but no reason. He also has human flesh, which in this context means flesh which is able to endure temptation, sin, suffering and death. Here we meet, for the first time in a confessional document, the word *subsisting*. This was to have a great future in medieval theology, where *subsistence* was used to describe the objective being of the Person as opposed to the objective being (*substance*) of the Nature. But it has a humbler purpose here. Soul and flesh could exist separately, as in the post-mortal state, but neither could be called a man on its own. On the other hand, Man was more than just a compound of two substances;

he had a reality in his own right. To put it another way, he *subsisted* as Man and did not merely exist as soul and flesh lumped together.

This Jesus, in his two natures, had an equality with God (Philippians 2:6) which he did not lose in the incarnation, yet at the same time he also had a humble dependence on the Father which was more than purely voluntary. This is important because the Manhood of Jesus was like that of any other man. In contrast to the Monophysites and even to the orthodox in the East, the Athanasian Creed rejects the notion of *theosis*, or deification, according to which the flesh of Christ was transformed by grace into the nature of God. At this level, Jesus retained the inferiority necessary to ensure that he was a real human being, and the quality of his Manhood remained the same until it was taken into the Godhead.

Having established the double nature of Christ, the author goes on to expound how it is that he is only one Person:

> Who, although he be God and Man, yet he is not two, but one Christ;
> One, not by conversion of the Godhead into flesh, but by taking of the Manhood into God;
> One altogether, not by confusion of Substance, but by unity of Person.
> For as the reasonable soul and flesh is one man, so God and Man is one Christ.

Once again we find a neat balance between Antioch and Alexandria. The notion that God and Man are joined in Christ would have sounded perfectly correct to Nestorius, but Nestorianism is excluded by the insistence that the union involved a taking of Manhood into God. Such a phrase would in turn have delighted the soul of any Monophysite, but the idea that the Manhood was somehow deified is excluded by the third statement which rules out a confusion of Substance and focuses on the Person as the subject of the unity. What we are left with is Chalcedonian orthodoxy of a kind which is not polemical but conciliatory. The truth of each position is acknowledged and welded together in a higher synthesis which offers us a model of ecumenical agreement without compromise.

The somewhat curious comparison between the soul and flesh of man on the one hand and the God and Man of the incarnation on the other needs to be thought about carefully if confusion is to be avoided. What the author is saying in effect, though not in words, is that the incarnate Christ also *subsists* as God and Man together, which means that one or the other, though they may conceivably exist in separation, are not by themselves Christ. His Person unites the two natures in the same way that our persons unite the two elements of our own nature in a functioning subsistence which has a reality and identity of its own.

What did this Christ come to do? The author of the Creed explains:

Who suffered for our salvation, descended into hell, rose again the third day from the dead.
He ascended into heaven, he sitteth on the right hand of the Father, God Almighty; from whence he shall come to judge the quick and the dead.

In the light of the elaborate discussion of the Trinity and the incarnation, the section on the work of Christ seems remarkably bare and unsophisticated. There is no direct mention of Christ's death, a feature which we noted in the Nicene Creed, and no mention of the atonement, beyond the vague expression *for our salvation*. How can we explain this? The answer seems to be that the atonement had not yet been fully worked out in relation to the rest of the system. No-one denied that Christ was the true Paschal Lamb, and we know from the Liturgies that the concept of sacrifice was well understood, so well in fact that the *finished* work of Christ on the cross was in danger of being obscured by notions of a repeated offering every time Communion was celebrated.

Such ideas were to become current during the Middle Ages, and they became major points of controversy at the Reformation. The Eastern Church did not participate in these later developments, which is one reason why it has never understood what the differences between Protestants and Roman Catholics really are. Within the Western Church, various theories of atonement have done the rounds, and none has ever received explicit formal recognition as the only permissible doctrine. Even denominations which *have* expounded a highly developed understanding of the atonement seldom make it a point of doctrine on which a disagreement with other Christians would constitute a bar to communion with them.

Nevertheless, there is one theory which has tended to prevail over the others, and which may properly be called the standard view of the orthodox, both Catholic and Protestant, in the West. This is the so-called *penal substitutionary theory* of the atonement, first elaborated by Anselm of Canterbury (d.1109) and touched up at the Reformation. Anselm held that Christ took our place on the cross, bearing our sins and propitiating by his sacrifice the wrath of God. Nowadays we are so familiar with this teaching that we do not see that it is closely bound up with the Athanasian Creed, which Anselm used as his basic definition of orthodoxy. For the sacrifice of Christ on the cross was not the death of a man to appease the anger of God, despite the fact that it is often caricatured in this way and condemned as immoral. What happened at Calvary was that the Son offered sacrifice as the divine High Priest whose human nature was the victim, presented without spot or blemish to the Father. The acceptance of the sacrifice and the vindication of Christ in the resurrection, like the voluntary obedience of the Son in the first place, can only be understood in the context of the love which the Father had for the Son and vice versa. The Spirit who implants that love in our hearts implants both justice and mercy, law and gospel, the vision of the Holy and the experience of forgiveness. The two belong together in the unity of the Trinity, without which nothing in our Faith makes any real sense.

The author of the Creed does not teach us this, but his work was to be the indispensable foundation stone on which it was later to be worked out. Meanwhile he has another interest to bring before us before concluding:

> At whose coming all men shall rise again with their bodies, and shall give account for their own works.
> And they that have done good shall go into life everlasting, and they that have done evil into everlasting fire.

The New Testament basis for such statements is not hard to find, since both Pauline and non-Pauline passages can be cited in support. The main source for this verse was probably 1 Corinthians 3:10-15, which speaks of the judgment awaiting even the righteous; but the anonymous author of the *Quicunque Vult* may have been thinking of Romans 2:5-11, 2 Corinthians 5:10, Matthew 16:27 and even Revelation 2:23. The difficulty comes in that there is no corresponding emphasis in the Creed on man's inability to save himself and his need to depend wholly on the grace of God. This lack has led some scholars to suggest other, extra-biblical sources of this teaching. An obvious one is Pelagius, whom Augustine opposed on the doctrines of grace, and whose views were championed to some extent in the monastic circles from which this creed emerged. Is it therefore Pelagian in its apparent emphasis on salvation by works?

Here we must take into account the fact that just as the author had no very developed theory of atonement, so he did not consider this question of works in the light of a doctrine of justification. The account to be given of the works is a statement of fact, not a plea for forgiveness. The rest of the Creed makes it perfectly plain that faith is the basis of salvation – that is the whole point of its composition. What these lines mean is that God expects a work of sanctification in our lives as the inevitable fruit of salvation. Our works manifest what we are; and when God discloses them, it will become apparent where we have put our trust. Then judgment will be pronounced, and the great separation between good and evil will be consummated for ever.

We who look at these lines from hindsight have reason to regret their ambiguity, but we should not blame the author, for whom the issues brought into focus by the Reformation were less than clear. The Reformers did not reject the Athanasian Creed, whose teaching they fully accepted, but they were careful to add a corresponding emphasis on justification by faith, in the various doctrinal articles and confessions which they composed. Perhaps the greatest pity is that by the sixteenth century it was no longer possible to amend or add to the traditional creeds in a way which would make such points perfectly plain. If this is so, there has been a loss on both sides which the whole Church in its wisdom might do well to put right for the future.

Meanwhile we can do no more than finish off what lies before us:

This is the Catholic Faith, which except a man believe faithfully, he cannot be saved.
Glory be to the Father, and to the Son, and to the Holy Ghost;
As it was in the beginning, is now, and ever shall be, world with out end. Amen.

At the end we return to the beginning, though now it is with the explicit acknowledgement that the Faith must be held *faithfully*. In other words, the spirit of right believing must be one with the Spirit of right belief. How sadly true it is that a man can hold the Faith whole and undefiled, yet do so in a way which betrays its inner spirit and power. The author of the Athanasian Creed did not advocate a bigoted defence of orthodoxy which automatically excommunicated all who disagreed with him. The Faith was not his, it was *Catholic*, revealed as universal and obligatory for all men, regardless of their own opinions. At the same time it was also his, if he received it and held it in the spirit of faithfulness which is the hallmark of any true Christian. Properly balanced Christianity – this is the essence of the orthodoxy of the Athanasian Creed, and the substance of its appeal to Christians today.

The doxology at the end is easy to pass over without comment, but is not an optional extra. Confession of the Faith is an act of worship, the rehearsal of what we believe in an attitude of praise and thanksgiving to God. It is easy to think that the creeds are technical and dull, and many congregations would much prefer to sing a chorus or listen to someone give a personal testimony than to recite a statement of belief. The Athanasian Creed has certainly gone out of fashion for reasons of this kind, and the other creeds survive to the extent they do mainly because, like modern sermons, they are short.

The consequences, however, are devastating. Ordinary people no longer know precisely what they believe. They have no yardstick to test what they hear, unless they know the Bible inside out. As a result we live in a day when heresy flourishes in high places, yet few people are sufficiently concerned either to call the offenders to account or to provide a reasoned alternative. The gospel of Christ is mocked in the Church, because we have lost our taste for doctrine and our knowledge of what it is we believe.

Conclusion

The Athanasian Creed represents the high point which ancient theology reached in its search for systematization. Later on there were to be more ambitious endeavours, as in the work of John of Damascus, but by then we are already on the threshold of the Middle Ages. That is another tale, but we must not leave the ancient world, without considering the wider context in which the problem of theological confession was situated.

There are many writers whose works could be cited in this regard, but perhaps none is more peculiarly suitable than Maximus the Confessor (c. 580-662). Maximus was a son of the aristocracy of Constantinople and spent his youth in the public service. He lived through the crisis caused by the rise of Islam, and participated actively in the theological debates of his time, suffering persecution for his opposition to Monotheletism. He was also 'catholic' in the best tradition of ancient society, at a time when it was crumbling or had disappeared. He knew Rome at first hand, and was even aware of a difference over the *Filioque*, though he did not understand it fully or regard it as divisive. At the other end of the scale he was an avid reader of the pseudo-Dionysius, and did much to give his works the honoured place which they were to occupy in medieval theology.

Maximus is not especially well known, nor was he very original – a common failing of his age. Yet he pieces together for us ideas which floated about in different guises throughout antiquity, and which in his works find a logical synthesis every bit as important for our understanding as the one we have examined in the Athanasian Creed.

In his search for an integrated vision of his world, Maximus sensed that the cosmic order rested on three basic laws. Others had said the same before in their different ways, and perhaps they had put something more accurately or more profoundly than anything he was capable of. But if so, his forerunners had hit upon things in passing, as a sideline in the pursuit of some doctrinal point or other. With all or most of that behind him, Maximus was free to examine the structure itself. This is what he found.

The first order of reality was the *law of nature*. This law was as old as mankind, planted in the heart of Adam and remaining there still, in spite of all the vicissitudes of human history and human sin. St Paul had referred to it, as when he wrote that the conscience was the accuser of the heathen, or said that a man would have his hair short and a woman have hers long. The philosophers had understood it, and their speculations were attempts to solve what lay behind the order of things. Of course, they had got it wrong, but they were not to blame for their ignorance. Some indeed had come so close to the truth that it was almost possible to think of them as Christians before Christ.

Moreover, the law of nature was not an accident, or second best. It was fundamental to any spiritual understanding. If there were no order in the universe, how would one speak of God? What appeal could be made to moral principles, if these were totally unknown to the pagan world? In so many fields of science, the Christian had no source of information other than the one provided by the collective intellect of antiquity. God did not want his children to abandon all this, but rather to use it as the basis of a right worship, in a cosmic liturgy which would glorify him in every aspect of creation. The pagan world was to be redeemed in and for Christ, so that his Kingdom should extend over all things, a Kingdom in which every knee would bow and every tongue confess that he alone was Lord.

The second level of reality which Maximus saw was the *law of Scripture*. The law given to Adam was a wonderful thing, but it did not bring a man salvation. For all their greatness, the Greeks had to turn in the end to the Jews to find the one thing needful. Scripture did not contradict nature, but built on it. The gospel could not be arrived at by guesswork; only God, in the latter days, had revealed himself in his Son.

This was the miracle beside which all else paled into insignificance. Even the transfiguration, resurrection and ascension of Christ himself were only the planned outworking of the incarnation. What amazed Maximus is that God should have come into the world at all, to save men from their sins. No pearl of great price could match this treasure, no wisdom could equal the glory which God had bestowed on the human race when he entered it himself. All the humanism of Greece had nothing to compare with this, and Christ Pantocrator, reigning down from the dome of a thousand churches, reminded the believer of the glorious destiny which awaited mankind at his side.

But the third level of reality is the most interesting and in some ways most important of all. This was the *law of grace*, the free favour of God bestowed on his elect. Nature was given to all, Scripture was open and available to all. But grace was given to the few, in the secret place of the heart where no man could see. By the law of grace the Scriptures lived, and by it nature could be seen for what it really was. It was not to be worshipped as the pagans did, but used to further the heavenly worship and the spread of the Kingdom of God.

In different ways at different times, scholars and theologians would take up these themes again, and work them out in detail. Should a Christian pursue a career in the world? Did science contradict the gospel? Was it enough to read the Bible in order to be saved? How could a man receive the grace of God?

These questions have come and gone across the span of Christian history, provoking dissension, causing new patterns of life and worship to be formed. Yet at the heart of the matter the issues are still the same, and Christ is still the answer. Like Maximus, we who follow after cannot retrace our steps and write again the history of God's plan. We can only take it, cherish it, seek to understand it and finally offer it up to him who is our life, at one in praise with the heavenly throng assembled around the throne of God.

8

Envoi

When did the formative period of orthodox Christian doctrine come to an end? School history texts love to simplify things by fixing dates to mark off cultural epochs, while professional historians delight in poking fun at them. Everybody knows that Rome fell in 476, that William the Conqueror landed in 1066 and that Columbus discovered America in 1492. These events stand out as historical landmarks, but did they really change anything? Nobody who watched the imperial insignia being shipped off to Constantinople in 476 was conscious that the Western Empire had 'fallen'; on the contrary, as far as most people were concerned, the unity of Christendom under one emperor was being formally restored. An English peasant would not have taken much notice of the Battle of Hastings, which hardly affected his everyday existence, and Columbus's discovery was widely regarded at the time as an expensive failure by merchants and adventurers who were trying to get to India.

Historical periods take shape more slowly and imperceptibly than most people realize and they dissolve in much the same way. The attitudes and achievements which characterize a particular age or civilization are largely creations of subsequent generations, who reflect on their past in a particular way; only rarely do we find that there were contemporaries who shared a similar understanding of the world they were living in. Christianity came to maturity in the final phase of Roman power, and when the Empire broke up, the Church was the only social institution able to step into the vacuum. The famous eighteenth-century historian Edward Gibbon regarded 'barbarism and religion' as the twin causes of Rome's decline and fall, but no responsible historian today would accept such a naive idea. Rome was rotten at the core long before Christianity could challenge its rule, and the Church did more to rescue ancient civilization than to destroy it.

In fact Christians bewailed the barbarian invasions as much as the pagans, and were equally reluctant to fraternize with their new rulers, most of whom were Arians. The process of conversion was a slow one, but it was undertaken, and in the end the Church captured those who had come to loot and destroy it. Nowhere was Latin spoken more purely than in Anglo-Saxon England, and no people showed a greater missionary zeal for the Faith than those one-time heathen marauders, whose devotion to Rome and its Church became a byword for piety in the Middle Ages.

The passing of an age cannot be discerned in events like these, but must be sought out at a deeper level. The famous Belgian historian, Henri Pirenne, sensed as much when he wrote that the Mediterranean civilization of Greece and Rome, fortified and reinvigorated by Christianity, did not come to an end until the Arab invasions. It was when Syria, Egypt, North Africa and Spain fell to Islam that the ancient world was torn apart and its culture destroyed. Rome and Constantinople continued much as before, but Antioch, Alexandria and Carthage sank into an oblivion from which they have never recovered.

After the eighth century, Christianity moved northwards, leaving its southern frontier more or less where the Arabs had fixed it. The Muslim Turks would later take Asia Minor, and Christians would regain the Iberian Peninsula, but these minor changes merely confirmed that the Church's destiny was to be linked with the rise of Europe as a cultural entity. The seat of gravity moved away from the Mediterranean to the northern plains, where cities like Paris and Kiev eventually replaced Antioch and Alexandria as the intellectual centres of the Faith.

In the West, cultural and religious pre-eminence passed to the French, so much so that for both Greeks and Arabs 'Frank' was a standard synonym for 'Latin' or 'Westerner'. Their debased form of Latin became the *lingua franca* of the East at the time of the Crusades, and even today a Greek who is converted to the Roman Church may be accused of having become a 'Frank'. At a more serious level, the intellectual revival spearheaded by Charlemagne eventually made possible the rise of the great cathedral schools at Laon, Orléans, Chartres and above all Paris. The Middle Ages was the age of France *par excellence*, and it was there that the achievements of medieval civilization reached their peak. The Sorbonne became the university of Europe, the chief citadel of theological orthodoxy. Gothic architecture, later to be exported by English missionaries to India and the Far East as the 'typically Christian' art form, was born at St Denis. The finest stained-glass in the world still graces Chartres Cathedral, despite the vicissitudes of time. French hegemony was not seriously challenged until the sixteenth century, when it faced a two-pronged attack – from the Italian Renaissance and from the German Reformation.

France met the challenge by producing its greatest theologian, John Calvin, who blended the warm passion of a Luther with the cool logic of a Macchiavelli to produce the seed of a new civilization, which is the third age of Christianity in the West. Rejected by his own nation, Calvin and his theology went to the Dutch and the English-speaking peoples, whose society and world influence still rest on ideas first propounded in the Genevan theocracy.

In Russia, a very different form of Christianity took root. The theology of the Russian church was mystical, and found its greatest outlet in the spiritual experiences of the 'old men' (*startsi*), whose influence over the lives of the people was hypnotic long before Rasputin made it notorious. Apocalyptic visions and mad dreams of utopia have dominated the Russian tradition, in a way which seems strange to the more rational faith of the West. Peter the Great was attracted to a secularized form of Western rationalization and introduced it into Russia, where it was eventually triumphant in the October Revolution of 1917. But Soviet communism, for all its atheistic and secular ways, looked much more like the visionary Orthodoxy of Holy Russia than like the ideas of a German professor whose world was the Reading Room of the British Museum. In spite of all the persecution, Stalin's daughter became a professing Christian, as did many of the most prominent Russian intellectuals, and the Church received a good deal of discreet patronage from the regime. Reconciliation between church and state was finally achieved in 1988, since when Marx has withered away while the Christian Church has gone from strength to strength in the new and post-Communist Russia.

The shift from a Mediterranean to a European base was accompanied by a change of attitude towards the theological tradition. Until the eighth century most theologians thought of themselves mainly as exponents and defenders of the orthodoxy defined by the great ecumenical councils. They saw themselves as partisans of men like Athanasius, Augustine or Cyril of Alexandria, contending for the same beliefs as they had done and engaging the same enemy. As a result, their conservatism was always more than merely deference to ancient tradition. As long as the ancient heresies were alive, they needed a living orthodoxy to combat them.

It was only when they were finally vanquished, or lost to Islam, that orthodoxy settled into a series of formulae held intact by the brittle strength of *rigor mortis*. By the time of Charlemagne, leading theologians were doing little more than appealing to the authority of past masters, quoting from them rather than thinking for themselves. This was not simply blind deference to the past, or intellectual laziness; these men were convinced that God had spoken in times past to the Fathers of the Church, and that it was their duty to repeat what God had said for the benefit of future generations.

Of course, life never stands still, and the Middle Ages gave birth to a theological development which went far beyond the achievement of antiquity. What distinguished it from the earlier period was the conscious awareness that a certain framework had been put in place and had received the sanction of the universal Church. It was no longer possible to dispute the nature of God, or the one person and two natures of Christ. Instead, debate raged on issues which the ancients had not fully worked out. Predestination, for example, was a favourite theme of the Carolingian divines in the ninth century, and it was through them that the doctrine reached Luther and the other Reformers.

The Carolingians also developed theories of transubstantiation and of papal supremacy in the Church – much to the embarrassment of Rome! It was only in the eleventh century that the papacy began to adopt these ideas and it never succeeded in imposing them on the universal Church. Both doctrines were attacked in different quarters throughout the Middle Ages, and it was not until the Council of Trent (1545-63) that Rome was able to enforce conformity to its will – after having lost nearly half its flock. Sixteenth-century Reformers claimed, with considerable justice, that it was they who were the true upholders of the Catholic Church, and it is encouraging to note that in our own time Roman Catholic scholars, liberated at last from the bondage of Trent, are taking a new and sympathetic look at the first Protestants. It may even be that if the Reformed churches continue their slide into liberalism and theological indifference, twenty-first century Roman Catholicism may become the true heir and repository of the teaching of Luther and Calvin!

The medieval controversy about transubstantiation is apt to obscure a more important development, which was the elaboration of the theory of atonement known as penal substitution. What Christ did on the cross had always lain at the heart of Christianity, but it had never been explained in a very precise manner. In ancient times, the main idea was one of liberation – by his death and resurrection Christ took man from darkness into light, from death into life, and from evil into righteousness. This idea is once more widely current in our own time, and is certainly not false; but it has certain defects which the profound theological inquiry of the Middle Ages brought to light.

In an understanding of atonement which emphasizes liberation or victory, there is a tendency to regard the sacrifice of Christ as a means to an end, not an end in itself. When this happens, it becomes difficult to explain why God chose the way of the cross to effect the salvation of mankind. There must have been an easier, less cruel way for him to have opened the gates of death and given us eternal life!

The doctrine of penal substitution is concerned above all to explain the purpose of Christ's suffering. He died because he became sin for us, and sin demanded the full punishment of God's law. Many people have claimed that this is immoral, but it is hard to see why. Christ did not deserve to suffer, but he voluntarily assumed our sins and suffered in our place. It is we who have deserved it, and those who find the substitution idea immoral have probably not yet considered the weight of their own sin. *Nondum considerasti quantum sit pondus peccati* – Anselm's famous rebuke to his pupil Boso rings true to experience today as much as it did then.

It is to Anselm that we owe further elaboration of this doctrine because it was he more than anyone who understood its relevance to the Trinity. When the Son performed his great work on the cross, who was the main object of his labours? Origen had thought it was the devil, to whom the ransom for the souls of men must be paid. The liturgy ascribed to Hippolytus suggests that we men are the main object of his attention: 'He opened wide his arms for us on the cross', as the *Alternative Service Book 1980* renders it (Third Eucharistic Prayer). But here Anselm had a deeper understanding of the ways of God than his predecessors in the Faith. He knew that on the cross, the Son was offering himself primarily *to the Father*, as the satisfaction which his justice demanded for sin. Christ's work of atonement thus goes to the very heart of God, linking his righteousness and his faithfulness in the bond of love which is the Holy Spirit.

Luther took Anselm's teaching one step further by concentrating on the penal aspect of Christ's substitution. He understood that Christ, in paying the price of sin, set us free to live a new life unhampered by the guilt and bondage of the past. He thus combined something of the liberation theory with Anselm's teaching about satisfaction to produce a more complete doctrine. Finally, it was Calvin, the 'theologian of the Holy Spirit', who understood that true Christian experience could only be the experience of the liberating power of the atoning work of Christ. Others had known this before, of course, but Calvin's theology made it an inescapable necessity. The Holy Spirit of the Father and the Son brought to the heart of the believer *both* conviction of sin before the holiness of God *and* assurance of redemption by the shed blood of Christ. The Trinitarian pattern of Christian experience has found no higher expression than this.

Can we, then, say that with the Reformers we have reached the final stage of Christianity before our Lord's return? There are many who believe we have, and the continuing vitality of Evangelical Protestantism adds considerable weight to this feeling. It is easy to look at the world around us, imagine that Christianity is everywhere on the defensive, and conclude that the end is nigh. Yet here, as elsewhere, caution is required. The Christian Church has faced crises before, most obviously in the seventh and eighth centuries, when the combined forces of Islam and barbarism threatened to destroy it. The world religion which had known its hour of triumph at Constantinople in 381 was cowering behind the walls of that same city only three centuries later, which is roughly the same span of time which separates us from the last creative period of Protestant orthodoxy. We may stand at the end of time; on the other hand, we may be on the threshold of further triumphs of the cross.

What has gone wrong in the Church? In the Dark Ages, Christians faced enemies from without; today the chief danger comes from within. Our churches and theological faculties are dominated by men who in earlier times would have been excommunicated for heresy. Our society has lost the effective application of Christian standards, even while retaining some semblance of public religiosity. The recent revival of Judaism (in Israel) and of Islam as powerful socio-political forces does not seem to have affected the Christian Church, whose leaders prefer to acquiesce in the modern way of things rather than challenge it. Christian experience, though quite widespread at the popular level, is uninformed and uncontrolled by theology, which in many eyes is a suspect discipline.

There can be no doubt that the main reason for a sense of discouragement and failure among modern Christians is the apparent inability of orthodox theologians to address our age in a way which is both incisive and compelling. Orthodoxy has been so defensive and so sterile for such a long time now that many lively Christians regard it as an irrelevance or even as a hindrance to effective evangelism. Dogmatism is a term of abuse even among conservative Evangelicals, which is understandable when so many allow their convictions about peripheral issues like church government or political involvement to dominate their thinking and break their fellowship. The central themes of the gospel are subtly pushed aside as 'matters on which we are agreed' and they are neither expounded nor discussed in the light of contemporary thinking.

Nowhere is this failure more apparent, or more catastrophic, than in the field of pastoral theology. The modern world is inundated with theories of group dynamics and techniques of psychoanalysis. Central to these is the idea of the *person* which has recently become a major concept in secular thought. Yet almost no-one, Christians included, has penetrated the meaning of this term to discover its theological roots. How odd to be told, even by Christian theologians, that the language and concepts of classical orthodoxy are no longer meaningful to 'modern man', when the biggest word of them all is constantly being bandied about by a whole army of social analysts!

Modern sociology and psychology are in desperate need of a sharp and sustained critique from the standpoint of Christian orthodoxy. The hollowness of contemporary secular thinking in these areas has been demonstrated by Paul Vitz in his important book, *Psychology as Religion*. Himself a converted psychologist, Vitz demonstrates how a secularized, non-dogmatic Christianity has produced theories of self-awareness which concentrate on a selfish desire for 'fulfilment' and in the end destroy those who sell themselves to them. Vitz does not examine the theological significance of the word *person*, but this lack has been supplied by Jean Galot, whose writings have been introduced to the English-speaking world by Eric Mascall. Galot maintains that classical orthodoxy, with its clear distinction between *person* and *nature*, needs to be reactivated in order to provide a Christian answer to modern secularism. We agree.

Today we need to reassert that *personhood* does not mean individuality but a *capacity for relationship*. Dogs and cats are individuals, but they are not persons, and no person can find his or her fulfilment in isolation or selfishness. The members of the Trinity show us what being a person means – the Father gives himself by offering his Son in love for the world, the Son gives himself by being sacrificed in love to the Father for the world, and the Holy Spirit gives himself by presenting the Father and the Son to us in love. Self-sacrifice is the only way to perfect self-fulfilment and happiness in the peace of God.

The Trinity teaches us, moreover, that our existence as persons is dependent on the inner being of God. It is because we are created in his image and likeness that we have a capacity for relationship, which means that our primary relationship must always be with him. In the Trinity we see the sacred tie of kinship (Father and Son) perfectly balanced by the equally sacred but non-familial tie between the first two Persons and the Holy Spirit. The ancients knew that a love relationship between two was imperfect; it required a third to give it balance and fulfilment. Love between two would be self-devouring and destructive, but the third Person, dwelling in complete equality with the other two, provides the balance needed for a complete expression of the essence of God.

The Trinity provides the context for the redemption of mankind, because, in the Person of the Son, God has united manhood to himself. This is not universalism, not because there is no compulsion in love – there is – but because the compulsion of love speaks to persons, not to categories. It is not mankind as a species which is saved, but Tom, Dick and Harry, Emma, Jane and Elizabeth. God calls us by our name; we are his in a personal relationship which can triumph even over death and hell.

In the Person of Jesus Christ, God has taught us what it means to be human. Perhaps the greatest theological question facing us today concerns the consciousness of Christ, his self-awareness as a man. How can we find room for a human psychology in Jesus, the Son of God? The answer of orthodoxy is plain: Jesus is the single, divine subject of two consciousnesses, one human and one divine. When he fell unconscious on the cross he did not cease to be the Son of God, consciously making atonement for us. His self-awareness was not the mark of his personhood, but an attribute of his nature, something which he could lose without ceasing to be himself.

Today we are assailed by a concept of 'personality' which is false precisely because it is rooted in human nature, not in human personhood. 'Personality' means the sum and mixture of attributes which make up our individuality, but these can be changed beyond recognition without affecting the *person*. *Persons* are men and women as they have been created in the sight and in the image of God. We are distinguished by our names, not by our natures, and it is significant that we know God, too, by his name, and not by his nature.

The world we live in is at war, locked in a spiritual battle between the Spirit of God and his spiritual adversaries of many shapes and sizes. Christians who know the mind of the Spirit have a weapon to use in this warfare – the great armoury of Christian orthodoxy, with which the Holy Spirit himself has equipped the Church of Jesus Christ. Some of this armour may be rusty; much of it has seldom been used. But Christians have the assurance of Christ that nothing in his revelation is irrelevant or out-of-date. May God grant that by his Spirit those whom he has called may rise to do battle against the gods of an unbelieving age, and claim the victory which is ours through our Lord Jesus Christ.

Appendix A:

Modern translations of the creeds

The translations of the great creeds which appear in the text of this book are those of the Book of Common Prayer and reflect the religious English which until recently was common to all the churches of the English-speaking world. In recent years attempts have been made to recast the texts in a modern idiom, more readily understood by worshippers today.

The first impetus for this came from the Roman Catholic Church, which authorized services in the vernacular from 29 November 1964. Various English language liturgies were produced, which caused confusion as some of the differences were quite considerable. In order to harmonize usage, the Vatican set up an International Committee on English in the Liturgy (ICEL) which produced its first work in 1967. The success of ICEL led to the formation of an interdenominational body known as the International Consultation on English Texts (ICET) in 1969. ICET enlarged the work of ICEL, and submitted draft proposals for modern translations of well-known prayers and the two main creeds in 1971. These proposals were subsequently modified in 1975, and the revised forms are slowly winning acceptance in the churches. In the Church of England's *Alternative Service Book 1980*, the ICET text of the Apostles' Creed appears unaltered, and the Nicene Creed is reproduced with only one minor change.

The ICET texts are set out below, with the main changes from the classical versions printed in italics:

The Apostles' Creed

> I believe in God, the Father Almighty,
> *creator* of heaven and earth.

I *believe* in Jesus Christ, his only Son, our Lord.
  He was conceived by *the power* of the Holy *Spirit*
  and born of the Virgin Mary.
  He suffered under Pontius Pilate,
  was crucified, died, and was buried.
  He descended *to the dead*.
  On the third day he rose again.
  He ascended into heaven,
  and is seated at the right hand of the Father.
  He will come again to judge the *living* and the dead.

I believe in the Holy *Spirit*,
  the holy catholic Church,
  the communion of saints,
  the forgiveness of sins,
  the resurrection of the body,
  and the life everlasting. Amen.

This is a very conservative translation, with only a few changes from the earlier text. Obvious archaisms like *Ghost* and *quick* have been removed, and the second article has been given greater prominence by the addition of *I believe* instead of simply *and*. This change is not supported by the ancient credal tradition, but appears to be a variant form which was used in France from about the early eighth century. In the first article, *creator* replaces *maker* in order to give a more accurate rendering of the Latin.

There are only two points of doctrinal significance which need to be mentioned. The first is the statement that Jesus was conceived by the *power of* the Holy Spirit. This is intended to clarify the Spirit's role in the virginal conception of Christ, but it is not very successful. *Power* could suggest a rather more distant involvement on the Spirit's part, almost as if Jesus had been conceived by a divine operation working under remote control. This is not intended, but the addition of these unnecessary words must be regretted.

A rather different problem is posed by the words *he descended to the dead*. The Latin original reads *descendit ad inferna, he descended to the lower* (world), and says in the next line that he rose *from the dead* on the third day. The translators obviously wanted to get away from the crude conception some people have of *hell*, but it is doubtful whether their version is an improvement. The Latin word *inferna*

undoubtedly had a pejorative connotation of the sort which attaches
to the English word *infernal*. The note of humiliation and sorrow is
completely lacking in the modern text, an unfortunate development
which is true neither to the original nor to the teaching of the New
Testament.

The Nicene Creed

We *believe* in one God
    the Father, *the Almighty*,
    maker of heaven and earth,
    of *all that is*, seen and unseen.

We *believe* in one Lord, Jesus Christ,
    the *only* Son of God,
    eternally begotten of the Father,
    God from God, Light from Light,
    true God from true God,
    begotten, not made,
    of one Being with the Father.
    Through him all things were made.
    For us men and for our salvation
    he came down from heaven;
    by the power of the Holy Spirit
    he became incarnate from (ASB 1980:of) the Virgin Mary,
    and was made man.
    For our sake he was crucified under Pontius Pilate;
    he suffered *death* and was buried.
    On the third day he rose again
    in accordance with the Scriptures;
    He ascended into heaven
    and *is seated* at the right hand of the Father.
    He will come again in glory to judge the living and the dead,
    and his kingdom will have no end.

We believe in the Holy Spirit,
    the Lord, the giver of life,
    who proceeds from the Father (*and the Son*).
    With the Father and the Son he is worshipped and glorified.
    He has spoken through the Prophets.

We believe in one holy, catholic and apostolic Church.
We acknowledge one baptism for the forgiveness of sins.
We look for the resurrection of the dead,
and the life of the world to come. Amen.

Once again there are few changes of any real importance. The plural form has been restored throughout, which is a return to the original Greek text, and the *Filioque* clause has been put in brackets, to indicate that it was a later insertion. Moves have been made to drop it altogether, but it appears as part of the text, without brackets, in the *Alternative Service Book 1980* and elsewhere. At the beginning of the second article, *only-begotten* has been shortened to *only*, apparently to avoid repetition of the word *begotten*. This is unfortunate because it obscures the theological point which *only-begotten* (Greek: *monogenes*) is meant to secure. The term was introduced in opposition to the adoptionism of Paul of Samosata, who held that Jesus was the only Son of God, but that he was a man whom God had adopted to be his Son.

In the next line, *eternally begotten* is a phrase which recalls Origen, though care must be taken not to interpret it in the sense of an eternal process of begetting. This possibility is mentioned by ICET and justified by a reference to Athanasius, but it will not do. The Son of God is perfectly begotten in eternity, not forever emerging from the Father.

In the first article, *the Almighty* is marked off to indicate that it is a noun, not an adjective. This is true, but it is not very helpful, as we have seen, to regard it as a translation of *Pantocrator*. The creed is slightly defective at this point, and care must be taken not to suggest that the Father is somehow superior to the other two Persons of the Trinity. The same objection applies to the awkward phrase *all that is*. It would have been better to have said *everything*, because the word *is*, in this context, refers to *being*. The Son *is*, and the Holy Spirit *is*, but neither is a creature of the Father!

Likewise, care must be taken in translating the famous word *homoousios* in the second article. *Of one Being* is etymologically correct, but it obscures the theological argument. Here it is customary to use the word *substance* instead of *being*, because although the word 'substance' now has unfortunate materialistic overtones, it avoids the suggestion that the Persons are any less real than the Nature of God.

This may seem like a small point, but the history of debate shows how important it is to maintain the objective being of the Persons, if we are not to fall into the modalism which is supposed to characterize Western Trinitarianism!

The greatest change occurs in the description of the Virgin Birth. Here the fear expressed above, that the *power* of the Holy Spirit might lend itself to misinterpretation, is apparently realized. In the original text, the Spirit's parental function is clearly parallel to that of Mary, but here it is possible to maintain that Mary alone is the parent, whom God by the power of his Spirit enabled to bear a Son by parthenogenesis. The result would be no more than a miraculous or unusual *human* conception, which does not do justice to the Christian doctrine of the incarnation.

The other changes occur in the paragraph on the crucifixion, resurrection and ascension. They have less serious implications, but deserve some comment. *Death* is added on the ground that it is implied in the Greek, though not explicitly stated. This is probably true, though it would have been better to have put *died*, as in the Apostles' Creed, and the earlier revision of 1971. Death was not the only thing Christ suffered; he suffered and then he died. His death was a welcome release from suffering, a point which is missed completely in this translation.

In accordance with the Scriptures is a valiant attempt to render the Greek preposition *kata*, though there is a danger that the note of prophetic fulfilment may be obscured. The creed states that the Scriptures *foretold* the events of Christ's passion, not merely that they relate them as having already happened. A minor point concerns the heavenly session of Christ, who *sits* in an active sense and is not *seated* (in a passive sense) at the right hand of the Father. It is important to insist that his mediatorial work on our behalf, as well as his rule of the world, are continuing, not finished, like his work of atonement on the cross. The point is a subtle one, but it should not be obscured.

The Athanasian Creed has not been translated by ICET, nor does it appear in the *Alternative Service Book 1980*, probably because it is little used nowadays. A modern translation has however been made by Roger Beckwith, and is printed in his booklet, *Confessing the Faith in the Church of England Today*, Latimer Studies 9 (Oxford, 1981), pp. 32-33. It is reprinted here with permission:

The Athanasian Creed

Whosoever wishes to be saved
before all things it is necessary that he hold the catholic faith,
which faith, if anyone does not keep it whole and *unharmed*,
without doubt he will perish everlastingly.
Now, the catholic faith is this,
that we worship one God in Trinity, and Trinity in Unity,
neither confusing the Persons
nor dividing *the divine Being*.
For there is one Person of the Father, another of the Son,
and another of the Holy Spirit,
but the Godhead of the Father, the Son and the Holy Spirit is all
    one,
their glory equal, their majesty co-eternal.
Such as the Father is, such is the Son
and such is the Holy Spirit:
the Father uncreated, the Son uncreated
and the Holy Spirit uncreated,
the Father infinite, the Son infinite
and the Holy Spirit infinite,
the Father eternal, the Son eternal
and the Holy Spirit eternal;
and yet they are not three Eternals
but one Eternal,
just as they are not three Uncreateds, nor three Infinites,
but one Uncreated and one Infinite.
In the same way, the Father is almighty, the Son is almighty
and the Holy Spirit almighty,
and yet they are not three Almighties
but one Almighty.
Thus, the Father is God, the Son is God
and the Holy Spirit is God,
and yet there are not three Gods
but one God.
Thus, the Father is the Lord, the Son is the Lord
and the Holy Spirit is the Lord,
and yet not three Lords
but one Lord.

Because, just as we are compelled by Christian truth
to confess each Person singly to be both God and Lord,
so we are forbidden by the catholic religion
to say, There are three Gods, or three Lords.
The Father is from none,
not made nor created nor begotten;
the Son is from the Father alone,
not made nor created, but begotten;
the Holy Spirit is from the Father and the Son,
not made nor created nor begotten, but proceeding.
So there is one Father, not three Fathers; one Son, not three Sons;
one Holy Spirit, not three Holy Spirits.
And in this Trinity there is no before or after, no greater or less,
but all three Persons are co-eternal with each other and co-equal.
So that in all things, as has already been said,
the Trinity in Unity, and Unity in Trinity, is to be worshipped.
He therefore who wishes to be saved
let him think thus of the Trinity.

Furthermore, it is necessary to everlasting salvation
that he should *faithfully* believe the incarnation of our Lord Jesus
    Christ.
Now, the right faith is that we should believe and confess
that our Lord Jesus Christ, the Son of God, is both God and man
    equally.
He is God from the *Being* of the Father, begotten before the worlds,
and he is man from the *being* of his mother, born in the world;
perfect God and perfect man,
having both *man's* rational soul and human flesh;
equal to the Father as regards his divinity
and inferior to the Father as regards his humanity;
who, although he is God and man,
yet he is not two, but one Christ;
one, however, not by the conversion of the Godhead into flesh
but by the taking up of the humanity into God;
utterly one, not by confusion of human and divine *being*
but by unity of Christ's one Person.
For just as the rational soul and the flesh are one man,
so God and man are one Christ;
who suffered for our salvation,

descended to *Sheol*, rose from the dead,
ascended to heaven, sat down at the right hand of the Father,
from where he will come to judge the living and the dead;
at whose coming all men will rise again with their bodies
and will give an account for their own actions,
and those who have done good will go into life everlasting
and those who have done evil into everlasting fire.
This is the catholic faith
which, if anyone does not believe it faithfully *and firmly*, he
cannot be saved.

The text is well translated, and faithful to the meaning of the original. Most of the words italicized in the text are no more than translational variants, which scarcely affect the meaning. Only three call for any comment. *Faithfully*, at the beginning of the third section, might suggest *sincerely*, instead of *rightly*, which would be unfortunate, since it is quite easy to be sincerely wrong. *Sheol* has replaced *hell* in order to avoid the caricature associated with the latter term; the disadvantage is that few people know what it means. Lastly, *being* is used to replace *substance* in a way which is sometimes ambiguous. The Son is *God from the Being of the Father*, but it is not clear whether this refers to the Person of the Father or to his Nature. It would probably have been better to have used *nature* if *substance* would not do, though that has difficulties as well.

Translating ancient theological texts into modern idiom is not easy, especially since our language is not attuned to the theological subtleties of classical Christian thought. Faced with having to make the awkward choice between strict accuracy and easy intelligibility, the translator is sure to fall between two stools at some point or other. In general, however, accuracy has not been sacrificed, and this is surely right. The creeds were intended to be precise statements of faith, and loyalty to them demands that we respect this intention. May God grant us wisdom to understand what they mean and make their truth live again in the hearts and lives of men.

Appendix B:
The major credal documents of the Early Church

The major credal documents of the Early Church are easily available in translation, but the original texts are seldom readily accessible to the non-specialist. Below are the major texts which are discussed in this book, given in the original language, whether Greek or Latin.

The Apostles' Creed

The text is set out in parallel columns. On the left is the creed as reconstructed from the evidence of Rufinus (c. 400), on the right is the Received Text, or *Textus Receptus*, which first appears in exactly its present form in the writings of Pirminius, founder and first abbot of the monastery of Reichenau, which was founded in 724. For purposes of comparison, a Greek translation of this text is appended. The words in italics are those which appear in the *Textus Receptus* but are absent from Rufinus.

Credo in Deum Patrem omnipotentem	Credo in Deum Patrem omnipotentem *creatorem caeli et terrae*
et in Christum Iesum filium eius unicum, dominum nostrum	et in *Iesum Christum* filium eius unicum, dominum nostrum
qui natus est de Spiritu Sancto et Maria virgine	qui *conceptus est* de Spiritu Sancto *natus ex* Maria virgine
qui sub Pontio Pilato crucifixus est et sepultus	*passus* sub Pontio Pilato, cruci-fixus, *mortuus* et sepultus *descendit ad inferna*
tertia die resurrexit a mortuis	tertia die resurrexit a mortuis
ascendit in caelos	ascendit *ad* caelos
sedet ad dexteram Patris	sedet ad dexteram *Dei* Patris *omnipotentis*

unde venturus est iudicare vivos
    et mortuos
et in Spiritum Sanctum
sanctam ecclesiam
 	
remissionem peccatorum
carnis resurrectionem. Amen.
	inde venturus est iudicare vivos
	    et mortuos
	Credo in Spiritum Sanctum
	sanctam ecclesiam *catholicam*
	sanctorum communionem
	remissionem peccatorum
	carnis resurrectionem
	et vitam aeternam. Amen.

ΕΛΛΗΝΙΚΗ ΜΕΤΑΦΡΑΣΙΣ ΤΟΥ Β΄ ΚΕΙΜΕΝΟΥ

Πιστεύω εἰς Θεὸν πατέρα παντοκράτορα, **ποιητὴν οὐρανοῦ καὶ γῆς.**
Καὶ εἰς Ἰησοῦν Χριστόν, τὸν Υἱὸν αὐτοῦ τὸν μονογενῆ, τὸν Κύριον ἡμῶν
    τὸν **συλληφθέντα** ἐκ Πνεύματος Ἁγίου, γεννηθέντα ἐκ Μαρίας τῆς παρθένου
    παθόντα ἐπὶ Ποντίου Πιλάτου, σταυρωθέντα, **ἀποθανόντα** καὶ ταφέντα
    κατελθόντα εἰς τὰ κατώτατα (εἰς τὸν ᾅδην)
    τῇ τρίτῃ ἡμέρᾳ ἀναστάντα ἀπὸ τῶν νεκρῶν, ἀνελθόντα εἰς τοὺς οὐρανούς
    καθεζόμενον ἐν δεξιᾷ τοῦ **Θεοῦ** Πατρὸς τοῦ **παντοκράτορος**
    ἐκεῖθεν ἐρχόμενον κρῖναι ζῶντας καὶ νεκρούς.

Πιστεύω εἰς τὸ Πνεῦμα τὸ ἅγιον, ἁγίαν **καθολικὴν** ἐκκλησίαν
    ἁγίων κοινωνίαν, ἄφεσιν ἁμαρτιῶν, σαρκὸς ἀνάστασιν, καὶ ζωὴν αἰώνιον. Ἀμήν.

The Niceno-Constantinopolitan Creed

On the left is the text approved by the Council of Nicaea in 325 (the so-called Faith of the 318 Fathers). On the right is the text of the present 'Nicene' Creed, as it appears in Greek, without the *Filioque* clause. This text (the so-called Faith of the 150 Fathers) is meant to have been approved by the 150 bishops gathered at Constantinople in 381, but its first certain attestation dates from the Council of Chalcedon in 451.

ΤΑ ΤΗΣ ΠΙΣΤΕΩΣ ΣΥΜΒΟΛΑ

ΝΙΚΑΙΑΣ – Ν (325)	ΚΩΝΣΤΑΝΤΙΝΟΥΠΟΛΕΩΣ* – C
Πιστεύομεν εἰς ἕνα θεὸν πατέρα, παντοκράτορα πάντων ὁρατῶν τε καὶ ἀοράτων ποιητὴν καὶ εἰς ἕνα κύριον Ἰησοῦν Χριστὸν τὸν υἱὸν τοῦ θεοῦ γεννηθέντα ἐκ τοῦ πατρὸς μονογενῆ τουτέστιν ἐκ τῆς οὐσίας τοῦ πατρός θεὸν ἐκ θεοῦ φῶς ἐκ φωτός θεὸν ἀληθινὸν ἐκ θεοῦ ἀληθινοῦ γεννηθέντα οὐ ποιηθέντα ὁμοούσιον τῷ πατρί δι᾽ οὗ τὰ πάντα ἐγένετο τά τε ἐν τῷ οὐρανῷ καὶ τὰ ἐπὶ τῇ γῇ τὸν δι᾽ ἡμᾶς τοὺς ἀνθρώπους καὶ διὰ τὴν ἡμετέραν σωτηρίαν κατελθόντα καὶ σαρκωθέντα	Πιστεύομεν εἰς ἕνα θεὸν πατέρα, παντοκράτορα ποιητὴν οὐρανοῦ καὶ γῆς ὁρατῶν τε πάντων καὶ ἀοράτων καὶ εἰς ἕνα κύριον Ἰησοῦν Χριστὸν τὸν υἱὸν τοῦ θεοῦ τὸν μονογενῆ τὸν ἐκ τοῦ πατρὸς γεννηθέντα πρὸ πάντων τῶν αἰώνων φῶς ἐκ φωτός θεὸν ἀληθινὸν ἐκ θεοῦ ἀληθινοῦ γεννηθέντα οὐ ποιηθέντα ὁμοούσιον τῷ πατρὶ δι᾽ οὗ τὰ πάντα ἐγένετο τὸν δι᾽ ἡμᾶς τοὺς ἀνθρώπους καὶ διὰ τὴν ἡμετέραν σωτηρίαν κατελθόντα ἐκ τῶν οὐρανῶν καὶ σαρκωθέντα ἐκ πνεύματος ἁγίου καὶ Μαρίας τῆς παρθένου

ἐνανθρωπήσαντα

παθόντα
καὶ ἀναστάντα τῇ τρίτῃ ἡμέρᾳ

ἀνελθόντα εἰς οὐρανοὺς
καὶ ἐρχόμενον κρῖναι ζῶντας καὶ νεκρούς

καὶ εἰς τὸ ἅγιον πνεῦμα.

καὶ ἐνανθρωπήσαντα
σταυρωθέντα τε ὑπὲρ ἡμῶν ἐπὶ Ποντίου
Πιλάτου
καὶ παθόντα καὶ ταφέντα
καὶ ἀναστάντα τῇ τρίτῃ ἡμέρᾳ κατὰ τὰς
γραφὰς
καὶ ἀνελθόντα εἰς τοὺς οὐρανοὺς
καὶ καθεζόμενον ἐν δεξιᾷ τοῦ πατρός
καὶ πάλιν ἐρχόμενον μετὰ δόξης κρῖναι
ζῶντας καὶ νεκρούς
οὗ τῆς βασιλείας οὐκ ἔσται τέλος
καὶ εἰς τὸ πνεῦμα τὸ ἅγιον
τὸ κύριον, τὸ ζωοποιόν
τὸ ἐκ τοῦ πατρὸς ἐκπορευόμενον
τὸ σὺν πατρὶ καὶ υἱῷ συμπροσκυνούμενον
καὶ συνδοξαζόμενον
τὸ λαλῆσαν διὰ τῶν προφητῶν
εἰς μίαν ἁγίαν καθολικὴν καὶ ἀποστολικὴν
ἐκκλησίαν
ὁμολογοῦμεν ἓν βάπτισμα εἰς ἄφεσιν
ἁμαρτιῶν
προσδοκῶμεν ἀνάστασιν νεκρῶν καὶ ζωὴν
τοῦ μέλλοντος αἰῶνος. Ἀμήν.

* 381?

The Chalcedonian Definition

This short paragraph is an extract from a much longer confessional statement approved at the Council of Chalcedon on 22 October 451.

Ἑπόμενοι τοίνυν τοῖς ἁγίοις πατράσιν ἕνα καὶ τὸν αὐτὸν ὁμολογεῖν υἱὸν τὸν κύριον ἡμῶν Ἰησοῦν Χριστὸν συμφώνως ἅπαντες ἐκδιδάσκομεν τέλειον τὸν αὐτὸν ἐν θεότητι καὶ τέλειον τὸν αὐτὸν ἐν ἀνθρωπότητι Θεὸν ἀληθῶς καὶ ἄνθρωπον ἀληθῶς τὸν αὐτὸν ἐκ ψυχῆς λογικῆς καὶ σώματος ὁμοούσιον τῷ πατρὶ κατὰ τὴν θεότητα καὶ ὁμοούσιον ἡμῖν τὸν αὐτὸν κατὰ τὴν ἀνθρωπότητα κατὰ πάντα ὅμοιον ἡμῖν χωρὶς ἁμαρτίας πρὸ αἰώνων μὲν ἐκ τοῦ πατρὸς γεννηθέντα κατὰ τὴν θεότητα ἐπ' ἐσχάτων δὲ ἡμέρων τὸν αὐτὸν δι' ἡμᾶς καὶ διὰ τὴν ἡμετέραν σωτηρίαν ἐκ Μαρίας τῆς παρθένου τῆς Θεοτόκου κατὰ τὴν ἀνθρωπότητα ἕνα καὶ τὸν αὐτὸν Χριστὸν υἱὸν κύριον μονογενῆ ἐν δύο φύσεσιν ἀσυγχύτως ἀτρέπτως ἀδιαιρέτως ἀχωρίστως γνωριζόμενον οὐδαμοῦ τῆς τῶν φύσεων διαφορᾶς ἀνῃρημένης διὰ τὴν ἕνωσιν σωζομένης δὲ μᾶλλον τῆς ἰδιότητος ἑκατέρας φύσεως καὶ εἰς ἓν πρόσωπον καὶ μίαν ὑπόστασιν συντρεχούσης οὐκ εἰς δύο πρόσωπα μεριζόμενον ἢ διαιρούμενον ἀλλ' ἕνα καὶ τὸν αὐτὸν υἱὸν καὶ μονογενῆ Θεὸν λόγον κύριον Ἰησοῦν Χριστὸν καθάπερ ἄνωθεν οἱ προφῆται περὶ αὐτοῦ καὶ αὐτὸς ἡμᾶς Ἰησοῦς Χριστὸς ἐξεπαίδευσεν καὶ τὸ τῶν πατέρων ἡμῖν παραδέδωκε σύμβολον.
– ἐν Χαλκηδόνι τῇ 22ᾳ Ὀκτωβρίου τοῦ 451.

The Athanasian Creed

1. Quicunque vult salvus esse, ante omnia opus est ut teneat catholicam fidem
2. quam nisi quis integram inviolatamque servaverit, absque dubio in aeternum peribit.
3. Fides autem catholica haec est, ut unum Deum in trinitate et trinitatem in unitate veneremur
4. ·neque confundentes personas neque substantiam separantes
5. alia est enim persona Patris, alia Filii, alia Spiritus Sancti

6. sed Patris et Filii et Spiritus Sancti una est divinitas, aequalis gloria, coaeterna maiestas.

7. Qualis Pater, talis Filius, talis et Spiritus Sanctus.

8. increatus Pater, increatus Filius, increatus Spiritus Sanctus

9. immensus Pater, immensus Filius, immensus Spiritus Sanctus

10. aeternus Pater, aeternus Filius, aeternus Spiritus Sanctus

11. et tamen non tres aeterni sed unus aeternus

12. sicut non tres increati nec tres immensi, sed unus increatus et unus immensus

13. similiter omnipotens Pater, omnipotens Filius, omnipotens Spiritus Sanctus

14. et tamen non tres omnipotentes, sed unus omnipotens.

15. Ita Deus Pater, Deus Filius, Deus Spiritus Sanctus

16. et tamen non tres dii, sed unus est Deus

17. ita Dominus Pater, Dominus Filius, Dominus Spiritus Sanctus

18. et tamen non tres domini, sed unus est Dominus

19. quia sicut singulatim unamquamque personam et Deum et Dominum confiteri christiana veritate compellimur

20. ita tres deos aut dominos dicere catholica religione prohibemur.

21. Pater a nullo est factus, nec creatus, nec genitus

22. Filius a Patre solo est, non factus, nec creatus, sed genitus

23. Spiritus Sanctus a Patre et Filio, non factus, nec creatus, nec genitus, sed procedens

24. Unus ergo Pater, non tres Patres; unus Filius, non tres Filii; unus Spiritus Sanctus, non tres Spiritus Sancti

25. Et in hac trinitate nihil prius aut posterius, nihil maius aut minus

26. sed totae tres personae coaeternae sibi sunt et coaequales

27. ita ut per omnia, sicut iam supra dictum est, et trinitas in unitate et unitas in trinitate veneranda sit

28. qui vult ergo salvus esse, ita de trinitate sentiat.

29. Sed necessarium est ad aeternam salutem ut incarnationem quoque domini nostri Iesu Christi fideliter credat

30. est ergo fides recta ut credamus et confiteamur quia dominus noster Iesus Christus Dei filius et deus pariter et homo est.

31. Deus est ex substantia Patris ante saecula genitus, et homo est ex substantia matris in saeculo natus

32. perfectus deus, perfectus homo ex anima rationabili et humana carne subsistens

33. aequalis Patri secundum divinitatem, minor Patri secundum humanitatem.
34. Qui licet deus sit et homo, non duo tamen sed unus est Christus
35. unus autem non conversione divinitatis in carne, sed adsumptione humanitatis in deo
36. unus omnino non confusione substantiae, sed unitate personae
37. nam sicut anima rationabilis et caro unus est homo, ita deus et homo unus est Christus.
38. Qui passus est pro salute nostra, descendit ad inferna, surrexit a mortuis
39. ascendit ad caelos, sedet ad dexteram Patris, inde venturus iudicare vivos et mortuos
40. ad cuius adventum omnes homines resurgere habent cum corporibus suis et reddituri sunt de factis propriis rationem
41. et qui bona egerunt ibunt in vitam aeternam, qui mala in ignem aeternum.
42. Haec est fides catholica, quam nisi quis fideliter firmiterque crediderit, salvus esse non poterit.

For further reading

The literature available on the subject of the Early Church is vast, and much of it is accessible only to specialists. This is particularly true of source material, which in many cases has not been translated out of the original languages. For those able to consult these, the most important collection is the great nineteenth-century work carried out under the direction of Jean-Paul Migne. This is divided into two sections, according to language, and is frequently referred to as *Patrologia Graeca* (PG) or *Patrologia Latina* (PL), without further detail.

Since the time of Migne, most of the major theological works of antiquity have been re-edited, and a number of additional ones have been published. *Sources Chrétiennes* is the most widely known series of recent editions, and now contains over 400 volumes, each with the original text and a French translation.

For those restricted to English translations, the most easily available series is that of the *Ante-Nicene Fathers*, together with *The Nicene and Post-Nicene Fathers*, currently published by Eerdmans. Also available is the series *Ancient Christian Writers*, published under the auspices of the Catholic University of America, and *The Ante-Nicene Christian Library*, available from T. and T. Clark.

For specialized items on individual writers, it is best to consult a dictionary of Church History or a bibliographical guide. The best of these are J. Quasten's four-volume *Patrology* (Spectrum, Utrecht, 1950-86), and the German *Patrologie* edited by B. Altaner and A. Stuiber (9th edition, Herder Verlag, Freiburg im Breisgau, 1978).

A very limited number of texts is available in other collections. Augustine's *City of God* has appeared in Penguin, as has his *Confessions*. The *Loeb Classical Library* has a number of authors in bilingual editions, as *The Oxford Early Christian Texts*.

The texts of the creeds and conciliar documents of the Church can be found in H. Denzinger's famous *Enchiridion Symbolorum*, published by Herder, or in *Conciliorum Oecumenicorum Decreta*, edited by the Istituto per le scienze religiose, Bologna, 1973. This has now been republished as *Decrees of the Ecumenical Councils*, with an accompanying English translation edited by Norman Tanner (Sheed and Ward, 1990). A similar collection in Greek can be found in I. Karmiris, *Ta dogmatika kai symbolika mnemeia tes orthodoxou katholikes ekklesias*, published by Apostolike Diakonia, Athens, 1960.

There is no readily available handbook in English, though J.N.D. Kelly, *Early Christian Creeds* (London, 1972) and the same author's *The Athanasian Creed* (London, 1964) give both the text and a translation of all the major creeds, together with a long and very learned exposition of their origin and development. Another important source is the two-volume collection of texts edited by J. Stevenson, *A New Eusebius*, which covers the period up to 337, and *Creeds, Councils and Controversies*, which takes up the story down to 461. There is also a new study of some authors by Frances Young, *From Nicaea to Chalcedon* (SCM, 1983).

For those who may wish to follow up material relating to particular chapters, the following books can be recommended:

Chapter 1

P. Hazard, *The European Mind 1680-1715* (Penguin, 1964), and P. Gay, *The Enlightenment: An Interpretation* (Wildwood House, 1973), give a good picture of the growth of modern secular thinking. Also important are B. Reardon's works, *Religious Thought in the Nineteenth Century* (Cambridge, 1966), and *From Coleridge to Gore: Religious Thought in the Victorian Age* (Cambridge, 1971). To these must be added Owen Chadwick's *The Secularization of the European Mind in the Nineteenth Century* (Cambridge, 1975), and John Kent's study, referred to in the text, *The End of the Line?* (T. And T. Clark, 1981).

Chapter 2

The main work is H. Freiherr von Campenhausen, *The Formation of the Christian Bible* (A. and C. Black, 1972). To this may be added A. Souter, *The Text and Canon of the New Testament* (Duckworth, 1954); B. Metzger, *The Text of the New Testament* (Oxford, 1968); J.A.T. Robinson, *Redating the New Testament* (SCM, 1976), and many others. For the Old Testament, see R. T. Beckwith, *The Old Testament Canon of the New Testament Church* (SPCK, 1985), and for a recent study of Biblical interpretation in the patristic period, see G. L. Bray, *Biblical Interpretation: Past and Present* (IVP, 1996), which contains a full bibliography of the subject.

Chapter 3

The story of Christian mission is told by E.M.B. Green, *Evangelism in the Early Church* (Hodder and Stoughton, 1970), and W.H.C. Frend, *Martyrdom and Persecution in the Early Church* (Oxford, 1965). Also by the same author is his massive *The Rise of Christianity* (Darton, Longman and Todd, 1984).

On the conflict with pagan philosophy there are many specialist studies, but see especially C.N. Cochrane, *Christianity and Classical Culture* (Oxford, 1940); E.R. Dodds, *Pagan and Christian in an Age of Anxiety* (Cambridge, 1968); G.C. Stead, *Divine Substance* (Cambridge, 1977); G.L. Prestige, *God in Patristic Thought* (SPCK, 1952), and J. Pelikan, *The Emergence of the Catholic Tradition* (University of Chicago Press, 1971). See also S. Pétrement, *A Separate God: The Christian Origins of Gnosticism* (Harper Collins, 1990), which appeared in French in 1984.

Also of importance is *The Cambridge History of Later Greek and Early*

Medieval Thought (Cambridge, 1970), and E. Gilson, *A History of Christian Philosophy in the Middle Ages* (Sheed and Ward, 1955), which gives extensive coverage of the early period as well. Readers of French will derive much profit from E. von Ivánka's *Plato Christianus. La réception critique du platonisme chez les Pères de l'Eglise* (Presses Universitaires de France, 1990), which originally appeared in German (Einsiedeln, 1964).

On Origen, see Henri Crouzel, *Origen* (T. and T. Clark, 1989) and J. W. Trigg, *Origen: The Bible and Philosophy in the Third-century Church* (SCM, 1983). Dionysius the Areopagite is covered by Andrew Louth, *Denys the Areopagite* (Geoffrey Chapman, 1989), and his complete works are now available in the series *The Classics of Western Spirituality* (SPCK, 1987).

Chapter 4
The standard work is J.N.D. Kelly, *Early Christian Creeds* (A. and C. Black, 1972) and the same author's *Early Christian Doctrines* (5th edition, A. and C. Black, 1977). Kelly's treatment is so authoritative and exhaustive that few readers will want to look elsewhere, though some will find B. Lonergan, *The Way to Nicea* (Darton, Longman and Todd, 1976) useful as well, and R.P.C. Hanson, *Tradition in the Early Church* (SCM, 1962) has an excellent discussion of the meaning of *regula fidei*. See also his later work, *The Search for the Christian Doctrine of God* (T. and T. Clark, 1988).

Chapter 5
Church-state relationships in the Roman Empire have not received the same amount of attention as the theological controversies of the same period. The most important works, apart from W.H.C. Frend's book on martyrdom and persecution (see under Chapter 3), are R.M. Grant, *Early Christianity and Society* (Collins, 1978); J.M. Hornus, *It is not Lawful for me to Fight* (Herald Press, 1980); and P. Brown, *The Cult of the Saints* (SCM, 1981).

On monasticism, see D. Chitty, *The Desert a City* (Mowbrays, 1966); O. Chadwick, *John Cassian* (Cambridge, 1968); and R. Murray, *Symbols of Church and Kingdom* (Cambridge, 1975). For later political developments, consult J. Richards, *The Popes and the Papacy in the Early Middle Ages 476-752* (Routledge and Kegan Paul, 1979); W. Ullmann, *A Short History of the Papacy in the Middle Ages* (Methuen, 1972); W.H.C. Frend, *The Rise of the Monophysite Movement* (Cambridge, 1972); E. Barker, *Social and Political Thought in Byzantium* (Oxford, 1957).

On society in general, see Peter Brown, *Society and the Holy in Late Antiquity*, (University of California Press, 1982), and also *The Body and Society*, (Columbia University Press, 1988), by the same author.

Chapter 6
The standard work in English is R.V. Sellers, *The Council of Chalcedon* (SPCK, 1952). The earlier history of Christology is thoroughly catalogued

in A. Grillmeier, *Christ in Christian Tradition* (Mowbrays, 1975). A recent publication of interest is D.S. Wallace-Hadrill's *Christian Antioch* (Cambridge, 1982).

For post-Chalcedonian developments, see in addition to W.H.C. Frend on the Monophysites (see Chapter 5), J. Meyendorff, *Christ in Eastern Christian Thought* (Saint Vladimir's Seminary Press, 1975); P.T.R. Gray, *The Defense of Chalcedon in the East 451-553* (E.J. Brill, 1979); R. Chesnut, *Three Monophysite Christologies* (Oxford, 1976); P. Gregorios, ed., *Does Chalcedon Divide or Unite?* (WCC, 1981).

Chapter 7

J.N.D. Kelly, *The Athanasian Creed* (A. and C. Black, 1964) is the standard work on the subject, which has been little studied at the popular level. For an examination of the *Filioque* dispute, see L. Vischer, ed., *Spirit of God, Spirit of Christ* (WCC, 1981); also G.L. Bray, 'The *Filioque* Clause in History and Theology', *Tyndale Bulletin* 34, 1983.

On Maximus the Confessor there is a recent book by Andrew Louth (Routledge, 1995). The most readily available study is H. Urs von Balthasar, *La liturgie cosmique* (Aubier-Montaigne, Paris, 1947).

Chapter 8

There are many excellent studies of medieval theology, apart from the ones listed above. Special mention may be made of J. Pelikan, *The Spirit of Eastern Christendom 600-1700* (University of Chicago Press, 1974), and his *The Growth of Medieval Theology 600-1300* (University of Chicago Press, 1978). On Anselm, there is the excellent monograph by G. R. Evans, *Anselm and Talking about God* (Oxford, 1980), as well as a number of older studies.

An attempt to revitalize classical orthodoxy can be found in E.L. Mascall, *Theology and the Gospel of Christ* (SPCK, 1977); also his *Whatever Happened to the Human Spirit?* (SPCK, 1980). Also important are J. Galot, *Who is Christ?* (Gregorian University Press, 1981), and A. Grillmeier, *Mit ihm und in ihm* (Herder, 1975).

INDEX